I0121553

THE WISCONSIN ONEIDAS AND
THE EPISCOPAL CHURCH

The Wisconsin Oneidas *and the* Episcopal Church

A CHAIN LINKING TWO TRADITIONS ⇥

EDITED BY
L. Gordon McLester III,
Laurence M. Hauptman,
Judy Cornelius-Hawk, and
Kenneth Hoyan House

INDIANA UNIVERSITY PRESS

This book is a publication of

Indiana University Press
Office of Scholarly Publishing
Herman B Wells Library 350
1320 East 10th Street
Bloomington, Indiana 47405 USA

iupress.indiana.edu

© 2019 by L. Gordon McLester III, Laurence M. Hauptman,
Judy Cornelius-Hawk, and Kenneth Hoyan House

All rights reserved
No part of this book may be reproduced or utilized in any form or by any
means, electronic or mechanical, including photocopying and recording, or by
any information storage and retrieval system, without permission in writing
from the publisher. The paper used in this publication meets the minimum
requirements of the American National Standard for Information Sciences—
Permanence of Paper for Printed Library Materials, ANSI Z39.48-1992.

Manufactured in the United States of America

Library of Congress Cataloging-in-Publication Data

Names: McLester, L. Gordon, editor. | Hauptman, Laurence M., editor. |
Cornelius-Hawk, Judy, editor. | House, Kenneth Hoyan, editor
Title: The Wisconsin Oneidas and the Episcopal Church : a chain linking two
traditions / edited by L. Gordon McLester III, Laurence M. Hauptman, Judy
Cornelius-Hawk and Kenneth Hoyan House.
Description: First edition. | Bloomington : Indiana University Press, 2019. |
Includes bibliographical references and index.
Identifiers: LCCN 2018025854 (print) | LCCN 2018029263 (ebook) | ISBN
9780253041401 (ebook) | ISBN 9780253041371 (hardback : alk. paper) | ISBN
9780253041388 (pbk. : alk. paper)
Subjects: LCSH: Oneida Indians—Missions—Wisconsin—History. | Episcopal
Church—Missions—Wisconsin—History.
Classification: LCC E99.O45 (ebook) | LCC E99.O45 W73 2019 (print) | DDC
266/.309775—dc23
LC record available at https://lccn.loc.gov/2018025854

1 2 3 4 5   24 23 22 21 20 19

*We thank the Creator for guiding us in
the telling of this important story.*

Right Reverend Father:
"We are now about to do what we could not do
when last you visited us.
A chain of friendship is to be formed,
which we trust will never be broken.
We now extend to you the hand of the nation.
We acknowledge you, and will hereafter hold on
to you as our loyal Bishop. Our eyes will turn to you, and
to you alone for counsel and advice in all our spiritual affairs.
May the chain now thrown around us, never become dim.
May it bind us together in peace and friendship,
as long as life shall last.
Father, your children will take care to keep it bright."

ADDRESS OF FOUR ONEIDA CHIEFS, INCLUDING DANIEL BREAD,
TO BISHOP JACKSON KEMPER, CONSECRATION OF ONEIDA HOBART
EPISCOPAL CHURCH, SEPTEMBER 29, 1839. QUOTED IN JULIA KEEN BLOOMFIELD,
THE ONEIDAS (NEW YORK: ALDEN, 1907), P. 221.

CONTENTS

ACKNOWLEDGMENTS

THE EDITORS WOULD LIKE TO THANK THE ONEIDA Nation of Indians of Wisconsin's Business Committee for its support of this project as well as its past sponsorship of history conferences. Over the years, its membership has supported various efforts to document Oneida history, including projects to videotape and digitize hundreds of interviews with tribal elders. Some of these interviews, along with stories collected by the WPA Oneida Language and Folklore Project from 1938 to 1942, provided valuable source material for this book.

Both the clergy and membership of the Oneidas' Church of the Holy Apostles and the office of the diocese of Fond du Lac must be thanked for their major contributions to this project. Vicar Rodger Patience and Deacon Deborah Heckel, the Oneidas' Church of the Holy Apostles' vestry council, its altar guild, and numerous church members, especially Betty and John Dennison and Abby Jean Webster, need to be acknowledged for their assistance. The editors would also like to thank the Right Reverend Matthew Gunter, the bishop of the archdiocese of Fond du Lac, and diocesan archivist Matthew Payne for their encouragement of this project from its inception. The Historical Society of the Episcopal Church provided a small planning grant at the initial stages of this project.

Others must also be acknowledged. Dr. Gary Dunham, director of Indiana University Press, encouraged this unique undertaking of academics, Episcopal clergy, and Oneida local historians and elders from the first time it was proposed. The editors of *New York History*, especially Dr. Thomas Beal, graciously allowed the reprinting of an award-winning article on Susan Fenimore Cooper that appeared in their journal in 2013. Because of his special knowledge of the WPA Oneida and Language Project, Dr. Herbert Lewis, professor emeritus of anthropology at the University of Wisconsin at Madison, helped the editors choose interviews from this collection for inclusion in this book. Other scholars, especially Drs. Jack Campisi and Anthony Wonderley, have significantly added to the quality of this project with their insightful writings.

The technical support for this project came from several sources. The editors depended on the expertise of Bob Roszoff and Allen Condra, who videotaped parts of two conferences and numerous interviews with Oneida elders and then transferred these presentations into a digital format. Dan Hawk helped secure and transmit photographs for the project. Dana McLester, the treasurer of the Oneida Indian Historical Society, helped edit the PowerPoint presentations for showing at the same two conferences and advised the editors about images that are used in this book. Victoria Jicha helped the editors with her careful proofing of the manuscript. Our dear friend David Jaman of The Villages, Florida, provided the editors with good cheer, excellent wit, and expert computer skills as he has done before in all five previous books in this series.

The Editors
November 1, 2017

ABBREVIATIONS

APS	American Philosophical Society
ARCIA	*Annual Reports* of the [United States] Commissioner of Indian Affairs
BL	Beinecke Library
BIA	Bureau of Indian Affairs
CCF	Central Classified Files
COLL	Collection
EW	Eleazer Williams
GBAR	Green Bay Agency Records
HC	Hamilton College, Clinton, New York
ICC	Indian Claims Commission
JAJ	John Archiquette Journals
JAPR	John Archiquette Police Reports
JFC	James Fenimore Cooper
JR	*Jesuit Relations and Allied Documents*
M	Microcopy
MR	Microfilm Reel
MSS	Manuscript Collection
NA	National Archives
NYIA	New York Indian Agency
NYSA	New York State Archives
NYSL	New York State Library
OIA	Office of Indian Affairs
OLFP	Oneida Language and Folklore Project
ONIW	Oneida Nation of Indians of Wisconsin
REV	Reverend
RG	Record Group
Rt. Rev.	Right Reverend/Bishop
SK	Samuel Kirkland

SPG	Society for the Propagation of the Gospel in Foreign Parts
Stat.	*United States Statutes at Large*
USGPO	United States Government Printing Office
UWGB	University of Wisconsin at Green Bay
Very Rev.	Very Reverend/Senior Priest
WHC	*Wisconsin Historical Collections*
WHS	Wisconsin Historical Society
WHSARC	Wisconsin Historical Society Area Research Center
WPA	Works Progress Administration
YU	Yale University

PREFACE

*T*HE *WISCONSIN ONEIDAS AND THE EPISCOPAL CHURCH: A Chain Linking Two Traditions* is a unique collaboration by local Oneida historians, community members, and an academic that dates back forty years. The present book is the fifth volume in a series on the history of the Oneida Nation of Indians of Wisconsin that began in the mid-1980s. After completing what they intended to be their last book in the series in 2010, two of the editors—L. Gordon McLester III and Laurence M. Hauptman—realized that they had given Oneida Christianity, both the Episcopal and Methodist religious traditions, too little emphasis in their previous writings. Consequently, they recruited two new editors—Kenneth Hoyan House and Judy Cornelius-Hawk—to help them prepare a sixth volume, this time on the Episcopal mission.[1]

The present work builds on recent writings that go beyond generalizations about missionary interactions with Native peoples. It does not present the missionary as a hero bringing "civilization" or as the auxiliary of the conqueror and destroyer of Native traditions; however, it does recognize that Christianity, nevertheless, had and has real meaning to many American Indians. In our analysis, we explore both sides of the interaction, with special attention to the Oneida perspective in the encounter. The book includes articles about their relationship with the Episcopal Church as well as first-person accounts illustrating this link. The writings are by five academic historians, including one of the editors; by seventeen prominent Wisconsin Oneidas, including three of the four editors; and by seven members of the Episcopal clergy, including two Oneida nuns, a distinguished historian-theologian from the Nashotah House Episcopal Seminary, a diocese archivist, and the wife of a missionary. Moreover, one of the editors of this volume and twelve of the twenty-four authors represented here are women.

The Wisconsin Oneidas and the Episcopal Church: A Chain That Links Two Traditions emphasizes that there were three main factors that allowed for the Episcopal tradition to take root within the community. First and foremost, personal bonds, more than theology, developed between the Episcopal clergy and the Wisconsin Oneidas, allowing these Native Americans to accept the Christian message brought by outsiders. At times, their Episcopal bishop or missionaries in Wisconsin were defenders of the Oneidas against outside whites attempting to get at their lands and resources. At other times, these clergy provided certain benefits that the Oneidas, a savvy, practical-minded people, saw as beneficial—a school, a hospital, a women's lace-making project that provided a source of income and national recognition for their artistry, and so forth. Second, the clergy incorporated the Episcopal faith into an Iroquoian cultural and religious framework—the Condolence Council ritual—that they could understand and one that had a long-standing history among the Six Nations. Third, the Episcopal tradition allowed a level of agency by the Oneidas themselves. As shown in the article on Susan Fenimore Cooper included in this book, Oneidas modified the very form of the Episcopal faith in their territory by using their language in the *Gloria in Excelsis* and the *Te Deum* as well as by employing Oneidas in their singing of Christian hymns. In other words, the relationship was a two-way arrangement, and the church had to accommodate the wishes of those being missionized to some degree.

The title of the book was carefully chosen to capture the essence of the Wisconsin Oneidas' relationship with the Episcopal Church, although on numerous occasions there have been severe breaks in the chain linking these Native Americans with the clergy. Since Jackson Kemper's bishopric began in the mid-1830s, the relationship has not been a total one-way street with the clergy completely dominating and imposing their will on the Indians, as was too often the case in missionary history. It is no accident that contemporary Wisconsin Oneidas use the metaphor of the Covenant Chain to describe their historic relationship with the Episcopal Church. The original Covenant Chain was first established in the seventeenth century and was composed of a complex series of alliances between the Iroquois League, then composed of the Five Nations—Oneidas as well as Mohawks, Onondagas, Cayugas, and Senecas—and the Anglo-American colonies, and was fashioned diplomatically in belts of wampum. These agreements were supposed to be mutually beneficial and respectful to both parties and were later symbolized by an iron chain that tended to rust. Subsequently, the metaphor became a silver chain, one that had to be periodically polished/renewed to once again bind the parties in efforts at cooperation and alliance.[2]

The Oneida mission, founded in 1816 with roots going back more than a century, was the very first "foreign" mission of the Episcopal Church, predating others by a decade. The Wisconsin Oneidas have had four Episcopal churches to meet the spiritual needs of their growing population in Wisconsin since the beginning of their migration out of New York. It is important to note that when the Oneidas first came to Wisconsin in the 1820s and 1830s, they brought with them two already established Christian traditions: the Protestant Episcopal and the Methodist religions. At that time, although they were heavily influenced by Hodinöhsö:ni´ beliefs, no Iroquois longhouse, whether inspired by the Good Message of Handsome Lake that arose in 1799–1800 or the earlier Great (Binding) Law, was brought with the Oneidas to Wisconsin. Although traditional revivalist movements came to the fore in the 1920s and today play a significant role in community life, the Oneidas' longhouse that exists in Wisconsin was formally established in the late 1960s and early 1970s.

In 1825, after arriving from central New York, the Oneidas built their "Log Church" about ten miles southwest of Green Bay in the vicinity of Duck Creek. This church structure was the first Protestant church in the Old Northwest Territory. In 1838, their second church, a Gothic-styled wooden structure, the first non–Roman Catholic church consecrated in the Old Northwest Territory, held its first religious services. As late as 1847, the Oneida mission was only one of three parishes of the Episcopal Church in Wisconsin Territory. Volunteering their labor to quarry stone and secure funding over a two-decade period, the Oneidas built their third church, the "Hobart" or "Stone Church," one with a steep roof, heavy buttresses, and low massive walls designed by priest and architect Charles Babcock and opened in 1886; this house of worship was consecrated by Bishop Charles Chapman Grafton in 1897. When this church was struck by lightning and its interior destroyed by fire in the summer of 1920, the Oneidas rebuilt the interior around the surviving stone wall frame and opened the new structure. In June 1922, the church was reconsecrated by Bishop R. H. Weller and renamed the Church of the Holy Apostles. Today, the church is one of thirty-seven parishes in northeastern Wisconsin under the spiritual leadership of the bishop of Fond du Lac, whose diocese office is headquartered at Appleton, Wisconsin. Its importance in the state and nation was best recognized by one Native American, not an Oneida, who described the church, with its majestic gray tower, as "the cathedral for all Episcopal Indians."[3]

The Wisconsin Oneidas and the Episcopal Church: A Chain That Links Two Traditions begins with an introductory essay by an Oneida local historian and a diocesan archivist who reflect on the nature of the historical links between this Native community and the Episcopal Church. Then the book is divided into four parts. Part I contains three essays, one focusing on the Oneida world before the arrival of missionaries; one on Jesuit, Anglican, and Presbyterian proselytizing efforts; and, finally, one on the controversial Eleazer Williams, who Bishop John Henry Hobart chose to serve the spiritual needs of the Oneidas at the Episcopal Church's first Indian mission. The authors in Parts II of the book describe the Episcopal Church involvement in Oneida community life from the mid-1830s into the first decade of the twentieth century. It includes articles on the Episcopal clergy; on the special bond between Kemper and Oneida leadership as well as the bishop's influence on Susan Fenimore Cooper; on Oneida connections to the Nashotah House Seminary; on two Oneidas—Chief and Priest Cornelius Hill and John Archiquette—and their roles as both tribal and church leaders; on Christmastime at the mission; on church-sponsored health care delivery; and on a successful Episcopal-sponsored lace-making project. Part III is composed of accounts by seventeen Oneidas reflecting on the Episcopal Church's influence on the community over the past one hundred years. These reminiscences clearly show that what Wisconsin Oneidas valued most were the good works by individual Episcopal clergy, including Oneida priests and nuns themselves, who often engendered respect and approval for their actions while preaching Christ's path to salvation. In Part IV, Christopher Vecsey puts the previous sections into a larger perspective, comparing the Wisconsin Oneida experience with the scholarly literature on other Native American communities. Vecsey's article is followed by the editors' concluding words about the history of this lengthy and extraordinary link between the Wisconsin Oneidas and the Episcopal Church.

The editors are quite aware of the criticisms, both in the scholarly literature and in the media, of the Episcopal/Anglican Church over the past half a century. In 1974, the late Vine Deloria Jr., the noted scholar and activist and himself a former seminarian who was brought up in the Episcopal religious tradition among the Standing Rock Lakota, pointed out that major cultural, economic, political, and social problems in Native American communities resulted from the severing of traditional religious life.[4] In 1999, Edmond Browning, presiding bishop of the Episcopal Church in the United States, and Native American leaders, including the chief of the Mattaponi Nation of Virginia, acknowledged this and issued the Jamestown Covenant, one of faith and reconciliation, where the church asked for forgiveness in some of its past policies and treatment of indigenous peoples. In July 2009, the General Convention of the National Episcopal Church meeting in Anaheim, California, passed Resolution 2009-D035, which repudiated and renounced the Doctrine of Discovery that was applied by Henry VIII and the Anglican Church in the early years of colonization of the Americas; in the same resolution, members called on US officials to endorse the United Nations Declaration of Indigenous Rights. Moreover, the editors are also aware of revelations since the late 1980s of rampant abuse of Native American children at residential schools administered by the Anglican Church of Canada. After this scandal was widely reported, Primate Archbishop Michael Peers made a formal apology in 1993. In 2005, the Canadian government and indigenous communities established a mechanism for students to seek financial compensation. The Canadian Truth and Reconciliation Commission was created in 2008, and its final report was issued in 2015.[5]

While presenting the positive side of the church's relations with the Oneidas, *The Wisconsin Oneidas and the Episcopal Church: A Chain That Links Two Traditions* does not attempt to cover up the failings of the Episcopal clergy. The authors make it clear that both sides of the chain from the first used each other for their own purposes, be they economic, political, or religious. Jack Campisi, the foremost ethnohistorian on the Oneidas, has said that Episcopal clergy "advised the council, and, in turn accepted direction and advice from it."[6] These same missionaries and bishops were the Oneidas' representatives to the national church, raised funds for Indian needs, brought medical care, taught at the mission school, developed self-help projects that benefited the tribal economy, and periodically served as cultural brokers between the Oneidas and local, state, and federal officials to defend the

Oneidas against outside threats. On the other hand, Campisi has also brought out that the Episcopal mission weakened the Oneida clan system and discouraged certain aspects of Iroquoian culture, including membership in medicine societies. He has pointed out that the Oneida mission school had an assimilationist focus and that its teachers insisted on the use of English and not the Oneida language, a policy that was strictly enforced at times.[7]

The editors benefited substantially from the Wisconsin Oneidas' long tradition of preserving their history both orally and in print form. Indeed, the records that the Wisconsin Oneidas have amassed over the years are second to none in Indian Country. From 1938 to 1942, thousands of pages of Oneida history were collected in the WPA Oneida Language and Folklore Project administered by Morris Swadesh, Floyd Lounsbury, and Harry Basehart. Unlike the WPA's massive Indian-Pioneer History of Oklahoma, Oneida Native speakers, not non-Indians employing English, interviewed community members.[8] Moreover, since 1987, L. Gordon McLester III has administered twelve conferences on every aspect of Wisconsin Oneida history, much of which has been videotaped, transcribed, and digitized. Under contract from the Oneida Nation Business Committee, he has also conducted more than five hundred interviews of Oneida elders ranging in length from one to eight hours. They contain information about, among other things, events, genealogy, holiday celebrations, people, places, and traditions. In addition to these oral conferences and oral history projects, the Wisconsin Oneidas have an extensive Cultural Heritage Department that publishes on a variety of subjects, including on famous Oneidas, cultural and religious traditions, federal Indian policies, and treaties.

About one-fourth of the material presented in this collection was delivered at two major conferences. On August 24, 2014, the Wisconsin Oneidas held a conference celebrating the 175th anniversary of the consecration of their Episcopal Church, now named the Oneida Church of the Holy Apostles. At this gathering, Rt. Rev. Matthew Gunter, bishop of Fond du Lac, helped renew a bond between the Episcopal faith and the Oneidas that dated back to the first years of the eighteenth century. On June 14–17, 2016, the diocese of Fond du Lac and the Historical Society of the National Episcopal Church held a conference entitled "Wondering, Witness/ Worship, and War: Historical Encounters Between the Episcopal and Anglican Church and Indigenous Peoples in North America" at the Radisson Hotel on the Wisconsin Oneida reservation. This Episcopal conference was organized in cooperation with the Oneidas' Church of the Holy Apostles and the Oneida Nation of Indians of Wisconsin.

The day before the formal presentation of papers, a votive mass in honor of chief and Episcopal priest Cornelius Hill was held at the Church of the Holy Apostles, with Rev. Canon Robert Two Bulls providing the sermon. It was followed by Holy Communion with the *Gloria in Excelsis* and the *Te Deum* sung in Oneida and by a formal procession to the church cemetery, where the graves of prominent Oneida leaders and Episcopal clergy were formally consecrated. After that, the conferees made their way to Bishop Grafton Parish Hall, where the Oneidas themselves presented their own reminiscences about the church and those men and women clergy who served their nation.

Notes

1. For the previous books in the series, see Jack Campisi and Laurence M. Hauptman, eds., *The Oneida Indian Experience: Two Perspectives* (Syracuse, NY: Syracuse University Press, 1988); Laurence M. Hauptman and L. Gordon McLester III, eds., *The Oneida Indian Journey: From New York to Wisconsin, 1784–1860* (Madison: University of Wisconsin Press, 1999); Laurence M. Hauptman and L. Gordon McLester III, *Chief Daniel Bread and the Oneida Nation of Indians of Wisconsin* (Norman: University of Oklahoma Press, 2005); Laurence M. Hauptman and L. Gordon McLester III, eds., *The Oneida Indians in the Age of Allotment, 1860–1920* (Norman: University of Oklahoma Press, 2006); and L. Gordon McLester and Laurence M. Hauptman, eds., *A Nation Within a Nation: Voices of the Oneidas in Wisconsin* (Madison: Wisconsin Historical Society Press, 2010).

2. For the history and symbolism of the Covenant Chain, see William N. Fenton, *The Great Law and the Longhouse: A Political History of the Iroquois Confederacy* (Norman: University of Oklahoma Press, 1998), 7, 235–39, 301–3, 328–29, 349–357, 385–88, 391, 404, 408–9, 422, 427–28, 473, 478, 537, 545, 675–76, 717.

3. Quoted in Owanah Anderson, *400 Years: Anglican/Episcopal Mission Among American Indians* (Cincinnati, OH: Forward Movement, 1999), 38.

4. Vine Deloria Jr., *God Is Red* (New York: Grosset and Dunlap, 1974). For Deloria's other writings on religion, see his *For This Land: Writings on Religion in America*, ed. James Treat (New York: Routledge, 1999).

5. "Resolution 2009-D 035." In National Episcopal Church General Convention, *Journal of the General Convention of . . . the Episcopal Church, 2009* (New York: General Convention, 2009), 371–372; Truth and Reconciliation Commission of Canada, *Honouring the Truth, Reconciling the Future: Summary of the Final Report of the Truth and Reconciliation Commission of Canada* (Ottawa, Ontario, Canada, 2015), vi.

6. Jack Campisi, "Ethnic Identity and Boundary Maintenance in Three Oneida Communities" (PhD diss., State University of New York at Albany, 1974), 139.

7. Ibid., 137–40. The False Face Society was still active in 1941 at Oneida. See WPA OLFP interview of Eddie Metoxen in Herbert Lewis, eds., *Oneida Lives: Long-Lost Voices of the Wisconsin Oneidas* (Lincoln: University of Nebraska Press, 2005), 295–301.

8. Lewis, *Oneida Lives*; Jack Campisi and Laurence M. Hauptman, "Talking Back: The Oneida Language and Folklore Project," *Proceedings of the American Philosophical Society* 125 (1981): 441–48.

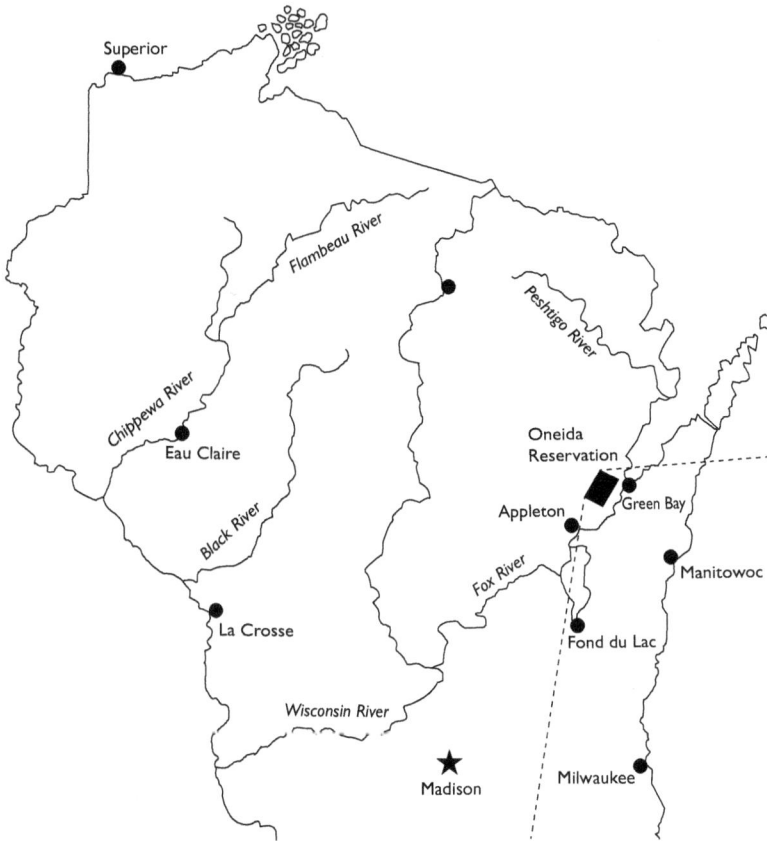

Map 1. The Oneida Nation of Indians of Wisconsin Today. In 1838, Oneida treaty lands were 65,540 acres, most of which were lost as a result of federal allotment policies between 1887 and 1933. In 2017, the Wisconsin Oneidas had 25,329 acres—14,481 acres of trust lands and 11,048 of tribal fee simple lands. Map by Laurence M. Hauptman.

THE WISCONSIN ONEIDAS AND
THE EPISCOPAL CHURCH

INTRODUCTION

L. Gordon McLester III and Matthew P. Payne

THE ONEIDA NATION OF INDIANS OF WISCONSIN, NEARLY eighteen thousand strong, was one of the original five nations of the Iroquois League that the Europeans first encountered in the sixteenth century. At one time, the Oneidas occupied a vast area of 5–6 million acres in what is now central New York. Today, the Oneidas are a federally recognized American Indian nation that has treaty rights with the US government dating back to 1784.[1] Its present reservation is composed of 25,329 acres—14,481 acres of tribal trust lands and 11,048 acres of tribal fee lands—in the environs of Green Bay situated in Brown and Outagamie counties, Wisconsin.[2] Besides the Oneida Nation of Indians of Wisconsin, there are three other Oneida reservation communities: in central New York; at Southwold, Ontario; and at the Six Nations Reserve at Ohsweken, Ontario, although the latter's connection to the other territories was largely severed because of its alliance to the British in the American Revolution. Moreover, there is also a sizeable urban Oneida community in Milwaukee, sometimes referred to as "the other Oneida."

The Oneidas are a highly resilient people who have skillfully adapted to changing circumstances and made new alliances throughout their history. In the colonial era, faced with epidemics such as smallpox, measles, and influenza as well as increasing battlefield losses, they adopted numerous Iroquoian, Algonquian, and Siouan peoples into their nation and made alliances at different times in the seventeenth and eighteenth centuries with three European empires: the Dutch, the French, and the English.

The story of the Oneida–Episcopal connection has lasted for over three hundred years! When the North American continent experienced the incursion of the Europeans, the Oneidas needed to make solid relationships to support peace and stability and preserve trade. In order to ensure their survival, the Hodinöhsö:ni', the Iroquois Confederacy of five and later six nations, through an elaborate ritual of forest diplomacy, made a series of alliances and treaties known as the Covenant Chain, reflecting three ideals: peace, friendship, and mutual respect. The parties to this Covenant Chain connection were considered to be similar to an extended family. These early alliances dissolved by the end of the colonial era and were replaced by treaty making with the newly formed US government. Subsequently, the metaphor of the Covenant Chain was employed to describe nongovernmental links. As early as 1811, the metaphor was used by John Henry Hobart, the third Protestant Episcopal bishop of New York, to link the church to the Indians.[3] Later, in the 1830s, the metaphor was used by Chief Daniel Bread, along with several other chiefs, to link the church to the Oneidas.[4]

The exact beginning of the Oneida–Episcopal connection is unknown. A year after the founding of the Society for the Propagation of the Gospel in Foreign Parts in 1701, an Anglican missionary priest reported to his church superiors that Native peoples had expressed a desire to form a relationship. The sachems of the Five Nations requested that the English monarch King William III "send them some to teach them Religion and establish traffic amongst them."[5] Over the next half a century, the Anglicans or Church of England (an ancestor of the Episcopal Church) introduced the Mohawks and Oneidas to their liturgical practices. However, unlike the ideal symbolized by the Covenant Chain, it was largely a one-way street, since the church's purpose was to Christianize so-called heathen peoples.[6]

Following the American Revolution, the Anglican Church, largely in disrepute due to its association with loyalism to the British cause during the war, had to transform itself. It did so by recasting Anglicanism into what became the Protestant Episcopal Church in the United States. The Oneidas, who allied themselves with the Patriot cause, suffered immensely during and after the war. As soon as the conflict ended, these American Indians faced intense pressures aimed to dispossess them from their central New York homeland.[7] With both the church and the Oneidas in crisis, a chain was again forged. At the 1811 ceremony, the oldest Oneida chief clasped the hand of Bishop Hobart in a formal ceremony renewing the covenant they had made at the beginning of the eighteenth century.[8] The energy to reconnect the links of the chain came from the Oneidas, who were once again in need of allies. By 1816, the bishop established a mission at Oneida, the first of its kind within the Episcopal Church. However, within the next two decades, the chain became rusty, caused in part by the nefarious actions of Eleazer Williams, lay catechist and later deacon assigned by Hobart to care for the spiritual needs of the Oneidas. Despite his success as a charismatic preacher in converting Oneidas, Williams nearly severed the chain by ignoring the Oneidas' best interests and collaborating with land speculators and government agents for his own self-aggrandizement.

As a result of the leadership of Bishop Jackson Kemper and Chief Daniel Bread, the missing links in the chain were restored in the late 1830s. There was a shine on the chain when the Oneida mission built the first consecrated Episcopal Church building in Wisconsin at Oneida, hosted the first ordinations to the priesthood at Oneida, and became a founding congregation of a new diocese. It glittered when

Chief Bread was given the seat of honor next to Bishop Jackson Kemper at the diocesan council and addressed a session in the Oneida language.[9]

Despite the extraordinary compassion and work of Bishop Kemper, missionaries and the dominant American culture had an inherent bias. Yes, there was friendship, peace, and common religious beliefs, but that did not mean equality in the Episcopal clergy's relationship with Native Americans. Clergy members assumed that they had the right to "civilize" Native peoples without recognizing the worth of these communities. This mental block prevented the true spirit of the Covenant Chain ideal—namely, that of two equal parties coming together in alliance and mutual respect. This myopia was often reflected in the writings of members of clergy. In 1877, John Henry Hobart Brown, the first bishop of the diocese of Fond du Lac, noted after a visit to Oneida: "The general result of my observations and inquiries is the opinion that the Church has not wasted love and money on the Oneidas, but that there has been steady, sure growth among them, of all the elements of Christian character and civilization."[10] Several decades later, Julia Keen Bloomfield, in her classic book *The Oneidas*, commented that the Sisters of the Holy Nativity would "labor for the advancement of the tribe in everything that helps towards civilization."[11]

Since the Indian New Deal of the 1930s, the Oneida Nation of Indians of Wisconsin, with its checkerboard land patterns created after the Dawes General Allotment Act of 1887, has attempted to reacquire reservation land for tribal ownership. In 1933, the Wisconsin Oneidas had fewer than ninety acres of tribally owned lands and approximately seven hundred acres of individually owned allotments.[12] After World War II, the link between church and Indian community was strengthened, especially when the bishops of the diocese of Fond du Lac began to realize that a new approach was necessary to once again strengthen the chain between the church and one of its historically important parishes. From the late 1940s onward, the Wisconsin Oneidas requested that some portion of Episcopal mission property be transferred to their control because of tribal needs for housing development, athletic fields, and community meeting space. Each time, the congregation and the diocese readily agreed to the transfer, even noting in the process that they were returning the land to its original owners. In 1948, the diocese of Fond du Lac provided ten acres of its Church of the Holy Apostles' lands for Oneida recreational purposes. Two decades later, the diocese awarded five acres to the Oneidas for athletic fields. In 1997, the diocese reached an agreement with Wisconsin Oneida and transferred two acres and the historic Bishop Grafton Parish Hall, which has served the mission since 1906; in return, the Oneidas made a formal commitment to restore the building. A decade and a half later, the diocese of Fond du Lac transferred land to the Wisconsin Oneidas to allow the development of a recreational trail connecting two shores of Duck Creek for biking and jogging.[13]

The diocese has supported the Oneidas in several major jurisdictional battles with their white neighbors. When a local municipality attempted to tax cemetery land three times starting in the 1950s and continuing to 2010, the diocese worked with the Oneidas to successfully resist these efforts. When the town of Hobart, carved out of Oneida treaty lands after the Dawes Act, took the position that Congress disestablished the Oneida reservation by the passage of allotment legislation from 1887 to 1910, the Episcopal Church gave clear support to the Oneidas' position that the original treaty boundaries of 1838 still existed and that all their federal trust lands contained there were not subject to outside local regulations and taxation. The Oneida position was later upheld by the courts.[14]

The connecting links have been strengthened in other ways. Four Wisconsin Oneidas have been ordained as full-fledged priests and deacons within the Episcopal Church, including three who have served at the Church of the Holy Apostles in the last thirty years. In 2011, Rt. Rev. Katherine Jefferts Schori, presiding bishop of the national Episcopal Church, visited the Church of the Holy Apostles and renewed the bond between the church and the Oneidas. Three years later, a conference celebrating the 175th anniversary of Bishop Kemper's consecration of the Episcopal Church was held on the Wisconsin Oneida reservation, at which time Matthew Gunter, bishop of Fond du Lac, paid tribute to the Oneidas. In 2016, the Tri-County History Conference, sponsored by the diocese of Fond du Lac, focused on the Episcopal Church's historic relationship with Native American communities and was held at the Oneidas' Radisson Hotel in cooperation with the Oneida Nation of Indians of Wisconsin. Church historians and clergy from all over Canada and the United States attended. Mass was performed at the Church of the Holy Apostles.

The Wisconsin Oneidas and the Episcopal Church: A Chain That Links Two Traditions clearly shows that good works by individuals and faith in the Creator/God by both Oneidas and Episcopal clergy were more important than esoteric aspects of theology. The two authors of this essay, one an Oneida community historian and the other a non-Indian archivist working for the diocese of Fond du Lac, share a common faith. Their working relationship is based on honesty and mutual respect, and they know that the spirit of God/Creator links them together. Both understand that human beings are not perfect and that there is always a need for self-reflection and reform to retain their friendship. Although they are different people from different cultures, they are, nevertheless, connected. That is the true meaning of the Covenant Chain as they see it.

Notes

1. The federal treaty with the Six Nations at Fort Stanwix, 7 *Stat.*, 15 (October 22, 1784).
2. Statistics about the Oneidas' present land base was provided by the Wisconsin Land Management Office, Oneida Nation of Indians of Wisconsin, February 17, 2017.

3. John Henry Hobart, *The Correspondence of John Henry Hobart* (New York: privately printed, 1911), cxliii.

4. See chapter 4 of this book.

5. C. F. Pascoe, *Two Hundred Years of the Society of the Propagation of the Gospel* [SPG]: *An Historical Account of the Society for the Propagation of the Gospel in Foreign Parts, 1701–1900. (Based on a digest of the Society's records)* (London: SPG, 1901), 73.

6. Laura M. Stevens, *The Poor Indians: British Missionaries, Native Americans, and Colonial Sensibility* (Philadelphia: University of Pennsylvania Press, 2010), 111; Daniel O'Connor, *Three Centuries of Mission: The United Society for the Propagation of the Gospel, 1701–2000* (London: Continuum, 2000), 34.

7. For the crisis that led to the transformation of the church, see Jennifer Clark, "'Church of Our Fathers': The Development of the Protestant Episcopal Church Within the Changing Post-Revolutionary Anglo-American Relationship," *Journal of Religious History* 18, no. 1 (1994): 27–51; David L. Holmes, "The Episcopal Church and the American Revolution," *Historical Magazine of the Protestant Episcopal Church* 79 (1978): 261–91. For the Oneidas in the American Revolution, see Joseph T. Glatthaar and James Kirby Martin, *Forgotten Allies: The Oneida Indians and the American Revolution* (New York: Hill and Wang, 2006). For the impact of the war on the Oneidas, see Karim M. Tiro, *The People of the Standing Stone: The Oneida Nation from the Revolution Through the Era of Removal* (Amherst: University of Massachusetts Press, 2011), 65–192; and Laurence M. Hauptman, *Conspiracy of Interests: Iroquois Dispossession and the Rise of New York State* (Syracuse, NY: Syracuse University Press, 1999), 1–97.

8. Hobart, *The Correspondence of John Henry Hobart.*

9. Harold Ezra Wagner, *The Episcopal Church in Wisconsin, 1847–1947: A History of the Diocese of Milwaukee* (Milwaukee, WI: Diocese of Milwaukee, 1947), 54. See also Breck's and Kip's excerpts in chapter 5 for two other descriptions of this convocation.

10. John Henry Hobart Brown, "The Oneida Indians," *The Church Magazine* (April 1877), 4.

11. Julia K. Bloomfield, *The Oneidas* (New York: Alden Brothers, 1907), 343.

12. Jack Campisi states that there were only 84.8 acres of Oneida lands held in common, while anthropologist Harry S. Basehart states that there were 733 acres held by individual Oneidas in fee simple by the New Deal. Jack Campisi, "Ethnic Identity and Boundary Maintenance in Three Oneida Communities" (PhD diss., State University of New York, Albany, 1974), 158; Harry S. Basehart, "Historical Changes in the Kinship System of the Oneida Indians" (PhD diss., Harvard University, 1952), 218.

13. Numerous discussions about returning land to the Oneidas can be found in various committee minutes, 1948–2016. Archives of the Diocese of Fond du Lac, Appleton, Wisconsin.

14. *Oneida Nation of Indians of Wisconsin v. Town of Hobart,* 2013WL5692337 (7th Cir. Oct.18, 2013).

PART I

CHRISTIANITY COMES TO ONEIDA COUNTRY

Editors' Introduction to Part I

In the first essay in Part I, Laurence M. Hauptman describes the Oneida world in central New York before the arrival of Christian missionaries. He defines the Oneidas' historic territory, outlines their role within the Iroquois League of the Five Nations, and briefly recounts some of their beliefs, including ones that corresponded to Christianity. He also stresses the Iroquoian importance of alliance—namely, the way the Five and later Six Nations brought outsiders, Indian as well as non-Indian, into their orbit through the mechanism of the Covenant Chain.

Karim M. Tiro then traces the early history of Oneida Christianity. The initial contact came in 1667, when Jesuit Jacques Bruyas arrived at the Oneida village of Kanonwalohale and established the St. Francis Xavier mission. Because he did not speak their native language, the Catholic missionary was successful only with the Oneida war captives who had an understanding of English and had previously been exposed to Christianity. Bruyas was followed by Jesuit Pierre Millet, who made inroads within the community until his presence was withdrawn in the mid-1680s because of severe tensions building between the Five Nations and the French. In 1701, the Society for the Propagation of the Gospel in Foreign Parts was established by the British monarchy, and it soon began organizing Anglican efforts to convert the Iroquois. In 1709, missionary Thomas Barclay was sent from England to Albany to establish a mission. He was followed by William Andrews, who moved the mission to Mohawk Country near the English outpost of Fort Hunter. Five years later, Andrews extended his proselytizing westward to the Oneida village of Oriske. Other Anglican missionaries followed Andrews, including Thomas Barclay Jr. and John Ogilvie, but they failed to convert a significant number of Oneidas; however, the Anglican missionary presence and Christianity were not completely lost on the Oneidas. Tiro describes how the missionaries' preaching actually led to the comingling of Christian and Iroquoian beliefs, with Christ as the Iroquoian Peacemaker, the Virgin Mary as Sky Woman, and angels as traditional spirit forces.

The Oneidas were exposed to the religious fervor of the Great Awakening from the 1740s until the American Revolution by Congregational ministers such as Gideon Hawley and Eleazar Wheelock, and, more importantly, by Samuel Kirkland, a Presbyterian missionary. Kirkland arrived at a time when the Oneida world was rapidly changing and facing multiple crises—battlefield losses in colonial wars, white encroachment, intratribal schisms, epidemics, and alcohol. Although the missionary served the key role of intermediary between the white and Indian worlds, his version of Christianity characterized the Indians as being cursed and facing a fiery hell. He was tolerated by some Oneidas, such as chiefs Skenandoah and Agwaelendongwas (Chief Good Peter), the latter who served as his assistant. However, in the quarter century before his death in 1808, Kirkland began to broker deals with land companies and to secure compensation at the expense of the Oneidas, and he became more interested in promoting his plans for Hamilton-Oneida Academy, now Hamilton College. The result was that the majority of Oneidas repudiated him even before his death in 1808.

Both the Anglican Church, by then referring to itself in the United States as the Protestant Episcopal Church, and the Oneidas had to rebuild after the American Revolution, a seminal event in both of their histories. Because many of the Anglican clerics in New York were Loyalists during the Revolution and refused to take oaths to the American Congress, they found themselves in disfavor during the war and in the years that immediately followed. Church leaders faced a crisis, forcing them to adapt and lead the church in new directions. At the same time, the Oneidas were in crisis as well, with most allying themselves with the American cause, unlike most within the nations of the Iroquois League, who served the British. The Oneidas, too, had to set out in a new direction and find new ways to cope with aggressive land speculators allied with Albany politicians who were knocking at their door after the Revolution. Indeed, from 1785 onward, the Oneidas were dispossessed of 99 percent of their central New York landholdings—millions of acres—in so-called state treaties.

Dissatisfied with Kirkland's complicity in tribal land losses, the Oneidas turned back to their Anglican religious roots after the missionary's death. Once again, the Oneidas needed intermediaries and allies because their world in central New York was coming apart. The millions of acres of Oneida lands were the necessary ingredient for the rise of the Empire State, since they were situated at a vital transportation crossroads that was essential for New York's economic growth after the Revolution. In order for New York State to expand east-west and north-south, private entrepreneurial interests in conjunction with Albany officials—be they Federalists, Jeffersonians, Clintonians, Democrats, or Whigs—and subsidized by public funds constantly picked away at Oneida lands from 1785 until the mid-1840s. By 1817, New York State began building the Erie Canal, which went right through Oneida lands. Now even more Oneidas believed that their fate was sealed. Already severely fractionated in their polity and religion, the Oneidas largely found it impossible to resist the pressures of land speculators and state and federal officials, leading a majority of the community to eventually migrate for its protection and survival west to Michigan Territory in the period 1822 to 1838, or to Ontario from 1839 to 1846.

In the last selection in Part I, Michael Oberg focuses on the controversial Mohawk Eleazer Williams and his role in bringing the Episcopal faith to the Oneidas. By the time Williams arrived in Oneida Country, some within the Indian leadership were already talking about moving out of central New York. Bishop John Henry Hobart encouraged the idea and saw the possibilities of extending the church's influence onto the frontier well beyond New York State. In 1816, Hobart, intent on extending the influence of the church, placed Williams as lay catechist at the newly established Oneida mission in New York. In Bishop Hobart's opinion, Williams, a descendant of the famous unredeemed captive Eunice Williams taken by the Mohawks in their 1704 raid on Deerfield, Massachusetts, was the perfect person to bring the faith to the Oneidas, since he had lived and been educated in both the Indian and white worlds; he was also familiar with both the Catholic and Anglican religious traditions and was a charismatic and fluent Native-language speaker. Despite his bizarre claim that he was the "lost dauphin" of the royal family of France, the Mohawk was a skillful preacher and soon succeeded in converting significant numbers of the Oneida "Pagan Party," later known as the Second Christian Party, to the Episcopal religion.

Williams was a schemer, an opportunist with little moral fiber, who worked for a decade and a half for the Ogden Land Company, which was intent on securing Oneida lands by "encouraging" Indian migration to Michigan Territory. Although he did not originate the idea of moving the Oneidas to the West, Williams conspired with agents of the Ogden Land Company to promote this plan. From 1820 onward, the Oneidas sent exploring parties to the West and ultimately decided to settle in Wisconsin, then the western part of Michigan Territory. After negotiating with the Menominees and Ho Chunks in 1821 and 1822, the Oneidas, along with the Stockbridge and Brothertown, were allowed to reside there. After the settlement of the Oneidas on their Duck Creek reservation and Hobart's elevation of Williams to deacon in 1824, the controversial Mohawk cleric, now married to a thirteen-year-old Menominee girl, turned his attention to other things, focusing on nonspiritual matters—namely, the acquisition of lands in the environs of Appleton. Many Oneidas broke with Eleazer Williams soon after their arrival in the West, and they later formally repudiated him in council, declaring him *persona non grata* in the early 1830s. The chain, now tarnished by Williams's actions and strange behavior, required polishing once again.

In need of allies to fend off Jacksonian Indian policies that threatened their removal from Wisconsin to Kansas, then part of Indian Territory, the Oneidas faced another crisis. Luckily for both the church and the Oneidas, Episcopal bishop Jackson Kemper, a compassionate and extraordinary churchman, arrived in Michigan Territory in 1834 and restored the damaged chain. The bishop became the Oneidas' greatest defender for the next four decades. Largely because of Kemper's influence, the majority of Wisconsin Oneidas remained within and allied to the Episcopal Church despite the 1834 arrival of a significant number of Oneida Methodists from New York led by Chief Jacob Cornelius.

1

THE ONEIDA WORLD BEFORE
CHRISTIANITY

Laurence M. Hauptman

THE ONEIDAS ARE ONE OF THE FIVE ORIGINAL nations of the Iroquois League or Confederacy, holding nine out of fifty sachemships within it. A sixth nation, the Tuscaroras, was incorporated into the League between 1711 and 1724. To the east of the Oneidas, the Mohawk Nation held sway, and to the west was the home-land of the Onondaga Nation, the central fire of the Iroquois League.[1] According to one estimate of the Oneidas before the smallpox epidemic of 1634, their population was between 1,500 and 1,800 individuals.[2]

The Oneidas' original homeland in today's central New York included approx-imately 5 to 6 million acres of land at the time of European contact. It stretched from the Saint Lawrence River valley to just beyond what is today the New York–Pennsylvania boundary line. At the heart of their estate was the short portage between the Mohawk River and Wood Creek, known as the Oneida Carrying Place, which was strategic for both the Hodinöhsö:ni´ and, later, for Euro-Americans. To the southeast are the headwaters of the Mohawk, which flows eastward until it joins the Hudson, which connects the Atlantic Ocean at New York City. On the north was Wood Creek, which, along with Fish Creek, Oneida Lake, and the Oswego River, was a major passageway to Lake Ontario and the rest of the Great Lakes. From Wood Creek, Oneida lands ran southeast along the Unadilla River to the Susquehanna and then to the second branch of the Delaware River. To the north, where great timber and wildlife resources abounded in the western Adiron-dacks, the Oneida homeland stretched from East Canada Creek to West Canada Creek near today's Poland, New York, and then west across the headwaters of the Black and Oswegatchie Rivers and northwest to the Saint Lawrence River following the shoreline of Lake Ontario southward to nearly the rift of the Onondaga River valley. It ran due south to a point five miles west of the outlet of Oneida Lake, one of the great fisheries of eastern North America, and then southeast to Chittenango Falls on Chittenango Creek and Cazenovia Lake. This territory then returned to its starting point via the headwaters of the Oswego River and the course of the Susquehanna.[3]

One of the central beliefs of Oneida existence, then and now, concerns a standing stone, an inanimate boulder unlike any other stone. The elders in central New York told the children stories about this magical stone and other Hodinöhsö:ni´ legends when storytelling was at a premium during the harsh winter months. It was supposed to bring good luck when Oneidas took the warpath. Unaided by human hands, it would suddenly appear every time the Oneidas would move their villages in their homeland. The Oneidas conducted their great councils around this sacred stone, where they resolved questions presented to them and worshipped the Creator.[4] Finally, when the village at Oneida Castle was founded, the stone remained there. Consequently, it is no coincidence that the Oneidas call themselves "Onyota´a:ká: the people of the standing stone."[5]

In the seventeenth century, the Oneida world was a matrilineal, matrilocal society organized into three clans—Wolf, Bear, and Turtle. Each clan was headed by a matron, and each clan appointed three chiefs. Clan mothers had control of chiefly titles. In the seventeenth century, the forest world was the province of men, and they handled diplomacy, the hunt, and war; however, in the clearing (or village), women had key roles in nominating male leadership, in horticulture, in child-rearing, and within the walls of the longhouse residence.[6] Longhouses were located within the Iroquois' palisaded villages and were directly associated with maternal lineages, since matrons owned the longhouses. These structures included three to five fireplaces and provided shelter for two nuclear families of five or six persons each. Longhouses were more than residential units. They became the Hodinöhsö:ni´ symbol of identity; hence, the Iroquois referred to themselves as the people of the longhouse.[7]

In 1634, the Dutch West India Company sent Harmen Meyndertsz van den Bogaert, a twenty-two-year-old barber surgeon, into Mohawk and Oneida Country to ascertain why fur supplies to the trading house at Fort Orange had declined. On December 30, van den Bogaert described an Oneida village in his journal. Referring to this palisaded village as a castle, he claimed that the community was "on a high hill, and was surrounded with two rows of palisades, 767 steps in circumference in which there are 66 houses, but built much better and higher than all the others." The Dutchman observed "many wooden gables on the houses which were painted with all sorts of animals" and indicated that the Oneidas, unlike other Indians he had previously encountered, slept "mostly on platforms" in their longhouses. He appeared to be startled by the substantial food supply within these longhouses in the dead of winter: "I saw houses with 60, 70 and more dried salmon" there.[8] It is clear from this description that Oneidas took advantage of the great fishing opportunities that existed a short distance from their villages. These included access to Fish and Wood Creeks as well as to the Mohawk, Oneida, and Oswego Rivers. Even more importantly was their proximity to Oneida Lake and to Lake Ontario, which provided a limitless food supply and opportunities to sell fish to other Native peoples as well.[9]

Despite the importance of fishing, the Oneidas were primarily horticultural-ists and supplemented their food supply by hunting. They raised maize, beans, and squash, referred to by the Iroquois as the "three sisters." Besides domesticated crops, they gathered wild plant foods, such as wild berries and nuts. As hunters, they sought out the white-tailed deer, which was their primary meat supply. Thus, as the van den Bogaert journal shows, their diet was quite diverse. The Dutchman described a vast variety of foods that were served in Mohawk and Oneida Coun-try, including bear, beaver, turkey, rabbit, venison, fresh and dried salmon, corn bread, baked and boiled pumpkins, dried blueberries and strawberries, sunflower seeds, chestnuts, and beans and corn, some cooked in bear fat and others cooked in turkey fat.[10]

Early contact with Europeans in the first four decades of the seventeenth cen-tury brought rapid changes to Oneida Country. Most devastating were waves of epidemic diseases, such as smallpox, that came as a result of contact. With the founding of trade at Fort Orange by the Dutch in 1614, Oneidas were slowly incor-porated into the world economy through their trade in deerskin hides and, more importantly, beaver skins. More than two decades before Jesuit missionaries came to Oneida territory, van den Bogaert's journal describes many of these changes. By that time, the Mohawks and Oneidas were already using European-introduced iron axes, brass kettles, nails, razors, scissors, and cloth and seeking these items out in trade.[11]

As one of the founding members of the Iroquois League, the Oneidas were affected by their relations with the other four nations. While the Iroquois League promoted cooperation that at times led to powerful alliances among its members, when consensus could not be achieved, individual nations often went their own way. Despite frequent warfare in the seventeenth century that included Iroquois conflicts with the Wenros (1638), Eries (1650–1680), Neutrals (1650–1651), Susque-hannocks (1675–1676), and Ojibwes (1696–1701), ethnohistorian Jack Campisi rightly points out that rarely did "all the Five Nations take the field in concerted action against a common enemy." He adds, "The League represented a higher level of integration, a shared symbol based on commonly held beliefs and values given voice through an elaborate ceremonial structure."[12] Unity, however, was encour-aged through seasonal ceremonies and common rituals. The Iroquoian ceremon-ial cycle included and still includes the Midwinter (January/February), Maple (March), Cornplanting (May), Strawberry (June), Green Corn (September), and Harvest (October) ceremonies.

Two major myths of the Iroquoian cosmology are the Earth Grasper, or the Woman Who Fell from the Sky (Sky Woman), and the Message of the Peacemaker, or the Origin of the League of the Iroquois. The first recounts the Iroquois version of the creation of the world through Sky Woman's fall from Sky World. It has been called "one of the great pieces of ancient oral literature of the Americas."[13] In its numerous versions retold over the centuries, the epic offers the reason for women's special role in Iroquoian society, describes the relationship of human beings to the natural world, explains the origins of Iroquoian horticulture and dance, and offers an explanation for why life is both a blessing and a hardship. The prominent anthropologist William N. Fenton described nine component parts of this epic: the description of the Sky World, the "uprooting of the life-giving tree," the "casting down of Sky Woman," water animals diving to save Sky Woman, "the establishment of the earth on the turtle's back," "Sky Woman's daughter gives birth to twins known as 'the Good-Minded and Evil-Minded," "Good-Minded, a culture hero, frees the animals pent up by his twin brother and procures maize," the twins battle in a Herculean manner, and, finally, the "banishment of Evil-Minded while Good-Minded and Sky Woman return to the Sky World, promising to return one day."[14]

The other epic, first recorded by Euro-Americans in 1743, is related to the Peacemaker's legacy—namely, how the Five Nations stopped feuding and joined in the Great Peace, thereby creating the Iroquois League. This is at the heart of what the Iroquois call, in the Oneida language, *Kayanla:kówa*, the Great Law of Peace and Power.[15] The Peacemaker, born of a virgin on the north side of a great lake, crosses these waters in a white stone canoe with the message from the Creator for the five nations to end their incessant internecine warfare. He meets grief-stricken Hiawatha, whose family had been killed by Onondaga chief Thadoda:ho'. After hearing the Peacemaker's message and receiving wampum brought by the Peacemaker to help him deal with his grief and wipe away his tears, Hiawatha accepts the assignment to help end conflict within the five nations. The importance of how grief is overcome becomes an important aspect of Iroquoian existence. The Peacemaker through his convert and missionary Hiawatha slowly convinces the Oneidas, Mohawks, Cayugas, and Senecas of the rightness of this plan, but he is stymied by Thadoda:ho' at Onondaga. Thadoda:ho', a cannibal, is reluctant to accept the message. He has earthly and evil thoughts and is often depicted by Iroquois artists as having snakes in his hair. Faced with opposition from the four nations and given assurances that the Onondagas would have a special place—more sachems within the league structure than other nations—the practical Thadoda:ho' agrees to end his cannibalistic ways, have the snakes combed from his hair, and join in with the other four nations. He accepts the Creator's message brought by the Peacemaker and his emissary Hiawatha, thus forming the Iroquois League of the Five Nations.[16]

In addition to the concept of the Peacemaker's virgin birth and his journey, the epic has other elements that parallel Christian theology. Similar to Christ miraculously walking on water, the Peacemaker is able to magically cross the waters in his stone canoe. Moreover, the theme of redemption, so much a part of Catholic theology, is included in this Iroquoian epic. Even evildoers and cannibals such as Chief Thadoda:ho´ have the ability to change and reform themselves.[17]

This epic is still repeated today by the Iroquois nations in the Condolence Council, a ritual for mourning and installing chiefs. The ritual is essential for understanding the Hodinöhsö:ni´, their beliefs, culture, and history, as well as the nature of Iroquois–Indian and later Iroquois–Euro-American diplomacy. In the colonial era, the Condolence was "the ritual paradigm that governed the proceedings [of forest diplomacy and] guided the behavior of Iroquoian and Algonquian speakers alike throughout the lower Great Lakes."[18] Both chiefs and colonial officials were mourned during this ritual. According to Fenton, in order to cement alliances, the Hodinöhsö:ni´ employed metaphors about "keeping the paths open by clearing rivers, rapids, and roads, polishing a chain and maintaining a perpetual fire to bind." He adds, "Perhaps the most famous metaphor was the Chain. Keeping the Chain of Friendship bright and free of rust required frequent meetings."[19] As we will see in later chapters, the metaphor was later carried to Wisconsin by the Oneidas in the third and fourth decades of the nineteenth century and had a direct bearing on the formation of the Oneida bond with the Episcopal Church. Moreover, the Wisconsin Oneidas' celebration of July 4 in the mid-nineteenth century had elements of the Condolence Council ritual as well.[20]

The ceremony, in effect, was used to reinvigorate Iroquois existence, renew political forms, restore society, and build or strengthen alliances. The Iroquois expectation was that all the guests and outsiders observe and respect these traditions and learn the proper etiquette and forms of the ritual. Fenton adds that through the seriousness and religiosity of the Condolence Council, the Iroquois attempted to manipulate the foreboding white world to their own advantage.[21] Perhaps this is overstating its role; however, in order for Iroquoian people to make sense of the "foreigner," they had to incorporate him or her into their cultural ways of doing things, which might or might not mean surreptitiously manipulating the situation.

Much like what the Peacemaker did for Hiawatha, the Condolence Council does for mourning dead chiefs, lifting up the minds of bereaved relatives, and installing successor sachems. The council consists of sixteen separate elements, including rites known as the Roll Call of the Founders, the Welcome at the Wood's Edge, the Recitation of Laws, the Requickening Address, the Six Songs of Requiem, and the Charge to the New Chief. Invited guests gathered at the wood's edge and were welcomed into the village, where the chiefs read the Roll Call of the Founders, recounting the sacrifices of past leaders. Dead chiefs were recognized for their service to the nation, mourned, and their successors raised and validated, "requickened" in the titles of the deceased, and charged in their new duties to carry out the people's will.[22] The ritual was followed by a feast. In addition to the social dancing that always followed the end of the ten-day period of the Condolence Council, a game of lacrosse, known as the Creator's game, was included as part of the rite. It was meant to entertain the Creator, but it also defused social tensions, discouraged internecine warfare, kept warriors fit, and encouraged the crowd to cheer players who were relatives of the deceased.

On the surface, one might inaccurately conclude that the coming of Christianity submerged the traditional Oneida religious traditions and altered them beyond recognition, especially after the Oneidas resettled in Wisconsin. Yet, Campisi states that the Good-Minded Twin, *Thaluhyawá:ku* in the Iroquoian creation epic, "became synonymous with Jesus Christ." He also points out that the Oneidas' tradition of collecting water before sunrise on Easter morning fit well within the Oneida traditions since they used their own version of holy water, *kanekká:nol*, for "therapeutic purposes."[23] In the accounts of the WPA Oneida Language and Folklore Project of the late 1930s, the False Face Medicine Society is described as continuing in the Wisconsin setting even into the twentieth century, and references to Oneida traditional herbalist practices are also described as persisting. In addition, the ceremonial bestowing of Oneida names continued during July 4 celebrations at Oneida into the mid-nineteenth century. Moreover, Oneidas brought to Wisconsin traditional all-night wakes accompanied by songs and eulogies in Oneida that often lasted three days. They also brought the traditional Iroquoian ten-day feast, at which time possessions of the deceased were distributed to kin and friends, to their new surroundings.[24]

Although clans declined and ceremonies were abandoned, the "few remaining features relative to health, spirits, and death persisted but were absorbed into the corpus of Christian belief."[25] I was to observe this firsthand on June 14, 2016. On that day, I attended a ceremony at the Oneidas' Church of the Holy Apostles graveyard. I stood silently in the crowd, observing a solemn ceremony. His Excellency Reverend Matthew Gunter, the bishop of Fond du Lac, consecrated the Oneida cemetery containing gravesites of Oneidas and their non-Indian missionaries since the nation's move from New York in the 1820s and 1830s. The bishop read the names associated with this historic parish, paying homage to them, almost as if he was recounting the Roll Call of the Founders in a Condolence Council ritual, a reminder that the past and present sometimes intersect in mysterious and long-forgotten ways.[26]

Notes

1. The best overview of Oneida ethnohistory is still Jack Campisi, "Ethnic Identity and Boundary Maintenance in Three Oneida Communities" (PhD diss., State University of New York at Albany, 1974).

2. William A. Starna, "The Oneida Homeland in the Seventeenth Century," in *The Oneida Indian Experience: Two Perspectives*, ed. Jack Campisi and Laurence M. Hauptman (Syracuse, NY: Syracuse University Press, 1988) 16.

3. Ibid., 25–28. The Oneidas' traditional territorial boundaries were confirmed after the American Revolution in the federal treaty with the Six Nations at Fort Stanwix, 7 *Stat.*, 15 (October 22, 1784).

4. Anthony Wonderley, *Oneida Iroquois Folklore, Myth, and History: New York Oral Narrative from the Notes of H. E. Allen* (Syracuse, NY: Syracuse University Press, 2004), 1–14, 24–31; Charles A. Huegenin, "The Sacred Stone of the Oneidas," *New York Folklore Quarterly* 8 (1957): 16–22.

5. Karim M. Tiro, *The People of the Standing Stone: The Oneida Nation from the Revolution Through the Era of Removal* (Amherst: University of Massachusetts Press, 2011), 1–2.

6. Campisi, "Ethnic Identity and Boundary Maintenance," 37–43; Elisabeth Tooker, "Women in Iroquois Society," in *Extending the Rafters: Interdisciplinary Approaches to Iroquoian Studies*, ed. Michael Foster, Jack Campisi, and Marianne Mithun (Albany, NY: SUNY Press, 1984), 109–23.

7. William N. Fenton, *The Great Law and the Longhouse: A Political History of the Iroquois Confederacy* (Norman: University of Oklahoma Press, 1998), 23–24.

8. Harmen Meyendertsz van den Bogaert, *A Journey into Mohawk and Oneida Country, 1634–1635*, trans. and ed. Charles Gehring and William A. Starna (Syracuse, NY: Syracuse University Press, 1988), 12–13.

9. Ibid., 12–22.

10. Ibid.

11. Ibid.

12. Campisi, "Ethnic Identity and Boundary Maintenance," 51.

13. Demus Elm and Harvey Antone, *The Oneida Creation Story*, trans. and ed. Floyd G. Lounsbury and Bryan Gick (Lincoln: University of Nebraska Press, 2000), 2.

14. Fenton, *The Great Law and the Longhouse*, 35.

15. Amos Christjohn and Maria Hinton, *An Oneida Dictionary*, ed. Clifford Abbott (Green Bay: University of Wisconsin at Green Bay, 1996), 597.

16. Fenton, *The Great Law and the Longhouse*, 51–103.

17. Ibid.

18. Ibid., 10.

19. William N. Fenton, "Structure, Continuity, and Change in the Process of Treaty-making," in *The History and Culture of Iroquois Diplomacy: An Interdisciplinary Guide of the Treaties of the Six Nations and Their League*, ed. Francis Jennings, William N. Fenton, Mary A. Druke, and David R. Miller (Syracuse, NY: Syracuse University Press, 1985), 22.

20. "Celebration of the Fourth of July at Oneida Settlement: Speech of Daniel Bread," *Green Bay Advocate*, July 4, 1854. For an analysis of how these Oneida Fourth of July speeches and commemorations fit into the Condolence Council paradigm, see Lawrence M. Hauptman and L. Gordon McLester III, *Chief Daniel Bread and the Oneida Nation of Indians of Wisconsin* (Norman: University of Oklahoma Press, 2005), 121–26.

21. Fenton, *The Great Law and the Longhouse*, 6.

22. Ibid., 135–223.

23. Campisi, "Ethnic Identity and Boundary Maintenance," 128.

24. Ibid., 127–31.

25. Ibid.

26. For more on the eulogy, the Roll Call of the Founders in the Condolence Council ritual, see Fenton, *The Great Law and Longhouse*, 190–202.

2

ONEIDAS AND MISSIONARIES, 1667–1816

Karim M. Tiro

THE STANDARD MODEL OF MISSIONIZATION IS AS STRAIGHTFORWARD as it is familiar: a missionary goes forth, instructs nonbelievers, wins their understanding and acceptance of his or her faith, and performs the necessary rituals of initiation. The process is repeated, perhaps with the number of converts increasing (the missionaries might hope) geometrically. However, a brief review of the introduction of Christianity among the Oneidas shows that missionization in fact followed a far more complex path. The cultural gap between seventeenth-century Europeans and Native Americans was wide and the ability to communicate across it limited. In the beginning, a missionary's ability to gain a hearing depended mostly on the community's misfortunes in the form of war or disease or a critical need for European goods. It was mostly the presence of these problems that gave Native people incentive to engage with missionaries and their alien practices and ideas. As a result, Native converts to Christianity did not abandon all, or even most, of their traditional beliefs. Despite the either-or connotations of the word *conversion*, it is misguided to think of the process as absolute or exclusive. In the indigenous North American worldview, belief was not a zero-sum game, and learning new ways did not automatically invalidate traditional ones.

The introduction of Christianity among the Oneidas can be considered to have unfolded in three distinct phases. The first was Roman Catholic. It began in 1667 and emanated from the Saint Lawrence Valley. The Oneidas' initial direct, sustained encounters with Christian missionaries began with the arrival of resident Jesuit priests dispatched from Quebec City, the capital of New France. These men had a limited impact on religious practice at the principal Oneida settlement, but they facilitated the involvement of numerous Oneidas in the establishment of the Catholic mission village of Kahnawake, across the Saint Lawrence River from Montreal.

The second phase originated in Albany in 1690 and lasted until after the Seven Years' War. This phase saw the spread of various Dutch, English, and German forms of Protestantism westward up the Mohawk River. These missionaries and settlers interacted most directly with the Mohawks who constituted the "Eastern Door" of the Iroquois Confederacy. Routine interaction between the Mohawks and the Oneidas ensured that the latter were not left untouched. Since missionaries were few and their presence sporadic, much of the work of sustaining Christianity in the Five (then Six) Nations during this period was left in the hands of Native converts. This permitted Mohawks to reinterpret Christianity from an Iroquois perspective and to indigenize it. The resulting practice was syncretic, merging rituals and concepts that were common to both while downplaying incongruities.

The third phase, which began in earnest shortly after the end of the Seven Years' War, was the most significant. It involved the near-constant presence of missionaries among the Oneidas. These missionaries were based in Connecticut, Massachusetts, and New Jersey and reflected the evangelical "New Light" wings of the allied Congregational and Presbyterian churches. These missionaries represented the first real effort on the part of American colonial society to engage Native Americans in religious matters. But if the evangelical and egalitarian orientation of New Light Christianity sparked colonists' interest in the state of Natives' souls generally, the motivation to save those of the Oneidas in particular had to do with the Oneidas' location, which lay directly in their preferred path of future settlement.

The Oneida experience also highlights the significant role women played in the success or failure of particular missions, especially early on in the religious encounter. Although European men usually were the purveyors of Christian ritual and doctrine, Native women were the key mediators and practitioners of Christianity in their communities during the seventeenth and eighteenth centuries. That they remained influential as followers and promoters of Christianity is certain, but the patriarchal influence of Euro-American culture caused Native women's religious authority to diminish in subsequent years.

* * *

The French relied on Natives to provision and defend the colony of New France and to supply the furs that made it an economically viable colony. Colonial leaders supported missionary activities insofar as these promised to strengthen ties with Native peoples. The Jesuits received particular favor. They had proven themselves highly motivated and systematic in their approaches to proselytizing Native peoples, in particular through their commitment to learning Native languages. The Jesuits also demonstrated a tolerance for other cultures that was not universally shared among Catholic missionary orders but was demonstrably effective in building relationships with Natives.[1]

France's relationship with the Iroquois, however, was extremely fraught. The French had aligned themselves with the Montagnais and Algonquin nations. These peoples were relatively close to the French settlements and had access to the thickest, most desirable furs. In aligning themselves with the Algonquians and Montagnais the French inherited the friends of these nations, like the Huron, but they also inherited their enemies. The Oneidas and the rest of the Five Nations Iroquois were among those enemies. Beginning in the 1640s, as the Iroquois attacked their enemies on all sides to secure captives to replace people lost to epidemic disease, conflict with the French intensified. The Iroquois were deeply suspicious of the French and resisted French missionization, sometimes even killing priests.

Ultimately, it was force that opened Iroquoia to Jesuit missionaries. After the Marquis de Tracy defeated the Mohawks in 1666, the Five Nations agreed to peace with the French.[2] One of France's demands was that the Iroquois allow Jesuits to come and reside among them. It was in this context that the French Jesuit Jacques Bruyas undertook the first sustained attempt to convert Oneidas to Christianity. He arrived at their principal village in September 1667. Bruyas had arrived in Quebec City from France only about a year earlier. This was his first real challenge in America. To fulfill the terms of their agreement with the French, Oneida men erected a house for the mission, which Bruyas named after Saint Francis Xavier. But Bruyas's efforts were hamstrung by his inability to communicate in the Oneida language. In January 1668, he wrote his superior, "What can a man do who does not understand their language, and who is not Understood when he speaks? . . . As Yet, I do nothing but stammer." Bruyas was left to focus on baptizing children and the very sick.[3]

The Oneidas initially saw Bruyas more as a potential hostage in the event of future conflict with the French than as a teacher. They did not see much purpose in altering their traditional practices to suit his preferences. Bruyas was challenged by those seeking to uphold traditional religious beliefs and practices. A woman claimed that a voice speaking from a pot foretold an attack on the community. This initiated daily "dancing, singing, and feasting." Bruyas complained that this was "a powerful deterrent to our prayers" and attributed the woman's revelation to "the Devil." He was similarly disturbed by the Iroquois practice of analyzing, and sometimes acting on, the content of dreams. Bruyas recognized this as deeply rooted in their culture and "very hard to cure."[4]

What saved Bruyas's mission from irrelevance was the reality that Christianity was, in fact, already present among the Oneidas. From 1626 to 1649, the Jesuits had missionized the Erie, Neutral, and Huron peoples around Lake Simcoe and Lake Huron, the country the French called "Huronia." While the same cultural and linguistic chasm existed between those peoples and the French, their economic relationships had been more cooperative, and some Natives had turned to the Jesuits for help in the wake of epidemic disease. The Jesuit response had been robust; between 1634 and 1650, the mission to Huronia involved no fewer than twenty-four Jesuit missionaries. Of those, ten worked for more than a decade and seven from twelve to eighteen years—long enough to gain the linguistic and cultural knowledge needed to translate Christian ideas.[5] When the Iroquois conquered these nations at midcentury, a significant minority of the captives they seized and adopted brought Christian ideas with them. As a result, the first Oneida Christians were not Oneidas who were converted to Christianity but rather Christian Algonquians, Eries, Neutrals, or Hurons whose personal identities had been converted to Oneida ones.

According to Bruyas's estimate, no less than two-thirds of the Oneida population was adopted.[6] While most of these individuals did not take any more interest in Christianity in their new homes than they had in their old, Bruyas found a small group living among the Oneidas who found solace in Christianity—or at least the continuity Christian worship provided between their present and former lives. Prior to Bruyas's arrival, a female Erie adoptee named Gandeacteua had fostered Christianity among the Oneidas by saying prayers and having others repeat them. Gandeacteua and her cohort welcomed Bruyas's ability to perform rituals and instruct them further. However, as historian Daniel Richter has pointed out, Christianity created strains within the community. To the extent that Bruyas discouraged his charges from participating in traditional rituals that were supposed to sustain the well-being of the family, clan, or community, he could be seen as promoting an agenda that was antisocial in its effects if not in its intent.[7]

It was likely for this reason that Gandeacteua and her husband, Tonsanhoten, as well as five others (some Oneidas by birth, some adopted) left the main Oneida town for the Saint Lawrence Valley in the winter of 1667–1668. In Iroquois society, and indeed in any society in which the principle of consensus is deeply valued, separation was a common solution to chronic disagreement. Under Jesuit auspices, Gandeacteua and Tonsanhoten founded a new community of Native Roman Catholics at Kentaké (La Prairie). In 1668, another small party departed Oneida to join the first settlers. Gandeacteua's community grew quickly. It moved to a location opposite Montreal in 1677 and became known as Kahnawake. Over the ensuing decades, Kahnawake developed into an important northeastern pole of Iroquois settlement. It drew Iroquois settlers from multiple nations but especially from the Mohawk, with which it ultimately became most closely identified. As historian Jon Parmenter has noted, this movement into a new area for ostensibly religious reasons had important strategic and environmental benefits for the Iroquois.[8]

Culturally, the Roman Catholic community of Kahnawake honored the tradition of female leadership and even amplified women's religious roles. The preponderance of women discussing Christian matters in the missionary reports at Kahnawake, Oneida, and elsewhere is striking. This perhaps reflects a tradition of women serving as cultural intermediaries—akin to the roles they played when they married traders—but also as community leaders. At Kahnawake, much of the religious activity was supervised by women, sometimes organized into single-sex societies. As Richter has observed, "The cult of the Virgin Mary, its veneration of female saints, and its sisterhoods of nuns appealed strongly to the matrilineal principles of Iroquois culture. Especially at Kahnawake, priests consciously built on that appeal by organizing female sodalities" and encouraging women to follow holy examples.[9]

Bruyas was reassigned in 1670 and replaced at Oneida by fellow Jesuit Pierre Millet in 1672. Like Bruyas, Millet primarily baptized only Oneidas who were dangerously ill. However, having already spent several years at Onondaga, Millet was more assertive, even confrontational. For example, in 1674, knowing that an eclipse was coming, he "challenged the elders and, in particular, some jugglers [shamans]" to predict its precise time. "The more I pressed them, the more they were abashed," he gloated.[10] This strategy—to convert or discredit influential men—had mixed results, winning some minds, perhaps, but probably fewer hearts. As had been the case with Bruyas's mission, Catholicism was better served by the efforts of a knowledgeable female convert. Millet reported that a convert named Félicité Gannondadik "was able to assume and ever to maintain a certain ascendancy over all the other Christians." A Huron by birth, Félicité had spent several years living in an Ursuline convent in Quebec City. Millet reported, "She thoroughly knows all the prayers, the chants of the Church, and the mysteries of our Faith; and she explains them so clearly that the men themselves willingly listen to her as their teacher."[11]

Millet remained until 1685, when he was withdrawn along with many other Jesuits as war between the Iroquois and the French was brewing. The concern for the safety of missionaries was not misplaced, but in Millet's case things played out differently than anyone might have anticipated. In the midst of King William's War, Millet, then on the northern shore of Lake Ontario, was captured by some Onondagas. His captors turned him over to his erstwhile Oneida hosts. Some Oneida clan matrons decided not only to adopt him but to do so as Odatshete, one of the League sachems. This made him nearly immune from harm by any ill-minded pro-English Iroquois. Returning to Oneida, Millet was pleasantly surprised to see material evidence of autonomous Christian practice in the form of crucifixes on graves and rosaries. Clearly, some of his followers had sustained Christianity in his absence.[12] Millet also encountered Oneidas asking him to baptize their children and hear their confessions. Beyond the purification symbolism, baptism was thought to have curative value. It was also a gesture of alliance with, and goodwill toward, Europeans and their god—a god who could presumably help with other problems, too.[13]

The Iroquois sought equilibrium in their relationships with the competing European colonial powers, and Millet's adoption was part of that balancing act. While it made the English apoplectic, it did not ultimately bend the Oneidas decisively toward Catholicism or the French. Over the course of the decades that followed, the large size of the Mohawk population at Kahnawake encouraged the Jesuits to concentrate their efforts there rather than at the peripheral missions like Oneida. Thus, Oneida engagement with Catholicism in the 1700s continued, but more indirectly, through ongoing family and trade connections with Kahnawake.

* * *

Protestantism made its way up the Mohawk River to the Oneidas only haltingly before the middle of the eighteenth century, and was also mediated to a significant degree by Mohawks. The first settlers at Fort Orange (which became Albany after the English conquest in 1664) were Dutch. Of all the European colonizing powers, the Dutch had demonstrated the least interest in converting the Natives. Perhaps this was a function of the broad tolerance that characterized the seventeenth-century Dutch Republic, or perhaps it was the fact that the Dutch did not practice a brand of Christianity that placed a high priority on evangelization. Or perhaps the Dutch near the mouth of the Mohawk were simply too busy minding the fur trade. Whatever the case, little transmission of Christianity took place until the English takeover. Mohawks and Oneidas at Fort Orange might attend a Christian ceremony or receive a very occasional visit from a clergyman in their villages, but little effort was made to instruct them.

In the 1680s, the Dutch Reformed dominie of Albany, Godfridius Dellius, made the first notable effort to proselytize the Iroquois. Although he did not spend much time with the Mohawks, he supervised the translation of some psalms, the Belgic Confession, and the Ten Commandments. The translator was Hilletie van Olinda, a woman with a Mohawk mother and Dutch father. Van Olinda had grown up among the Mohawk but was married to a Dutchman and lived in Schenectady. Given van Olinda's background, we may presume the translations were better able to convey theological concepts than if they had been made by a trader.[14] The limited nature of Dellius's missionary work made it unlikely that the two hundred Mohawks he claimed he had baptized by 1693 had a thorough understanding of the faith, although the sixteen he admitted to church membership, who included van Olinda, probably understood more. Most of these individuals lived at the far eastern end of the Mohawk River, closest to the Dutch settlements, or upriver at the nearest Mohawk town, Tiononderoge. The mission was interrupted, though, when Dellius and van Olinda were dismissed over their involvement in a huge land swindle that came to light in 1698.[15]

From that point onward, the Mohawks were served by clergymen based in Schenectady or Albany. Bernardus Freeman achieved some proficiency in the Mohawk language and used it to translate parts of the Book of Common Prayer.[16] However, he removed to Long Island in 1705, never to return. Johannes Lydius continued to perform services until his death in 1710. By this time, most Mohawks of

Tiononderoge had been baptized. About three dozen Mohawks expressed deeper commitment, regularly attending services or seeking further instruction. The earlier betrayal by Dellius and van Olinda might have given them pause, but the importance of remaining on good terms with the colonists only increased as the latter grew in numbers and power. This interfered with Mohawk subsistence activities and allowed alcohol to flow more freely into their villages. Some Mohawks hoped that adopting some of the colonizers' spiritual practices might improve relations with the newcomers—and counteract the ills that came with them.

Although the English disdained the Dutch mission effort, that did not prompt them to exert themselves much more forcefully.[17] When the Anglican Reverend Thomas Barclay assumed responsibility for an Anglican mission to the Mohawks in 1709, he deemed the Mohawks "so ignorant and scandalous that they can scarce be considered Christians." Barclay remained in the comfort of Albany and did not learn any Mohawk.[18] In 1712, Rev. William Andrews was appointed missionary to the Mohawks. Andrews had the benefit of the recently erected Fort Hunter, situated near Tiononderoge. The fort strengthened English–Mohawk ties of security and trade, and its chapel was equipped with communion silver gifted to the Mohawks by Queen Anne. But Andrews lived in the fort rather than in Tiononderoge itself and, like Barclay, did not learn Mohawk. Andrews's strategy was to use translators—one from English to Dutch and then another from Dutch to Mohawk. This was hardly a recipe for clear communication. As had been the case with his predecessors, a significant portion of whatever influence he enjoyed was a result of the activity of womenfolk. Andrews acknowledged that his message was mediated by "a great many very good [Mohawk] Women, . . . [who would] meet together at one of their Wigwams or houses and one or two of them that have better Memorys than the rest repeat over again what the[y] have heard to the others."[19]

When Andrews extended his efforts to the Oneidas in 1714, things went badly awry. He visited them to baptize children who had at least one parent professing Christianity. These were Mohawks or Oneidas who had been baptized by Catholic or Dutch Reformed clergy. Some of the children died shortly afterward, leading to claims that Andrews's malpractice had caused the deaths.[20] From that point onward, the Oneidas preferred to avail themselves of baptismal services from clergy among the German Palatine settlers who took up lands between the Mohawk town of Canajoharie and the easternmost Oneida settlement of Oriske. These small German settlements formed symbiotic trade and defense arrangements, first with the more proximate Mohawks but also later with the Oneidas.[21]

Andrews gave up his Mohawk ministry in 1719 because the Mohawks refused his attempts to alter their cultural practices, such as changing marriage ways to enforce fidelity and permanence. For the Mohawks, accepting some Christian rituals and practices was one thing, but abandoning their traditional ones was quite another. As his flock dwindled to only about two dozen, Andrews lamented,

"Heathens they are, and Heathens they will still be."[22] No successor to Andrews was appointed until Henry Barclay (son of Thomas) resumed the mission in 1734, staying on until 1746. Barclay was also hampered by a lack of linguistic proficiency, but the Mohawks responded well to his efforts to teach them to read and write in their own language. He was in turn replaced by Rev. John Ogilvie between 1750 and 1760. Neither of these men seem to have achieved notable success, and yet—just as Millet had observed among the Oneidas—an indigenous, autonomous Christianity persisted even in the absence of a missionary. In explaining this phenomenon, one scholar who has studied the Anglican mission to the Mohawk particularly closely, William Hart, has highlighted the activity of Mohawk catechists. Many of these catechists were also sachems and therefore particularly influential. Working in the absence of missionaries, they could—and did—interpret Christianity in indigenous terms. For example, they commingled conceptions of Christ and the Iroquois Peacemaker, the Virgin Mary and Sky Woman, the Christian Heaven and the Sky World, and angels and traditional guardian spirits.[23] Linguist Thomas McElwain's analysis of nineteenth-century Seneca hymns demonstrated that much of their specifically Christian content was altered in translation, that "non-Iroquoian feelings and expressions are largely omitted," and that "totally different sentiments have replaced eighteenth-century Anglican expression."[24] Under the tutelage of local Native practitioners, the Iroquois used Christianity independently to supplement their traditional beliefs with the goal of enhancing community well-being. They hoped that reading prayers, singing hymns, and getting baptized would foster cohesion, combat disease and alcoholism, and bring good hunting and harvests.

This syncretic, latitudinarian state of affairs was generally satisfactory to Sir William Johnson, who was appointed superintendent of Indian Affairs for the Northern Department in 1756. When it came to the Natives under his jurisdiction (and the tenants on his extensive estates, for that matter), Johnson was more concerned with securing their reliable support for Britain than he was with their spiritual lives. Johnson continued supporting the use of Mohawk catechists and schoolmasters and the translation of Christian texts into the Mohawk language.[25] A tributary of this stream of religious encounter flowed through Oneida country midcentury, and its relaxed attitude left much room for Native autonomy in interpreting and living Christianity. However, as the Seven Years' War drew to a close, it would be subsumed by a more powerful current emanating from different sources.

* * *

Beginning in the 1720s, the English colonies experienced a religious revival that would come to be known as the First Great Awakening. Christianity in the colonies became less doctrinal and more egalitarian and was observed with a new and overtly emotional fervor. The English colonies were now over a century old and, for the first time, the people of New England and the mid-Atlantic seaboard demon-strated sustained, widespread interest in converting Natives.[26] Their efforts began close to home, with the Algonquian peoples of southern New England, the Hudson Valley, Long Island, and New Jersey. However, the colonists quickly grew keen to expand their efforts into the backcountry—particularly regions they wished to settle in the near future.

New England's evangelical mission to the Oneidas began at the Susquehanna River town of Oquaga, where Oneidas predominated in a population that included Tuscaroras, Mohawks, Susquehannocks, and Tutelos in significant numbers. Oquaga was, as historian Laurence Hauptman has described it, a "refugee haven." Congregationalist missionary Elihu Spencer resided there in 1748–1749, assisted by Job Strong and Benjamin and Rebecca Kellogg Ashley. Of these, it was likely the interpreter, Rebecca Ashley, who most effectively introduced the town's residents to Christianity. Ashley had been born in Deerfield, Massachusetts, and taken cap-tive by Kahnawakes during the famous 1704 raid on that town. She spent the next twenty-three years at Kahnawake before returning to New England society. Ashley had previously served as an interpreter at the Mohican mission at Stockbridge, where she was particularly close to the Mohawks who resided there briefly. Never-theless, the Oquaga mission foundered, apparently as a result of the sectarian dif-ferences between Spencer and Benjamin Ashley, who professed a more radical Baptist faith. Particularly damaging was the fact that Benjamin Ashley convinced Rebecca to limit her service to Spencer to one speech per week.[27]

Yale-trained Congregationalist Rev. Gideon Hawley of Connecticut resumed the Oquaga mission in 1753, and he enlisted the services of Rebecca Ashley once again. Although Hawley learned Oneida, he could not preach or catechize without Ashley for much of the time he was there. Indeed, he praised Ashley as "a very good sort of woman and an extraordinary interpreter in the Iroquois language."[28] One of the principal figures in early American Calvinism, Rev. Jonathan Edwards, took a particular interest in the Oquaga mission—indeed, so much so that in 1755, he sent his ten-year-old son and namesake there to learn their language. How-ever, the Seven Years' War brought the mission to a halt once again the following year, and the missionaries were recalled to New England. Once again Christian practice did not lapse; it persisted under the leadership of a small cadre of con-verts, most notably Good Peter (Agwelondongwas), Isaac Dekayensese, and Adam Weavonwanoren.

As the war drew to a close, the missionaries returned, this time in greater numbers, and not just at Oquaga but at the new principal Oneida village, Kanon-walohale, as well. With the demise of New France, New Englanders looked still more eagerly to expand their settlements across the Hudson River and deep into Iroquoia. The Oneidas were now a particular focus of attention because Mohawks were leaving the region, principally for Canada. Hawley and Eleazar Wheelock, the director of Moor's Indian Charity School in Connecticut, received money from a land-speculating outfit, the Susquehannah Company, to encourage land sales and the creation of an academy to teach the Natives farming.[29] Between 1765 and 1769, as many as ten young Oneidas attended, before the Oneidas withdrew all the remaining children over concerns about their well-being. Wheelock also sent Algonquians connected with his school to the Oneidas. In the 1760s, these included Samson Occom (Mohegan), David Fowler (Montauk), Joseph Woolley (Delaware), and Joseph Johnson (Mohegan). Wheelock reasoned that, as Natives, they should have special cachet with the Oneidas and, as Natives, he could pay them significantly less than he would white missionaries. The Oneida response to these men was ambivalent. Most felt there was something not quite right about them: their manners and dress were distinctly colonial, they were inept hunters, and they did not speak Iroquoian languages. Historian Daniel Mandell also suggests that their emotional, "awakened" style of worship clashed with the more staid, Anglican-influenced ways. But it was beyond dispute that these Algonquians possessed Bible knowledge and had a thorough understanding of the Euro-American society that was on the march in the Oneidas' direction. As Brothertown Indian Thomas Commuck put it in 1855, the Oneidas valued Fowler's "'book learning,' and other useful knowledge he could offer of the 'pale faces.'"[30]

Wheelock sent Euro-American missionaries to the Oneidas as well. While most stayed for only a brief time, Samuel Kirkland, a Connecticut Presbyterian, arrived at Kanonwalohale in 1766 and would remain engaged with the Oneidas nearly until his death in 1808.[31] Kirkland had studied at Wheelock's school and the College of New Jersey (now Princeton). The Oneidas' acceptance of Kirkland had a strong pragmatic element: missionaries generally brought access to cash and goods. The Oneidas were particularly hopeful that Kirkland might get them a blacksmith—something that Sir William had denied them. The Oneidas also demonstrated an interest in having Kirkland assist them in building European-style cabins. Most importantly, Kirkland was another mediator who might help them better manage their relations with the Euro-Americans who were becoming increasingly numerous on their eastern border. As colonial politics grew increasingly contentious after the Seven Years' War, the Oneidas saw in Kirkland someone who might help them decipher the imperial crisis and perhaps even circumvent Sir William Johnson's domination. Kirkland and his backers were solidly in favor of the rebels, but we should not succumb to the erroneous notion that Kirkland "led" the Oneidas into their famous alliance with the Patriots. The Oneidas behaved as allies to the Patriots because they understood this to be the best strategy for remaining in secure possession of their homeland.[32]

For his part, Kirkland thought the Oneidas were in need of serious religious reform. He disapproved of many aspects of the Oneidas' syncretic religious practice and insisted they accept a Christianity closer to his own terms, even if this limited his popularity—which it did. The pro-Anglican sachem Tagawaron complained to Sir William Johnson about Kirkland's stricter baptismal standards. According to Tagawaron, Kirkland was "shutt[in]g up the way [i.e., path] to Heaven, or mak[in]g it very narrow."[33] An unapologetic Kirkland responded simply that "as to baptiz[in]g the child[re]n [of] drunkard[s], whoremongers, liars, thieves, profane, ignorant, foolish, I have no authority."[34] Kirkland likewise disapproved of the Oneidas' practice of holding feasts after performing baptisms. Feasts were an important component of Native ceremonies of healing and adoption. The resemblance of the "rebirth" of Christian baptism and the traditional Iroquois "requickening" of lost kinfolk underscored the connection, but Kirkland disputed the Oneidas' belief that feasting was an "essential part of the ordinance & without which it would avail nothing. They . . . practized feasting at Baptisms & for the most part dance & frolick the whole night."[35]

While Kirkland groused about the Oneidas' feasting, he happily fulfilled their requests to translate hymns into their language. The Oneidas had been exposed to Christian hymnody by Jesuit, Dutch Reformed, and Anglican missionaries, and integrated it with their own singing traditions. Schoolteacher David Fowler, a Montauk, had already noted in 1765 that "they take great Pleasure in learning to sing," and when Eleazar Wheelock's son, Ralph, visited the Oneidas in 1767, he was "surprized at the Proficiency they have made at which they Sang Several Sacred Hymns in their own Language."[36] Hymnody represented the fertile middle ground between Christian and indigenous religious practice and emerged as the center of Oneida Christianity. This was very much on display when Capt. Joseph Bloomfield's Continental Army regiment passed several days with the Oneidas at the end of July 1776. Bloomfield called the Natives "poor Savages" but credited them with "the sweetest, best & most harmonious singing I ever heard." He noted, "They carried all the parts of Music with the greatest Exactness & harmony."[37]

Unfortunately, the war that brought Bloomfield to Iroquoia wrought tremendous destruction there. By the end of the conflict, the Oneidas' population had been reduced by a third. Their towns were destroyed, and they were made refugees. To make matters worse, the functioning of the Iroquois Confederacy had been suspended during the conflict, and acrimony between Iroquois people who had taken different sides impeded its reestablishment. Kirkland had absented himself for the latter part of the war to become a military chaplain, but he returned to Kanonwalohale to share in the hardship of rebuilding. The reestablishment of his congregation was aided by the fact that two of his most stalwart converts, Good Peter and Skenandoah, were in positions of leadership. Kirkland made himself useful and gathered congregants together to help them cope with their misfortunes. His sermons regularly drew as many as two hundred Oneidas, including those in the "pagan" faction.[38] Although the members of that faction were more traditionalist in orientation, they were not rigidly exclusivist in their beliefs, and they were suffering the same difficulties. From Kirkland's sermons, they wished to learn the secret as to why white settlers, whom they associated with all manner of fraud, abuse, and liquor peddling, increasingly seemed so dominant.[39]

Postwar rebuilding took place under a constant threat of dispossession—a threat that proved all too real, as the Oneidas were deprived of nine-tenths of their land within a decade of the war's end. The Patriots had made little effort to conceal their hunger for Iroquois land before the war, and now they were in control. The state of New York and various land companies raced to strike deals with all the Iroquois nations. State officials, private speculators organized into companies large and small, and needy Euro-Americans showed up at Kanonwalohale to urge the Oneidas to sell or lease them land. The Oneidas hoped Kirkland would help them navigate this treacherous situation, as he had earlier pledged "not to purchase, accept of or one way own one foot of lands on the west side of the Hudson River." Kirkland even boasted to an associate that this "had done more to establish my character among the Indians than perhaps five hundred pounds in presents would have done."[40] But that was before the war, and this was now. In 1787 and 1788, Kirkland compromised his personal reputation—and that of his faith—by serving as a translator and lobbyist for the Phelps-Gorham Company, the Genesee Company of Adventurers, and the state of New York. In those capacities, he facilitated several land transactions that deprived the Oneidas and other Iroquois nations of millions of acres of land. As Kirkland began his land-dealing career, he preached a sermon in which he "observed that his Thoughts were too extensive, their Country so large that he could not collect himself, and urged the Propriety of selling a Part and then his Ideas would be more confined and he would preach better."[41] What Kirkland meant was that he thought the Oneidas could not become Christian until they lived the physically bounded, settled lives of Europeans. Most Oneidas did not accept the logic that Kirkland's opportunism was part of making them better Christians.

Kirkland's involvement in Iroquois dispossession set the stage for a competing mission operated by the Quakers that began in 1796. A visitor recounted how Blacksmith, a chief of the Pagan Party, summed up his distinction of Christian sects. He "stamped earnestly with his feet at the white preachers, whom he said, are 'Friendly to us till they get our trees and lands, and then they are no more our friends; but the Quakers are good people, and do not serve us so; I love the Quakers.'"[42] There were further contrasts, of course: Quakers did not attempt to transmit Christian doctrine, allowing the traditionalists greater spiritual autonomy. The Quakers' mission revolved around teaching Native American men to farm in the Euro-American fashion and women to spin wool. Unfortunately for the Oneidas, the promise that the Quakers showed as defenders of Native land rights did not prevent a treaty in 1798, and their interest waned. From the Quakers' perspective, the Oneidas did not take sufficient advantage of the agricultural and industrial assistance they were offering. In 1800, the Quakers relocated to Seneca country.[43]

That the Oneidas had permitted Kirkland to resume his mission perhaps had more to do with the Oneidas' need for a missionary who spoke their language than their personal regard for him. The Oneidas' continued interest in hymn singing demanded a bilingual minister. In April 1804—only a few months before poor health forced him to end his mission—Kirkland wrote in his journal that the celebrated Tuscarora "Capt. Cusick came to see me to assist me in translating & versifying several psalms & hymns with a view to get them printed."[44] In 1807, another Presbyterian arrived to replace Kirkland, Scottish-born Rev. William Jenkins. Despite Jenkins's support for the Oneidas' land rights, and his access to an Oneida translator, the Oneida Christian party complained about his inability to speak their language. In particular, they cited the crimp this placed in their singing. In December 1814, two Oneidas wrote that "altho they can sing now very well . . . they wish to learn new tunes." Jenkins personally documented the ongoing importance of hymnody earlier that year. Describing the passing of Oneida John Bread, he wrote that the dying man "requested some young men who watched with him through the night to sing a hymn in which he joined them. . . . Finding his death approaching, he took leave of all present—joined in singing another hymn, and immediately died, as one falling asleep."[45] To fill the job of bilingual songmaster, the Oneida turned to a new and promising candidate, a Kahnawake Mohawk raised among New England Congregationalists. His name was Eleazer Williams.

* * *

Eleazer Williams embodied all three phases of Oneida Christianity up to that point. He was an Iroquois man born into the Catholicism of a mission town founded by Oneidas. He had been raised in the Congregationalism that had spawned the Kirkland mission, and he now professed the Anglican Episcopalianism that had dominated Oneida Christianity for the first half of the eighteenth century. In the beginning, Williams seemed a superb candidate to foster the ongoing development of a syncretic Iroquois Christianity that was already 150 years old. Ironically, of all the missionaries whom the Oneidas received, Williams would arguably prove the most vexing.

At the very outset of the European–Native encounter, the only way for European ideology to be made assimilable by peoples of the Americas was for it to be thoroughly reinterpreted. In the opinion of many Europeans, the doctrine was fatally compromised in the process. A few argued to the contrary that the process was a salutary one: Christianity was, in fact, being stripped of its European superfluities and reduced to its essence. In any case, missionaries faced a stark choice: they could either persist and hope for better, or they could give up. Most gave up. Over time, however, Natives' widening interactions with Europeans and their descendants would work significant changes on their lives, societies, economies, and cultures. The path missionaries would have to walk would become less tortuous than that of Bruyas, Ashley, or Kirkland. But in 1814, Oneidas still prized a man who could speak—and sing—with them in their own language, thereby allowing them to understand and practice Christianity in their own way.

Notes

1. There is significant English-language literature on the Jesuit missions to the Iroquois. See James Axtell, *The Invasion Within: The Contest of Cultures in Colonial North America* (New York: Oxford University Press, 1985); Matthew Dennis, *Cultivating a Landscape of Peace: Iroquois-European Encounters in Seventeenth-Century America* (Ithaca, NY: Cornell University Press, 1995); Bruce G. Trigger, *Natives and Newcomers: Canada's "Heroic Age" Reconsidered* (Montreal: McGill-Queen's University Press, 1985). More recent significant sources are cited below.

2. Daniel K. Richter, *The Ordeal of the Longhouse: The Peoples of the Iroquois League in the Era of European Colonization* (Chapel Hill: University of North Carolina Press, 1992), 98–102; Reuben G. Thwaites, ed., *The Jesuit Relations and Allied Documents (JR)* (New York: Pageant, 1959), 73 vols., 51: 81.

3. *JR* 51: 131, 139, 221–35; Allan Greer, *Mohawk Saint: Catherine Tekakwitha and the Jesuits* (New York: Oxford University Press, 2005), 91–92.

4. *JR* 53: 253, 51: 125.

5. Bruce G. Trigger, *The Children of Aataentsic: A History of the Huron People to 1660* (1976; Montreal: McGill-Queen's University Press, 1987), 666; John L. Steckley, *De Religione: Telling the Seventeenth-Century Jesuit Story in Huron to the Iroquois* (Norman: University of Oklahoma Press, 2004).

6. *JR* 51: 123.

7. Daniel K. Richter, "Iroquois versus Iroquois: Jesuit Missions in Village Politics, 1642–1686," *Ethnohistory* 32, no. 1 (Winter 1985): 1–16.

8. On the movement of the Iroquois to the Saint Lawrence Valley, see *JR* 63: 149–55; Greer, *Mohawk Saint*, 89–101; Gretchen Green, "A New People in an Age of War: The Kahnawake Iroquois, 1667–1760" (PhD diss., The College of William and Mary, 1991); Jon Parmenter, *The Edge of the Woods: Iroquoia, 1534–1701* (East Lansing: Michigan State University Press, 2010).

9. Richter, *Ordeal of the Longhouse*, 125–26; Greer, *Mohawk Saint*, esp. chap. 6; Natalie Zemon Davis, "Iroquois Women, European Women," in *Women, "Race," and Writing in the Early Modern Period*, ed. Margo Hendricks and Patricia Parker (New York: Routledge, 1994), 243–58.

10. *JR* 58: 181

11. *JR* 58: 199, 55: 47, 52: 149.

12. *JR* 64: 85.

13. Samuel Kirkland, *The Journals of Samuel Kirkland: 18th-Century Missionary to the Iroquois, Government Agent, Father of Hamilton College*, ed. Walter Pilkington (Clinton, NY: Hamilton College, 1980), 73.

14. Eric Hinderaker, *The Two Hendricks: Unraveling a Mohawk Mystery* (Cambridge, MA: Harvard University Press, 2010), 40–44. For a survey of the Dutch-American missionaries, see Lois M. Feister, "Indian-Dutch Relations in the Upper Hudson Valley: A Study of Baptism Records in the Dutch Reformed Church, Albany, New York," *Man in the Northeast* 24 (1982):

89–113; Charles E. Corwin, "Efforts of the Dutch-American Colonial Pastors for the Conversion of the Indians," *Journal of the Presbyterian Historical Society* 12 (1925): 225–46 (esp. 239).

15. Hinderaker, *Two Hendricks*, 41–56.

16. Daniel K. Richter, "'Some of Them . . . Would Always Have a Minister with Them': Mohawk Protestantism, 1683–1719," *American Indian Quarterly* 16 (1992): 476.

17. On the Anglican missions, see Axtell, *Invasion Within*; John Wolfe Lydekker, *The Faithful Mohawks* (Cambridge, UK: Cambridge University Press, 1938); other significant sources appear below.

18. William Bryan Hart, "For the Good of Our Souls: Mohawk Authority, Accommodation, and Resistance to Protestant Evangelism, 1700–1780" (PhD diss., Brown University, 1998), 32.

19. Richter, "Some of Them," 478.

20. Hart, "For the Good," 196.

21. David Preston, *The Texture of Contact: European and Indian Settler Communities on the Frontiers of Iroquoia, 1667–1783* (Lincoln: University of Nebraska Press, 2002), 78–85, 103, 187–91.

22. Richter, "Some of Them," 472.

23. Hart, "For the Good," 223–25; William Bryan Hart, "Mohawk Schoolmasters and Catechists in Mid-Eighteenth Century Iroquoia: An Experiment in Fostering Literacy and Religious Change," in *The Language Encounter in the Americas, 1492–1800*, ed. Edward G. Gray and Norman Fiering (New York: Berghahn, 2000), 233–34, 244.

24. Thomas McElwain, "'The Rainbow Will Carry Me': The Language of Seneca Christianity as Reflected in Hymns," in *Religion in Native North America*, ed. Christopher Vecsey (Moscow: University of Idaho Press, 1990), 83–103, esp. 87–88; Terence J. O'Grady, "The Singing Societies of Oneida," *American Music* 9 (1991): 67–91.

25. Elizabeth Elbourne, "Managing Alliance, Negotiating Christianity: Haudenosaunee Uses of Anglicanism in Northeastern North America, 1760s–1830s," in *Mixed Blessings: Indigenous Encounters with Christianity in Canada*, ed. Tolly Bradford and Chelsea Horton (Vancouver: University of British Columbia Press, 2016), 41–43.

26. While missionary John Eliot pioneered "praying towns" for New England Algonquians in the seventeenth century, these did not enjoy broad popular support. For eighteenth-century evangelicalism and Native Americans, see William S. Simmons, "Red Yankees: Narragansett Conversion in the Great Awakening," *American Ethnologist* 10 (1983): 253–71; David Silverman, *Red Brethren: The Brothertown and Stockbridge Indians and the Problem of Race in Early America* (Ithaca, NY: Cornell University Press, 2010); Linford D. Fisher, *The Indian Great Awakening: Religion and the Shaping of Native Cultures in Early America* (New York: Oxford University Press, 2012).

27. On Oquaga, see Laurence M. Hauptman, "Refugee Havens: The Iroquois Villages of the Eighteenth Century," in *American Indian Environments: Ecological Issues in Native American History*, ed. Christopher Vecsey and Robert W. Venables (Syracuse, NY: Syracuse University Press, 1980), 128–39; Colin G. Calloway, *The American Revolution in Indian Country: Crisis and Diversity in Native American Communities* (New York: Cambridge University Press, 1995); Daniel Mandell, "'Turned Their Minds to Religion': Oquaga and the First Iroquois Church, 1748–1776," *Early American Studies* 11 (2013): 211–42; Joy A. Howard, "Rebecca Kellogg Ashley: Negotiating Identity on the Early American Borderlands, 1704–1757," in *Women in Early America*, ed. Thomas A. Foster (New York: New York University Press, 2015), 128.

28. Howard, "Rebecca Kellogg Ashley," 132–33 (quote 132).

29. Stephen Valone, "Samuel Kirkland, Iroquois Missions and the Land, 1764–1774," *American Presbyterianism* 65 (1987): 190–92; Colin G. Calloway, *The Indian History of an American Institution: Native Americans and Dartmouth* (Hanover, NH: Dartmouth College Press, 2010), 34–35.

30. Thomas Cummock, "Sketch of the Brothertown Indians," *Collections of the State Historical Society of Wisconsin* 4 (1859; reprint edition, 1906): 292. Citations refer to the 1906 edition.

31. Kirkland's career is examined in detail in Christine Sternberg Patrick, "The Life and Times of Samuel Kirkland, 1741–1808: Missionary to the Oneida Indians, American Patriot, and Founder of Hamilton College" (PhD diss., State University of New York, Buffalo, 1993); and Alan S. Taylor, *The Divided Ground: Indians, Settlers, and the Northern Borderland of the American Revolution* (New York: Knopf, 2006).

32. For contrasting views on Kirkland, the Oneidas, and the American Revolution, see Joseph P. Glatthaar and James Kirby Martin, *Forgotten Allies: The Oneida Indians and the American Revolution* (New York: Hill and Wang, 2006); Barbara Graymont, *The Iroquois in the American Revolution* (Syracuse, NY: Syracuse University Press, 1972); and Karim M. Tiro, *The People of the Standing Stone: The Oneida Nation from the Revolution through the Era of Removal* (Amherst: University of Massachusetts Press, 2011), 39–64.

33. Kirkland to Jerusha Kirkland, 5 August 1772, 32b, Samuel Kirkland Papers (SK MSS), Hamilton College Archives, Burke Library, Hamilton College.

34. Kirkland, *Journals*, 74–77; Steven West to the Oneida Converts, 25 June 1773, 42e, SK MSS, Burke Library, Hamilton College; Samuel Dunlop to the London Board, 2 July 1773, 43a, SK MSS.

35. Kirkland to Jerusha Kirkland, 24 March 1773, 39e, SK MSS.

36. Fowler to Wheelock, 15 June and 23 September 1765, *Letters of Eleazar Wheelock's Indians*, ed. James Dow McCallum (Hanover, NH: Dartmouth College, 1932), 94, 97; Kirkland, *Journals*, 97 quoted in Patrick, "Life and Times," 118, see also 113.

37. Joseph Bloomfield, *Citizen Soldier: The Revolutionary War Journal of Joseph Bloomfield*, ed. Mark E. Lender and James Kirby Martin (Newark: New Jersey Historical Society, 1982), 90.

38. Kirkland, *Journals*, 134–35.

39. David J. Silverman, "The Curse of God: An Idea and Its Origins among the Indians of New York's Revolutionary Frontier," *William and Mary Quarterly*, 3rd ser., 66 (2009): 495–534.

40. Quoted in Valone, "Samuel Kirkland," 193. On the postwar land pressures, see Barbara Graymont, "New York State Indian Policy after the Revolution," *New York History* 57 (1976); J. David Lehman, "The End of the Iroquois Mystique: The Oneida Land Cession Treaties of the 1780s," *William and Mary Quarterly*, 3rd ser., 47 (1990): 523–47; Tiro, *People of the Standing Stone*, 65–128; Laurence M. Hauptman, *Conspiracy of Interests: Iroquois Dispossession and the Rise of New York State* (Syracuse, NY: Syracuse University Press, 1999); Taylor, *Divided Ground.*

41. Franklin B. Hough, comp., *Proceedings of the Commissioners of Indian Affairs Appointed by Law for the Extinguishment of Indian Titles in the State of New York* (Albany, NY: Munsell, 1861), 141.

42. Dorothy Ripley, *Bank of Faith and Works United* (Philadelphia: J. H. Cunningham, 1819), 62.

43. On the Quaker mission, see Karim M. Tiro, "'We Wish to Do You Good': The Quaker Mission to the Oneida Nation, 1790–1840," *Journal of the Early Republic* 26 (2006): 353–76.

44. Journal of Samuel Kirkland, April to October 1804, fol. 1, Northern Missionary Society, Rutgers University Library.

45. Oneida Chiefs to Williams, 9 December 1814, Eleazer Williams MSS, MR 2, 394, Wisconsin Historical Society; *Report of the Directors of the Northern Missionary Society, 1814* (Albany, NY: Websters and Skinners, 1815), 10–11; on Williams and Oneida singing, see O'Grady, "Singing Societies of Oneida," 67–91.

3

FLAWED SHEPHERD

Eleazer Williams, John Henry Hobart, and the Episcopal Mission to the Oneidas

Michael Leroy Oberg

How do you save a pagan's soul? The question ate at Eleazer Williams throughout much of his life. Born in 1788 at Kahnawake, the Catholic Mohawk town along the Saint Lawrence River, Williams descended from the unredeemed Puritan captive Eunice Williams and from many generations of Mohawks. In 1800, his parents sent him to the Connecticut River valley, and in Longmeadow and other towns he received an education in Calvinism from Eunice's Anglo-American descendants. He briefly attended Moor's Charity School but, frustrated with a lack of funds and faith from his Congregationalist patrons, he departed soon thereafter for New York City, where he sought out John Henry Hobart, the Episcopal bishop for the diocese of New York.[1]

Hobart wanted to extend the reach of his church's missionary enterprise, and he saw in Williams—fluent and literate in Mohawk and English—a means to that end. Williams adapted readily to his new theological surroundings. Now immersed in a third Christian denomination, he had little interest in doctrinal differences. Other than a vague statement that Episcopalianism seemed a happy medium between Calvinism and Catholicism, he said little. A theological dabbler, he recognized early on that one's standards might be flexible and that one might be a Christian and believe many things. Ecumenicalism was not uncommon among Native American Christians, who often found themselves living hard by white ministers from different faiths. This flexibility would serve Williams well in his missionary work.[2]

An early attempt at establishing an Episcopal mission among the Mohawks at Kahnawake ended quickly and in failure in 1812. Williams had been gone too long from his devotedly Catholic natal community to make much headway. The war years followed, with Williams serving the United States in some capacity on its northern frontier.[3] After the war ended, he returned to New York to reacquaint himself with Hobart and to remind the bishop of his determination "to proclaim the unsearchable riches of Christ to my poor brethren."[4]

Hobart still had big plans for Williams, who made his First Communion and received Confirmation at Saint John's Church in New York City in May 1815. Two days later, Hobart addressed a letter to *The Churchman's Magazine*: "An opportunity offers of extending, under the most favorable circumstances, the blessings of civilization and religion among the Indian tribes, through the instrumentality of Mr. Eleazer Williams, a young man of Indian extraction." Hobart asked his readers for donations. Williams—talented, educated, and committed—could produce a translation of the Book of Common Prayer in the Mohawk language with the support of dedicated Christians. Hobart sent Williams on the road to raise money, and he met with "some of our worthy church people" over the course of three days in June. He visited Washington as well and met, he claimed later, with President James Madison and his secretary of state, James Monroe, as well as several senators and congressmen and the men who immediately oversaw the conduct of US Indian policy in New York State—federal agent Erastus Granger and interpreters Jasper Parrish and Horatio Jones. There is irony in this, for Jones and Parrish provided Williams, he claimed, with valuable information about the state of the Iroquois in New York. Williams knew the language, but he learned about the actual conditions in Iroquoia from the more experienced white men who oversaw their relations with a government that wanted to acquire their lands and transform their culture.[5]

Hobart next sent Williams out into the mission field, this time to Akwesasne, a Mohawk settlement upriver from Kahnawake. He would act as a lay reader, catechist, and schoolteacher for the Indians. All the signs seemed favorable. Even though Williams had raised less money during his brief fund-raising tour than his sponsors had hoped, the mission project still generated considerable interest. Bishop Hobart placed his hopes on the twenty-seven-year-old missionary and expected him to perform as well. Williams's mission had the blessings of both the church and state. He arrived at Akwesasne in the summer of 1815. Seven months later, he declared the mission a complete failure.

Williams had no shortage of excuses for what went wrong. Hobart remained patient and urged his protégé to look to the west. Just two months after the Battle of Plattsburgh in 1814, Williams received a letter from the New York Oneidas inviting him to come minister to them "in their own language." Dissatisfied with their present missionary, they hoped that Williams might help them "to learn the way to heaven and we wish also that our children may learn to read and write." Although still smarting from the Akwesasne failure, with the blessings of Bishop Hobart, Williams decided to take the Oneidas up on their offer.

Williams certainly knew something about the efforts of his mission predecessors who had previously tried to bring Christianity to the Oneidas. He knew of Samuel Kirkland, whose arrival there preceded his own by half a century, and about Samson Occom, the Mohegan missionary who played a leading role in the settlement of the Brothertown community from New England on the New York frontier. The Oneidas welcomed Occom, but the Mohegan missionary assumed "such an air of importance" that he offended the members of the community. His zeal, Williams believed, "was not sufficiently tempered with the mild and gentle spirit of the religion he taught." He treated his congregants "with great severity." Williams drew the obvious conclusion. Only when Occom relaxed and began to accept the Oneidas as they were did his audiences view him as "agreeable and exemplary, easy and unassuming in conversation." A decade after Occom died, Quaker missionaries arrived. They tried between 1798 and 1800 to bring civility, private property, and Christianity to the Oneidas before they left to devote their attention to the Senecas farther west. By this point, some Oneidas had begun, as they told the New York State legislature, "to abandon our Savage life—to adopt your mode of life in cultivating the land, to raise grain, to be sober, and many other good things."[6]

Occom died three decades before Williams arrived. The Quakers had given up and left the same year Williams arrived as a child in southern New England. The Seneca prophet Handsome Lake had some followers in Oneida Country, but Williams faced little competition from them. Kirkland died in 1808. William Jenkins, a Presbyterian and Kirkland's successor, and a man described by his critics as "weak, inefficient, and without influence," could not follow in his predecessor's footsteps. For one thing, unlike Kirkland, he could not communicate with his audiences in their own language. He attracted few adherents, and the Christian Party dwindled in numbers.[7]

Yet, visitors to Oneida Country reported signs of "incipient civilization." Oneida farmers cultivated fields in which they grew the traditional "three sisters"—maize, beans, and squash—while tending apple orchards and the sheep and cows they kept in nearby pastures. They gathered ginseng in the forests and sold it to passing traders. They fished on Wood Creek or on Oneida Lake for eels, salmon, and catfish. They preserved important parts of their traditional way of life but also selectively adopted elements of white culture that they believed might allow them to weather the crisis caused by the growing numbers of white settlers. Christianity, for those Oneidas who converted, was only one of these creative adaptations. It is important to point this out. The Oneidas could have lived well enough on their remaining lands, but those who coveted them would not leave the Oneidas alone, regardless of the changes they had made. New Yorkers across the board ignored the provisions of laws like the federal Trade and Intercourse Act.

Many New Yorkers also ignored their state's own laws designed to protect Indians from sharps, cheats, and alcohol vendors.[8]

By 1816, the year of his death, the great Oneida leader Skenandoah, a Christian who had tried to cooperate with the New Yorkers, concluded that his hope for intercultural peace and accommodation had failed. He attributed what he saw as the Oneidas' downfall to the anger of a Christian God who refused to protect the Oneidas from their relentlessly advancing white neighbors. "No Indian sleeps," he said shortly before Williams arrived in Oneida Country, "but those that sleep in their graves." He expected that soon white men would occupy his house and that they would drive the rest of the Oneidas from their homes.[9]

Consequently, Eleazer Williams arrived in a community at once divided over matters religious, under siege from those non-Indians who coveted their lands, and wracked by self-doubt and insecurity, in spring 1816. The Oneidas gave to him, according to one story, the name Sky Had Been Crossed, perhaps a reference to the dark clouds that hung over Oneida Country, both figuratively and literally, at the time of his arrival.[10]

Armed with a commission from Bishop Hobart to serve as a lay reader, catechist, and schoolmaster, Williams saw reasons for optimism. The state government, far more interested in the Oneidas' lands in the center of the state and at the strategically critical "Carrying Place" than it had been in those more marginal lands belonging to the Mohawks, supported him where earlier it had ignored his efforts in the North Country. Williams enjoyed the patronage of the Episcopal bishop of New York. Powerful supporters in Christian circles, both New England Congregationalists and New York Episcopalians, provided support as he commenced both his mission and his translation of the Book of Common Prayer into the Mohawk language. In addition to this and to his being "tolerably versed in the Christian system and theology," Williams, his supporters noted at the outset, had mastered "the Indian language, his mother tongue, besides being a natural orator and powerful speaker, the *sine qua non* of persuasion and success with the Indians." It was Williams, and not a grasping white man, who moved into Skenandoah's recently emptied house.[11]

Williams approached the Christian Oneidas first. He thought they possessed a shallow understanding of the doctrines of Christianity and believed that they "scarcely understood the meaning of *saving faith*." But Williams succeeded in winning some of these Christians over, and they told the Northern Missionary Society, Rev. Jenkins's sponsor, that they vastly preferred Williams to Jenkins. The directors of the society conceded that the new missionary "is capable of benefiting his brethren beyond almost any other man." They had already paid Williams to complete some translation work for them by the time they decided to recall Jenkins and turn their organization's attention toward Indians in the Michigan Territory.[12]

Williams, like other missionaries, may have exaggerated how far these Indians had fallen in order to boost his own achievements. His writings reveal the critical and discerning quality of their Christianity and their active, rather than passive, engagement with their missionary. They told him, shortly after he arrived, that they did not care for the prayers of the Episcopal Church. And this is where Williams excelled. Despite his later career as a professional Indian who assisted the government and business interests in pursuing the policy known as Indian removal, and later still as a confidence man touring northern churches as the dauphin, Williams was a gifted and talented shepherd to his new flock. He opted for flexibility and suggested to the Oneidas that if they learned the church's principles, they would find that "its doctrines were pure, its ceremonies few, proper & primitive, its method exact, and phrases were taken out of scripture with the purest antiquity." He was not heavy-handed. The choice remained theirs, he said. He would condemn no one who appeared truly pious, and "with this answer, they appeared to be satisfied."[13]

During his time in New York, Williams met regularly with small groups of troubled Christians. He tried to explain why different Christian denominations disagreed over ritual, ceremony, and belief. He explained to them the disputes that led to the Protestant Reformation. He addressed the fears of Presbyterian Oneidas, Kirkland's former followers, who worried that Episcopalianism bore too many similarities to Catholicism. He might have explained to them that he had been born into a Catholic community, at Kahnawake in 1788, and that, like Kirkland, he had been educated by New England Calvinists but had now embraced the doctrines of the Episcopal Church. These believers returned to their homes and discussed among themselves the best path to follow.[14]

Williams succeeded in strengthening and revitalizing the Christian Party, but his greatest success as a missionary—he would refer to this achievement for the rest of his life—came with the "Pagan Party." From the time of his arrival, Williams made the conversion of the Pagan Party the particular focus of his mission. He held councils with them. He explained to them "the *nature & design of Christianity*." They raised "many objections and arguments, some of which were against the religion of the white man." He succeeded in overcoming this opposition by integrating himself into the community. A "Collection of Occasional Prayers" cobbled together from the Book of Common Prayer and other sources reveals this: Williams copied into his papers a prayer to be delivered "On the Birth of a Child," another when that child grew ill, and yet one more when that child died. He shared in the pain of a community where diseases still took a toll on Indian lives, where suffering was not uncommon and injustice and dispossession were a part of life.[15]

As he taught the pagans that "God, the *Great Creator* of all things, doth uphold, direct, dispose, and govern all Creatures, actions & things, from the greatest even to the least, by his most wise and holy providence," Williams proved himself a patient catechist, willing to instruct the Oneidas in their native tongue on the rudiments of Christian faith.[16] He also captivated his audiences as a preacher. According to an account published in the *Boston Recorder* in 1818, Williams held his audiences in rapt attention. Men and boys seated themselves to his left; the women sat to his right. He read the service "in the Indian language," with a large part of the congregation, and especially the women, "repeating the responses and prayers in a very devout, distinct, and harmonious manner." Williams "displayed the gestures of eloquence and Christian zeal." The congregation, the Boston correspondent wrote, "listened with as much attention and solemnity, as any I ever witnessed."[17]

Williams claimed that he drew his inspiration as a catechist from Luke 14:23, and in his own view, at least, he spared no effort to "go out into the highways and hedges, and compel them to come in, that my house may be filled." He used spectacle to draw the Oneidas to services. He decorated the altar of the chapel with evergreens for the Christmas service in 1816, and, in "white robe, chanted at the altar of that Angelic hymn, *Gloria in Excelsis* and *Te Deum Laudamus*."[18] Williams translated English hymns and employed singing instruction to communicate his message, even if this meant that he spent less time teaching the Oneidas to read and write in English than his sponsors may have wished. He encouraged his audiences as well. If the pagan Oneidas tried "to denounce the sins of the devil, the world, and the flesh; if they sincerely believe all the articles of the Christian Faith, even though their faith be weak; and if it is the desire and purpose of their hearts to keep God's holy will and Commandments, and to walk in the same all the days of their lives, even though their obedience is marked with much imperfection," they could find eternal happiness. He assured them of this. They had to make the effort, but the effort required was not great. It could be done. They could avoid alcohol, if they chose, and find happiness. Their past sins could be forgiven. "Light is sown for the righteous," his audience would have heard when Williams preached on Psalm 97:11, "and gladness for the upright at heart." Converts, he said in a sermon on the 107th psalm, undertake "a change of their course, from the broad way that leads to Hell, to the narrow way that leads to Heaven," beginning "that great work, and Journey, their whole lives should be devoted to, and spent in."[19]

If they chose to stray from that path, Williams readily changed his tone. He demanded that his audiences listen closely to him, one observer recalled, and he "challenged them either to obey or refute the Gospel." Those who "deserted the standard under which they had enlisted to war" and "had drawn back from the engagements into which they had entered" stood in "the most debased condition of man." In his most fiery sermons, Williams expressed little patience for those who chose to ignore God's law. He did not describe eternal suffering or torment in a fiery Hell, but he did make clear to them the loneliness and pain that came with forsaking God. The suffering he described was one of isolation, of being left alone to confront the many dangers of a sinful world, a vision of torment that might have resonated with Oneidas.[20]

It is difficult to overestimate the importance of preaching, and Williams was indeed an extraordinarily talented preacher. All accounts agree on this. But this was only part of Williams's job, and he spent much more of his time with small groups of Oneida seekers and individual Indians who lived in fear. In these small encounters—these intimate performances—Williams made his greatest impact. He labored "day and night," he wrote, "to strengthen the faith" of the Oneidas and to "lead them in the path of virtue & piety."[21] He answered their questions, and he told them stories. Early in April 1816, for instance, he met with four "Pagan Chiefs," who asked Williams why Christians suffered. Some Oneidas and their New England Indian neighbors had chosen Christianity, but still they lost their lands, still they faced racism, and still they experienced poverty and the ravages of alcohol. New Yorkers injured Indians, whether Christian or not. Some Christian Indians had concluded that God cursed them—that they suffered God's wrath because of who and what they were. Why did Christians, they asked, the followers of a God that Williams said was both almighty and merciful, not live lives of comfort and contentment? It is unclear if Williams's answer helped them. "If we want to be partakers of Christ's holiness," he said, "we must also be partakers of his sufferings, and if we suffer with him patiently, we shall reign with him eternally."[22]

Williams challenged drunkards. The abuse of alcohol led to the violation, he told four Pagan Party members in May 1816, of each of the Ten Commandments. "What sin is it that a drunken man stands not ready to commit?" he asked. "Fornication, murder, adultery, incest, what not?" Alcohol transformed "a man into a beast" and made "him the shame & reproach of human nature." He had seen it happen too many times. Other observers, in other Indian communities, documented amply the devastation wreaked by alcohol. It imperiled souls and communities. "The intemperate man is his own tormentor, yea, his own destroyer, as appears by the many diseased & untimely deaths which surfeiting & drunkenness daily bring upon them."[23]

Conversations like these continued throughout the year. In July, Williams challenged the small number of Oneida pagans who followed the Seneca prophet Handsome Lake, an "idolator," an "imposter," and a "false prophet" in Williams's view. They asked Williams "why the Great Spirit had made known his mind & will to the white people and not to the Indians?" He told them that "it is enough for us . . . to know for certain that he is good & just in every thing he does, or permits to be done" and that "we may be assured sooner or later, every tongue shall confess and every soul acknowledge, the justice and equity of God's proceedings with mankind." Williams explained that God worked in mysterious ways but that Christians believed "the God we serve to be the most perfect of all beings." One of Williams's listeners asked about this perfection. Williams answered that God was great and all-powerful, and his "perfections" included "his eternity & providence, his holiness & justice, his wisdom & truth, his goodness & mercy" and "the unspeakable riches of his exceeding abundant grace & love."[24]

Williams thought believers needed some basic knowledge "in the Doctrines of our Divine Redeemer" for salvation, and he did not believe that "persons will be taught the things which essentially belong to their peace" by dreams and rituals. He could not excuse the sins of the unconverted and told the Pagans "that mens unbelief" could not "take off & extinguish the guilt of all their other sins." All he asked was that they do their best to follow God's laws and believe in him. The choice of whether to do so was theirs.[25]

In October 1816, a young Indian, "very melancholy," approached Williams. He was, he said, "sick with my sins, my soul is sick, I am seeking for its remedy—I want to be healed." Jesus could heal him, Williams said. He was the "great physician of souls, who is ever ready to heal all who apply to him with penitent hearts." Jesus will not refuse you, Williams told the young sinner. "Look at his cross & all those streams of blood flowing from his visage, side, hands, and feet—they will wash away our sins with true repentance." A month later another sinner, an Oneida Williams did not know, asked the missionary to help him. "Such a miserable creature as I am," the Oneida said, worthless, frightened, and in his own words "evil" and "polluted with sin and yes, a great sinner": how could he hope to repay "that love & that precious blood spilt on my account?" God's love was great, Williams told him, and it knew no limits. This comforted the stranger, who said that "I will now throw away my great pack of sins & search after this loving father and when I find him, I will follow him all the days of my life."[26]

We cannot know for sure whether these conversations actually took place. Williams wrote them down long after the fact. He may well have made up these conversations out of whole cloth. Given his lifelong desire to secure a livelihood, and his penchant for telling tales and playing roles, whether as missionary, cultural broker, diplomat, or dauphin, truth for him could be conditional and a means to an end. But much of the material Williams included in the autobiographical drafts that appear in his papers is devoted to the few short years he spent at Oneida Castle under Hobart's sponsorship, clearly an important period in his life. In 1818, he told a group of pagans "from the west" that "as I love you, I tell you the truth." He wished for nothing more, he told them, than "your soul's eternal happiness in the world to come." And in ministering to the Pagan Party at Oneida Castle, Williams achieved what he viewed as his greatest success and the achievement of which he remained most proud.[27]

In January 1817, the chiefs of the Pagan Party wrote to New York's governor De Witt Clinton: "We have abandoned our Idols and our sacrifices and have fixed our hopes on our blessed Redeemer." They informed the governor that they now believed in "God the Father, the creator and preserver of all things—as omniscient and omnipresent—most gracious and most merciful." They believed in Jesus, too, and that "all must believe in him and embrace him in order to obtain salvation." To provide evidence that they had accepted Christianity, the chiefs offered to Clinton unequivocally "our abjuration of paganism and its rites."[28]

It was quite a letter. Williams wrote it; not only does its language not ring true for Oneidas who spoke little or no English but Williams also used similar language in a letter he wrote to Bishop Hobart some years later touting his successes. The Christian newspapers in New York and elsewhere in the northeast reprinted the letter widely nonetheless, and Williams became something of a celebrity in mission circles for transforming the Pagan Party into the Oneida "Second Christian Party."[29]

Williams worked with forty to fifty children each day, he told his superiors and sponsors. He catechized them twice a day, and they did very well, he wrote. Williams knew that he could take credit for "turning some of them from darkness to light, and from Satan to true God." He received from fellow missionaries and his superiors in the Episcopal establishment "congratulatory letters of my success among the Oneidas, expressed in a language most encouraging and flattering to my feelings." Hobart himself left New York City to travel to the Oneida Country. A hundred Oneidas rode out to greet him, their horses lining the road as he passed by them. Hobart acknowledged the gesture, this greeting at the edge of the woods, as the gathered Oneidas asked him for his help. Despite their recent profession of faith, they announced to the bishop that "we are ignorant, we are poor, and need your assistance. Come, venerable father," they asked, "and visit your children and warm their hearts by your presence in the things which belong to their everlasting peace."[30]

The bishop replied with a message that offered to transcend the racial lines that separated Indians and whites on the New York frontier. God, he said, "hath made of one blood all the nations of the earth, and hath sent his son Jesus Christ to teach all and to die for them all that they might be redeemed from the power of sin." Hobart suggested, unlike his protégé, that the Oneidas learn not only Christian doctrine but also the "arts of civilization" and that they start working the land like their white neighbors. Hobart, it seems, knew little of how the Oneidas actually lived. Still, he held the congregation's attention. Williams thought it "an affecting sight to see the aged and venerable chiefs, councilors, matrons and warriors, with uplifted hands, and with countenances indicating their minds were deeply affected," renounce their paganism. Hobart concluded his visit by consecrating the Oneida chapel and confirming ninety-four new Christians.[31]

Hobart energetically supported missionary enterprise. He wanted devoted young Episcopalians to become missionaries, and he wanted other Episcopalians to support these efforts financially. In a summary of diocesan missionary activity, Hobart mentioned at the end of a long list of missionaries "Mr. Eleazer Williams,

[who] acts as a Catechist, Schoolmaster, and Lay Reader among the Oneida Indians." Writing as "An Episcopalian" in the *Onondaga Gazette* in summer 1817, either Hobart or one of his supporters trumpeted Williams's accomplishments: "Hundreds of those once-bewildered beings, who joined in the war song of murder on their foes, are now uniting in the anthems and responses of our church, singing praises to the Savior who had brought them out of heathenish darkness into marvelous light." With additional funding, Williams might expand his mission to the nearby Onondagas.[32]

Hobart returned to visit the Oneidas in fall 1818. The Indians thanked the bishop for sending Williams to them. Hobart baptized twenty-four children and confirmed eighty-nine more, all of whom Williams had "previously prepared." It was, according to the small number of non-Indians able to witness the visit, a powerfully emotional ceremony. "The reverence and devotion with which the Indians joined in the confessions; the supplications and praises of the Liturgy; the solemn attention with which they listened to the instructions and exhortations of the Bishop; the humility and thankfulness, evidenced by their prostration on their knees, and by their tears which flowed down the cheeks of several of them, with which they devoted themselves, in the apostolic 'laying on of hands,' to the God who made them, and the Savior who shed his blood for them, powerfully interested the feelings of all present." Hobart was impressed. "I have admitted Mr. Williams as a Candidate for Orders," he told the annual convention of the diocese, "and look forward to his increased influence and usefulness, should he be invested with the office of the ministry.[33]

Williams, one correspondent who visited him later that year reported, still lived in Skenandoah's old house. Two women, one of them his cousin, and two young men made up his household. We know nothing about these people, but "the deportment" of Williams's family, the correspondent wrote, "was such as the most refined in manners would have been pleased with." Williams, whom the correspondent noted "is too well known to need my encomiums . . . appears to be a lover of science, and his parlor was ornamented with a very handsome library." The congregation of nearly 150 sang hymns beautifully, listened to sermons with "much attention and solemnity," and seemed to be making extraordinary progress.[34]

It is a revealing profile, and it speaks to the challenges an Indian missionary working for a white missionary organization faced. To earn respect, to gain credibility among potential patrons and backers for his mission, Williams not only had to put in his time on the ground, come to where his congregants were, and share in the experiences of a pressed-upon Native community but also had to keep up an appearance of refinement and something very much approaching gentility. He headed a household. He understood white expectations of mannerly behavior, and he could act the part. Not merely literate, Williams was immersed in the world of print culture, his ample library standing in the parlor as evidence. The correspondent who wrote so enthusiastically about Williams's success and good work never hinted that this catechist and lay reader faced burdens white clergymen seldom worried about. He never appreciated that service as an Indian missionary compelled Williams to perform for audiences often far removed from the mission field.

Some Oneidas supported Williams, but others criticized him. After Hobart returned to Oneida again in fall 1819 to formally consecrate an Oneida church "that was most tastefully illuminated by the matrons of the nation," Williams addressed the misrepresentations of those "who were inimical to the mission, to the church, and to myself." He stood accused of maintaining his ties to Catholicism. Williams could have addressed what he viewed as a slander at any point, but he believed that the bishop needed to hear what he had to say. "As I was educated in the Roman Catholic Church, and an impression may be entertained that I am yet, in heart, attached to that communion," he told Hobart, "I here . . . sincerely & solemnly declare, that I am in principle & practice firmly opposed to the doctrines, discipline, and worship of the Romish Church, as far as they are contrary to the word of God." Charges of doctrinal laxness, of a willingness to lean toward an excess in ceremony, would continue to dog Williams,[35] but they were not enough to keep him from broadening his horizons and expanding the reach of his missionary enterprise.

In May 1819, Williams visited the Senecas, then engaged in a struggle with the persistent Ogden Land Company to hang on to their remaining lands and in an internal dispute over the presence of Christian missionaries on their reservations. He worked on the company's behalf. Williams met with Red Jacket, a leader "most violently opposed to the introduction of Christianity among his people," but he could not win him over. He did send the Seneca Jacob Jemison to Hartwick College, where a missionary organization had sprung up interested in educating and Christianizing the Indians. Williams also interpreted for Baptist missionaries who visited the Oneidas as well as the Stockbridge and Brothertown communities. He spoke at the Baptists' annual convention in Buffalo in early 1820. He traveled and he spoke, and accounts of his success and his words were carried in the pages of a vibrant and growing Christian press. An Indian who had converted other Indians to Christianity, his story spread and his influence grew.[36]

Williams wanted to stay at Oneida. The request for funds to construct a church that accompanied the cession of 1817 only makes sense if we consider this to be the case. But experience would prove a harsh teacher. Williams learned about the many interests who wanted the Oneidas to leave central New York for Arkansas or the Allegany—it did not matter much to them. He benefited personally from his relationships with state, federal, and Ogden Land Company officials, all of whom wanted the New York Indians "removed." But he also knew the racists and the thugs, the alcohol vendors and the judges who judged wrong, and like many other

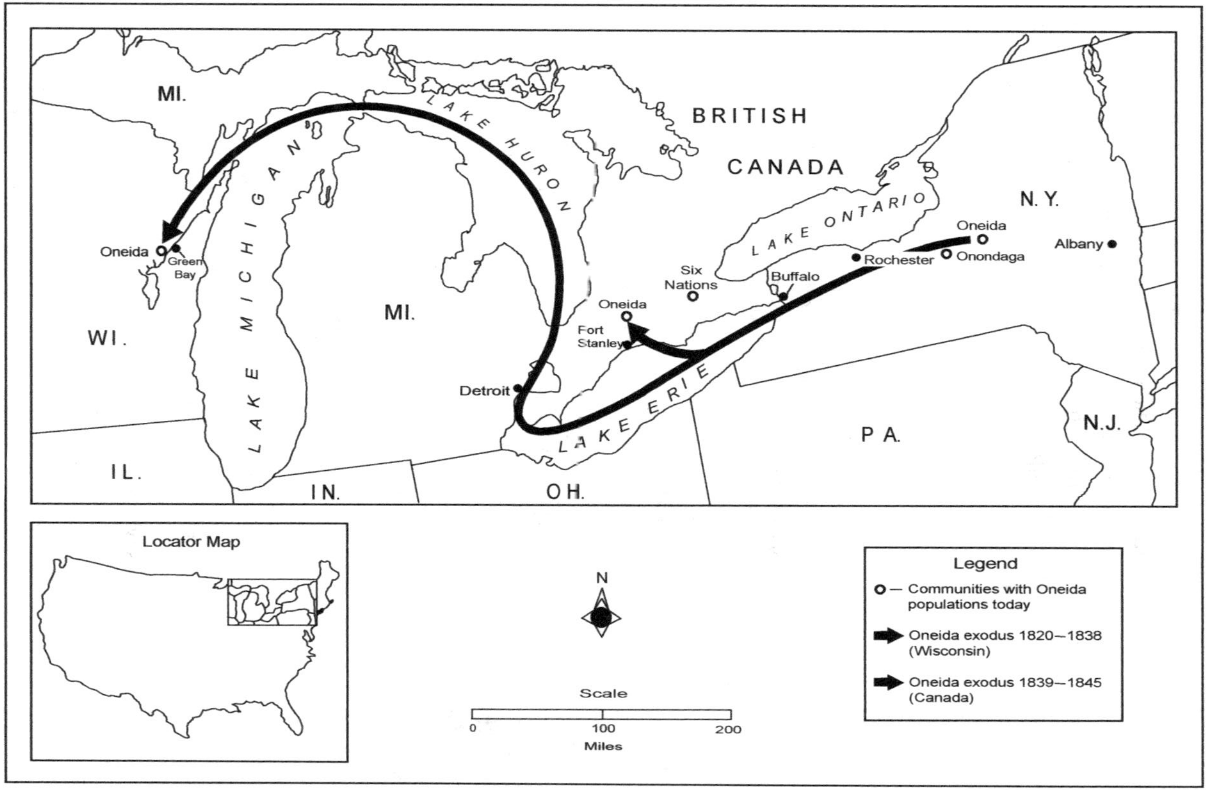

Map 2. Oneida Migrations Out of Their New York Homeland: Early 1820s to Mid-1840s. Map by Ben Simpson. Laurence M. Hauptman Collection.

Native peoples, at other times and in other places, he concluded that relocation to Green Bay might offer his followers a chance to outrun their problems and the white people who caused them. Williams led the first party of Oneidas to Green Bay early in the 1820s. Other Oneidas followed, so many that it is improper to attribute either credit or blame for the Oneidas' relocation solely to him. He helped the immigrants, at least at the outset, as New York Indians became pioneers, part of the great westward push of settlement that characterized the history of the nineteenth century. He established his Episcopal mission. His daughter was the first child baptized, and the first body buried, in the churchyard at Holy Apostles.

Notes

1. For an overview of Williams's life on which this essay is based, see Michael Leroy Oberg, *Professional Indian: The American Odyssey of Eleazer Williams* (Philadelphia: University of Pennsylvania Press, 2015); for Eunice Williams, see John Demos, *The Unredeemed Captive: A Family Story from Early America* (New York: Knopf, 1994).

2. Oberg, *Professional Indian*, 35.

3. For Williams's military service, see Oberg, *Professional Indian*, 37–45.

4. Eleazer Williams to "Respected Sir," n.d., Eleazer Williams (EW) Manuscript Collection (MSS), Microfilm Reel (MR) 2; Eleazer Williams, Autobiographical Writings, EW MSS, MR 3. Both in Wisconsin Historical Society Area Research Center (WHSARC), University of Wisconsin at Green Bay (UWGB). Oberg, *Professional Indian*, 50.

5. Eleazer Williams, Autobiographical Writings, EW MSS, MR 3, WHSARC, UWGB; J. H. Hobart, "Conversion of the Indian Tribes," *Churchman's Magazine*, May/June 1815, 101–2; and "Bishop Hobart's Address," *Christian Visitant*, December 23, 1815, 232; Oberg, *Professional Indian*, 51.

6. Historical Notes, EW MSS, MR 4, WHSARC, UWGB; James Taylor, Jonathan Thomas, and others to the Pennsylvania Yearly Meeting Indian Committee, 26 November 1798, Letters to the Pennsylvania Yearly Meeting, Indian Committee, Haverford College Library Special Collections, Haverford, PA; Jacob Taylor and Others to Brethren of the Oneida Nation, 6 January 1800, Letters to Pennsylvania Yearly Meeting Indian Committee; Petition of Oneida Indians to New York State Legislature, 27 February 1798, Legislative Assembly Papers, Correspondence and Reports Relating to Indians, 1783–1831, New York State Archives; On Occom's career, see David J. Silverman, *Red Brethren: The Brothertown and Stockbridge Indians and the Problem of Race in Early America* (Ithaca, NY: Cornell University Press, 2010), 55–67; W. Deloss Love, *Samson Occom and the Christian Indians of New England* (Syracuse, NY: Syracuse University Press, 2000).

7. Laurence M. Hauptman, *Conspiracy of Interests: Iroquois Dispossession and the Rise of New York State,* (Syracuse, NY: Syracuse University Press, 1999) 52–53; Albert G. Ellis, "Advent of the New York Indians into Wisconsin," WHC 2 (1856): 419; on Jenkins's subsequent career after he left Oneida, see the annual report of the board of directors of the Northern Missionary Society in *Christian Herald*, November 29, 1817. On Kirkland's limitations as a speaker of the Oneida language, see the commentary in Karim M. Tiro and

Cesare Marino, eds. and trans., *Along the Hudson and Mohawk: The 1790 Journey of Count Paolo Andreani* (Philadelphia: University of Pennsylvania Press, 2006), 70n69.

8. Julia K. Bloomfield, *The Oneidas* (New York: Alden, 1907), 150; Vivian C. Hopkins, "De Witt Clinton and the Iroquois," *Ethnohistory* 8 (Spring 1961): 114–16; Franklin B. Hough, *A History of St. Lawrence and Franklin Counties, New York, from the Earliest Period to the Present Times* (Albany, NY: Little, 1853), 174; Karim. M. Tiro, *The People of the Standing Stone: The Oneida Nation from the Revolution through the Era of Removal* (Amherst: University of Massachusetts Press, 2011), 121–22.

9. Skenandoah quoted in Hauptman, *Conspiracy of Interests*, 43–44, 47.

10. Tiro points out that the massive eruption of Mt. Tambora in Indonesia produced an ash cloud that caused darkened skies and that ruined harvests in central New York. Snow fell in June 1816, a year without a summer. See Tiro, *People of the Standing Stone*, 138–39.

11. Geoffrey E. Buerger, "Eleazer Williams: Elitism and Multiple Identity on Two Frontiers," in *Being and Becoming Indian: Biographical Studies of North American Frontiers*, ed. James H. Clifton (Chicago, IL: Dorsey Press, 1989), 122; Eleazer Williams to Dr. Stewart, 14 November 1817, EW MSS, MR 2, WHSARC, UWGB; Reginald Horsman, "The Origins of Oneida Removal to Wisconsin, 1815–1822," in *Oneida Indian Journey*, 57; Ellis, "Advent of the New York Indians," 419; Tiro, *People of the Standing Stone*, 138–39.

12. Extract of Minutes, Northern Missionary Society Meeting, 2 May 1816; James Mairs and Christian Miller, Committee Report to Northern Missionary Society, June 1816; Minutes of the Board, 4 September 1816, all in Northern Missionary Society of New York MSS, Rutgers University; Eleazer Williams's translation work appeared as Samuel Blatchford, *An Address Delivered to the Oneida Indians, September 24, 1810, Translated at the Request of the Board of Directors of the Northern Missionary Society by Eleazer Williams* (Albany, NY: Churchill and Abbey, 1815).

13. Eleazer Williams, Autobiographical Writings, EW MSS, MR 3, WHSARC, UWGB.

14. Ibid.

15. Eleazer Williams, "A Method of Daily Prayer," EW MSS, MR 6; "Occasional Prayers," EW MSS, MR 5. All in WHSARC, UWGB.

16. Catechism assembled by Eleazer Williams, EW MSS, MR 5, WHSARC, UWGB.

17. Eleazer Williams, Autobiographical Writings, EW MSS, MR 3, WHSARC, UWGB.

18. "Go out into the highways and hedges, and compel them to come in, that my house may be filled," Luke 14:23; Eleazer Williams, Autobiographical Writings, EW MSS, MR 3, WHSARC, UWGB.

19. Eleazer Williams, Autobiographical Writings, EW MSS, MR 3; Bible passages highlighted by Williams, EW MSS, MR 2; Sermon on Psalm 107:4–7, EW MSS, MR 5. Both in WHSARC, UWGB. Terence J. O'Grady, "The Singing Societies of Oneida," *American Music* 9 (Spring 1991): 67–91.

20. Ellis, "Advent of the New York Indians," 420. Eleazer Williams, Autobiographical Writings, EW MSS, MR 3; Sermon on John 8:34, EW MSS, MR 5. Both in WHSARC, UWGB. Tiro, *People of the Standing Stone*, 139.

21. Eleazer Williams, Autobiographical Writings, EW MSS, MR 3, WHSARC, UWGB.

22. Ibid.

23. Ibid.

24. Ibid.

25. Ibid.

26. Ibid.

27. Ibid.

28. Ibid; *Christian Herald*, March 1, 1817, 361.

29. *Christian Herald*, March 1, 1817, 361; Ellis, "Advent of the New York Indians," 420; Hauptman, *Conspiracy of Interests*, 56; Bloomfield, *Oneidas*, 146; Luna M. Hammond [Whitney], *History of Madison County, State of New York* (Syracuse, NY: Truair, Smith, 1872), 112.

30. Eleazer Williams to Bishop Hobart, n.d., EW MSS, MR 2; Eleazer Williams, Autobiographical Writings, EW MSS, MR 3. Both in WHSARC, UWGB; Ellis, "Advent of the New York Indians," 420; Frank W. Merrill, *The Church's Mission to the Oneidas* (Wisconsin Oneida Reservation: Oneida Episcopal Mission 1899), 12.

31. Merrill, *The Church's Mission*, 12; Eleazer Williams, Autobiographical Writings, EW MSS, MR 3, WHSARC, UWGB; Appendix to Eleazer Williams, *Prayers for Families and for Particular Persons, Selected from the Book of Common Prayer* (Albany, NY: G. J. Loomis, 1816), 20.

32. Clipping from the *Onondaga Gazette*, July 30, 1817, EW MSS, MR 3, WHSARC, UWGB; Hobart's survey printed in *Christian Journal and Literary Register*, March 19, 1817.

33. "Mission of the Protestant Episcopal Church in the State of New York to the Oneida Indians," *Christian Journal and Literary Register*, September 1, 1818; "Religion, from the *Utica Patriot*," *National Register: A Weekly Paper*, October 10, 1818; "Address by Bishop Hobart to the Convention of the Protestant Episcopal Church," *Christian Journal and Literary Register*, December 1, 1818; Bloomfield, *Oneidas*, 151; Charles Wells Hayes, *The Diocese of Western New York: History and Recollections*, 2nd ed. (Rochester, NY: Scranton, Wetmore, 1905), 49–51.

34. "Oneida Indians," *Religious Intelligencer*, December 26, 1818.

35. Eleazer Williams, Autobiographical Writings, EW MSS, MR 3, WHSARC, UWGB.

36. Ibid.; "Report of the Committee of the Board of the Hamilton Baptist Missionary Society," *Western New York Baptist Magazine*, February 1, 1820.

PART II

THE ONEIDA EPISCOPAL MISSION
The First Century in Wisconsin

Editors' Introduction to Part II

Oneida lands, totaling over 5 million acres in 1784, were the necessary ingredients for the rise of the Empire State. Their central New York lands were situated at a vital transportation crossroads that was essential for New York's economic growth after the Revolution. Road, canal, and railroad building made the Oneidas' lands accessible and brought with it a massive wave of white settlers. In order for New York State to expand east-west and north-south, private entrepreneurial interests in conjunction with Albany officials, be they Federalists, Jeffersonians, Clintonians, Democrats, or Whigs, and subsidized by public funds, constantly picked away at Indian lands. The Oneidas, already severely fractionated in their polity and religion, largely found it impossible to resist the pressures of land speculators and state and federal officials, leading a majority of the community to eventually migrate out of New York by the mid-1840s.

The Oneidas' position in Michigan Territory was precarious at best during the Jacksonian era. Although the Oneidas had negotiated agreements in 1821–1822 with the Menominees and Ho Chunks to what they thought was a vast land base of several million acres in Michigan Territory, their lands were reduced to 65,400 acres by a series of federal treaties from 1827 to 1838. To resist another Indian removal, Bishop Kemper worked with Chief Daniel Bread, who had emerged as the most prominent leader of the Oneidas at their Duck Creek reservation near Green Bay. The bishop also mentored a young Oneida lad, Cornelius Hill, who along with two other Oneidas was sent off to study at the Nashotah House Seminary. Hill, a son-in-law but a bitter rival of Chief Bread, later became the principal chief of the Oneidas as well as the first ordained Oneida deacon in 1895 and priest in 1903.

In addition to serving as both the spiritual adviser and protector of the Oneidas from outside pressures, the bishop had other positive effects on the Oneidas. By exploring the life of Susan Fenimore Cooper, in their award-winning essay reprinted with permission from *New York History*, L. Gordon McLester III, Judy Cornelius-Hawk, and Laurence M. Hauptman show how the bishop influenced the daughter of James Fenimore Cooper, the United States' first great novelist, to write about and take up the cause of the Wisconsin Oneidas and expose the threats these American Indians faced. As a distinguished nature writer and highly devout Episcopalian, Susan Fenimore Cooper came to the aid of the Oneidas, helping them raise funds to construct their new Episcopal Church, which opened in 1886.

Kemper also saw the need to train Episcopal clergy to serve American Indian communities. The bishop encouraged J. Lloyd Breck, William Adams, and John Henry Hobart Jr. to establish Nashotah House [Theological Seminary] in 1842. At the time of its founding, there were only two other Episcopal clergymen besides Bishop Kemper serving in Wisconsin Territory. Following the Cooper article, Very Rev. Steven Peay describes the founding of this historically important seminary, located on 460 acres of land at the foot of a hill overlooking two lakes, approximately thirty miles west of Milwaukee. The seminary training was in the Anglo-Catholic tradition. To this day, the Nashotah House continues to train priests for worldwide service.

Breck, who was ordained at the Episcopal Church at the Oneidas' Duck Creek reservation, was Nashotah House's first dean/superior, and William Adams, its librarian and most prominent teacher. Every day but Sunday, seminarians were required to help support the operations of the seminary by contributing four hours of work to maintain its operations. Students were assigned to different committees, including being responsible for Nashotah's carpentry, farming, and laundry. In the years of Breck's leadership, the seminary was an austere place with strict discipline handed down by the dean. Because of criticism of his management style, Breck was eventually forced to resign in 1849. Other deans that followed were less rigid, undoubtedly influenced by the beloved, well-respected Kemper. This historic seminary today stands as a tribute to him and his vision for the Episcopal Church.

Attached to Peay's article are excerpts from three Episcopal clergymen's accounts. The first was written by Father G. P. Schetky, who attended the seminary between 1845 and 1851, in which he describes daily life at the Nashotah House. At this time, three Oneidas, including the ten-year-old Cornelius Hill, along with their future missionary, Edward A. Goodnough, were in attendance. Father Schetky's diary also provides his impressions of a student visit to Episcopal Church ceremonies at the Wisconsin Oneida reservation. A second diary, one by Breck himself, sheds light on the connections between the Nashotah House and the Wisconsin Oneidas. Even by the late 1840s, the Oneidas' church was one of only three Episcopal parishes in all of Wisconsin. Breck describes his visits to the Oneidas at Duck Creek, and his account, as well as a third memoir authored by Rt. Rev. William Ingraham Kip, later the bishop of California, describes the special place of honor awarded to the Oneidas by Bishop Kemper at the first Episcopal Church convocation held in Milwaukee in 1847.

An article on two Oneida tribal leaders—Chief Cornelius Hill and John Archiquette—both of whom were major figures in the Episcopal Church at Oneida, follows. At a time when federal allotment policies were being formulated and implemented, both men's lives were intertwined with building, supporting, and defending the Episcopal faith on their Duck Creek reservation. The article clearly reveals the two Wisconsin Oneida leaders' unwavering commitment to the Episcopal mission in the waning decades of the nineteenth century and early years of the twentieth century. In the first section of this article, the authors focus on Chief Cornelius Hill's extraordinary life—from his birth in 1834, to his attendance at the Nashotah House in the mid-1840s, to his political battles with Chief Daniel Bread, to his ascendancy to the Episcopal deaconate in 1895 and to the priesthood in 1903, to his passing in 1907. In the second half of the article, the authors focus attention on John Archiquette, the captain of the Oneidas' federal police, tribal councilor, and Oneida vestryman who had an extraordinary fifty-year commitment to the church. Using the extensive collection of Archiquette papers at Yale University's Beinecke Library, the authors show that the police captain frequently ran afoul of federal authorities with his overriding commitment to his faith and his church.

The focus of the next section in Part II is on the Episcopal mission from the 1850s through the first decade of the twentieth century. Although not a church-appointed missionary, Ellen Goodnough, Reverend Goodnough's very dedicated first wife, assisted the Oneidas through bouts of famine, pestilence, and efforts to remove them to the Indian Territory. Until her death in 1870, Ellen Goodnough played a major role as an educator at the Oneida mission. Since she did not meddle in politics, in some ways she was more appreciated than her husband, especially by the Oneida women. In an excerpt from her diary reproduced from Julia Keen Bloomfield's *The Oneidas* (1907), the missionary's wife describes Christmastime at the mission.

Approximately fifteen months after the death of Edward Goodnough in 1890, Solomon S. Burleson came to serve the Oneida Indian mission. His previous service was in Minnesota under the Episcopal bishopric of Henry Whipple. Burleson convinced Rt. Rev. Charles Chapman Grafton, the bishop of Fond du Lac, of the need to improve health care among the Oneidas. His interest in this area was no accident, since Burleson's father had been a physician and the missionary himself had previous experience in Minnesota as a dentist. During Burleson's six-year tenure as a missionary, a chancel was added to the Hobart Stone Church, Chief Cornelius Hill was made a deacon, and the Hobart Stone Church was formally consecrated by Bishop Grafton.

In 1898, less than one year after Burleson's passing, the Episcopal Church opened its mission hospital on the Wisconsin Oneida reservation. A decade before the founding of the federal government's Indian Health Service, the Oneida mission hospital was already dealing with the scourges of tuberculosis, trachoma, measles, and influenza that periodically spread like wildfire in Indian communities throughout the Americas. In an excerpt from a biography of the missionary written by his sons, including H. L. Burleson, later the bishop of South Dakota, they describe their father's role as a health provider at Oneida. The Episcopal missionary encouraged Oneidas such as Nancy and Lavinia Cornelius and Josiah Powless to seek careers in the health professions. The two women became nurses, and Powless graduated from the Milwaukee Medical College in 1904.

Part II concludes with a first-person account, written by missionary Frank Wesley Merrill, describing the origins of Oneida lace making, an artistic tradition that is being revived today. Episcopal deaconess Sybil Carter initiated this project, which linked the lace traditions of northern Europe with Oneida women's traditional artistic skills. At the height of this effort, 150 people, mostly women, were involved in this self-help program, one fully endorsed by the Oneida Episcopal mission and aided by the presence of several different orders of nuns sent to serve the community. Making, packing, distributing, and selling lace, Oneidas won awards for their artistry, receiving high praise at local, state, and even world fairs. This artistic tradition is being revived today on the Wisconsin Oneida reservation. Missionary Merrill frequently traveled to the east to raise money for the mission. In his travels, he also helped facilitate the sale of lace, since the Sybil Carter Indian lace-making mission store and financial benefactors were headquartered in New York City. He also made stops at the United States Indian Industrial School in Carlisle, Pennsylvania, and at Hampton Institute in Virginia to check on the welfare of the hundreds of Wisconsin Oneidas attending the two boarding schools.

4

ANOTHER LEATHERSTOCKING TALE

Susan Fenimore Cooper, the Episcopal Church, and the Oneidas

Laurence M. Hauptman, L. Gordon McLester III,
and Judy Cornelius-Hawk

JAMES FENIMORE COOPER WAS THE UNITED STATES' FIRST great novelist, achieving a worldwide reputation during his lifetime His extraordinary novels—his massive body of work often referred to as the "Leatherstocking Tales"—evoke images of determined American frontiersmen such as Natty Bumppo and noble American Indians such as Chingachgook.[1] Susan Fenimore Cooper, the writer's daughter, spent her life in the shadow of this literary giant. Over the course of her life, she edited and prepared new editions of her father's masterpieces. Yet, she accomplished much on her own. Susan Fenimore Cooper was one of the founders of environmental literature, publishing the first book on nature writing by an American woman.[2] Her book, *Rural Hours*, influenced Henry David Thoreau and his classic *Walden*, published in 1854.[3] Cooper also wrote historical accounts of the American and French Revolutions, stories for children, a study of a prominent missionary, and a major article against women suffrage that employed religious arguments common in nineteenth-century America.[4] However, one aspect of her life has been neglected, namely her work with the hierarchy of the Episcopal Church on behalf of the Oneida Indians.[5]

From 1848 onward, the Oneida Indians fascinated Cooper. Later, she published a series of fourteen articles in which she roused church support to fend off their enemies. She also helped the Wisconsin Oneidas raise funds to build a new church to replace a smaller, dilapidated house of worship. Cooper's interest in their welfare gave impetus to other church efforts on behalf of the Oneidas. These included the Episcopal Church's establishment of a major self-help lace-making project that employed more than 150 women for more than three decades and support for the establishment of the first hospital on the Wisconsin Oneidas' Duck Creek reservation near Green Bay. Cooper also wrote a full-length history of these Native Americans, an unpublished manuscript now on deposit in the James Fenimore Cooper Collection at Yale University's Beinecke Library. In 1907, thirteen years after Cooper's death, Julia K. Bloomfield published *The Oneidas*, a book that was largely derived from Cooper's research and notes.[6]

By the middle of the nineteenth century, the Oneidas' association with the Episcopal Church was well established. Anglican missionaries had made their first appearance into Mohawk and Oneida Country in the first years of the eighteenth century. However, during the Great Awakening, missionary Samuel Kirkland established the Presbyterian Church in Oneida Country. Even before Kirkland's death in 1808, the Presbyterians were losing ground with the Oneidas because his attention was focused on building the Hamilton-Oneida Academy (the predecessor of Hamilton College) and on collaborating with land company agents who were acquiring tribal lands. After the War of 1812, the Episcopal Church hierarchy led by Bishop John Henry Hobart initiated a major effort at proselytizing the Oneidas. Eventually, the majority of Oneidas who migrated and resettled in the environs of Green Bay, converted to the Episcopal faith, and built the tribe's log church, the first Protestant congregation established in Michigan Territory.[7] Although the Methodist Church was important there from the 1830s onward, the Episcopal Church was at the center of Oneida political, economic and spiritual matters throughout the nineteenth and well into the twentieth century. In the nineteenth century, two of the most prominent tribal leaders of the Oneidas—Chiefs Daniel Bread and Cornelius Hill—were especially active in church affairs.[8]

Susan Fenimore Cooper was strongly influenced in the Episcopal faith by her mother, Susan Augusta Fenimore, who had come from a devoutly religious family. Moreover, Susan Fenimore Cooper's uncle was William Heathcote DeLancey, the first Bishop of western New York, serving from 1839 to 1865. A high churchman in the Anglo-Catholic tradition with an evangelical bent, DeLancey was a major figure in the Episcopal Church in America.[9] Cooper was especially active in the Episcopal Church's efforts. For much of her life, she lived across the street from Christ Church in Cooperstown, New York, the town founded by her grandfather Judge William Cooper. She was the leading force behind the founding of the Orphan House of the Savior for Boys and Girls, Thanksgiving Hospital that later merged with Mary Imogene Bassett Hospital that still serves as a regional medical facility, and the Susan Fenimore Cooper Foundation that provided vocational training for boys and girls.[10] At the time of her death, she was remembered more for her charitable contributions than for her literary achievements: she was a "prominent figure among the best and most useful and truly Christian women of this State. Every work and charity having for its aim and object the elevation of humanity, or the amelioration and improvement of the condition of the poor, the unfortunate, the outcast, had not only her sympathy and good will, but her active support. . . . She served her divine Master by a life mainly devoted to Christian charity; she literally wore herself out in the service of others. The world is better because she lived in it."[11] Eventually, this commitment to Episcopal philanthropic work led her to advocate for the Oneida Indians of Wisconsin.

Although Cooper was born in 1813 at her maternal grandfather's home in Mamaroneck, New York, she and her family are rightly equated with Cooperstown. This town, now identified as the baseball mecca, was the historic homeland of the Oneida Indians. Her grandfather, Judge William Cooper, taking advantage of Loyalist confiscations after the American Revolution, acquired land in the region and founded village named after him and became its most prominent and powerful citizen.[12] Although Judge Cooper's son, James Fenimore, later wrote about Native Americans, his focus in his most famous novel was the Mohicans (Mahicans), not Oneidas. At the time of Susan's birth, her father was serving at Oswego, New York in the United States Navy during the War of 1812. Ironically, the novelist's assigned duty was to help construct the *Oneida*, the first United States armed vessel to patrol Lake Ontario.[13]

Nothing else in Susan Fenimore Cooper's childhood would suggest that she would take a keen interest in Native American subjects or become an advocate for the Oneidas. Because of her family's prominence, Susan received a fine education from tutors; attended private schools; learned four languages; studied botany, history, literature, and zoology; and was accomplished in music, drawing, and dancing. Later, she spent eight years in France, where her father's Parisian residence attracted the likes of Sir Walter Scott and Samuel F. B. Morse; and three years in New York City before returning to Cooperstown in the 1830s.[14]

Cooper's most acclaimed book was *Rural Hours*, published anonymously by G. P. Putnam in 1850. During 1848 and 1849, she kept a journal of the seasonal changes in and around Cooperstown that described bird behavior as well as the growth and changes in plants in village gardens. She presented a deep concern for her surroundings, lamenting that European-introduced weeds threatened native plants.[15] Although she believed that the natural world existed for the benefit, pleasure, and use of humankind, Cooper, as scholars Rochelle L. Johnson and Daniel Patterson have observed, advocated an "argument for a sustainable balance between human culture and its natural surroundings." To her, "the ideal society" was a "rural one, carefully pointed between the receding wilderness and a looming industrialization."[16]

In her most famous work, Cooper wrote about her first contact with living Native Americans. In *Rural Hours*, she described a chance encounter with three Oneida women who had come into Cooperstown's environs. Her descriptions used the uncomfortable, racially charged language of the day, and her assimilationist conclusions, held by many reformers at the time, were based on the assumption that Native Americans would inevitably succumb to white man's 'superior' civilization; however, her writing revealed her empathy for them and her words were clearly intended to evoke sympathy and an understanding of their plight. To her, American Indians were an essential part of the fabric of the natural world whose continued existence was sadly threatened, much like what happened to indigenous plants faced with the invasion of European weeds.[17]

The three Oneida women made a lasting impression on Cooper since, at the time, she believed, much like her father, that the Native peoples were a vanishing race that had been displaced by "civilization." They had come to sell black ash baskets, but only one of them could speak English. The eldest, the grandmother, "was a Christian," but the other was (in Cooper's words) a "pagan." "Around their necks, arms, and ankles, they wore strings of cheap ornaments, pewter medals, and coarse glass beads, with the addition of a few scraps of tin, the refuse of some tin-shop passed on their way." She noted that the women were very reticent, "and they still kept up their true Indian etiquette of mastering all emotion." Unable to gather more information from them, she was most taken aback by "their whole appearance," which "was so much more Indian than we had been prepared for." Pleased with their visit, Cooper described the three women as being "gentle and womanly, so free from anything coarse or rude in the midst of their untutored ignorance."[18]

By the time of the appearance of these women near Cooperstown, most Oneidas had succumbed to the extreme pressures caused by land and canal speculation that led to the rapid non-Indian settlement of central New York. From the 1820s through the mid-1840s, most of central New York's Oneidas were to migrate to Wisconsin and Ontario, Canada. Thus not surprisingly, at the conclusion of the Oneida women's visit in 1848, Cooper noted that it was "painful, indeed, to remember how little has yet been done for the Indians during the three centuries since he and the white man first met on the Atlantic coast." Employing racially tinged language that was characteristic of the time, she bemoaned that this "savage race" was "almost invariably corrupted" right from the beginning of contact "with a civilized people; they suffer from the vices of civilization before they learn justly to comprehend its merits."[19]

Coming from a nineteenth-century world which defined western culture and values as far superior to that of the Indians, she saw missionaries as offering the Oneidas the gifts and benefits of "civilization." Thus, as late as the 1880s, Cooper continued to portray the Wisconsin Oneidas as a "half wild tribe," with "a mental condition of children."[20] Unlike her views of nature, which required the preservation of the beautiful world around Cooperstown, she believed that Native peoples were in need of being transformed for their own survival. To her, missionary wives such as Ellen Goodnough were especially needed to undo the "shiftless, untidy way of living in the Oneida cabins."[21]

Cooper, nevertheless, had been permanently affected by her 1848 encounter with the three Oneida women. Some of her past assumptions about Native Americans had been called into question and her deep religiosity and philanthropic activities were to lead her back to the Oneidas over the next decades. Her commitment to the Episcopal Church's missionary work motivated her to undertake an ambitious history that focused on these same Native Americans in both their New York homeland and on their later Wisconsin reservation. In the process, she would point out the Oneidas' contributions to the American experience, especially their key role helping Americans win independence from Great Britain. She would also describe the many injustices these Native Americans had to overcome, noting especially the troubled times during the Jacksonian removal era and the years immediately after the Civil War.[22]

Much like others in the Christian reform movement of Indian policy in the second half of the nineteenth century, Cooper saw the Oneidas as in need of protection since they were being overwhelmed by "the march of progress."[23] Although it may seem strange and contradictory today looking back and reading her overbearing and at times racist language, Cooper nevertheless recognized that these Native peoples were worthy Episcopalians and hardworking, intelligent farmers.[24] Cooper praised the Oneidas for being "shrewd observers of people" who were able to recognize the good intentions and benevolence of individuals.[25] She clearly identified with the work of Ellen Goodnough, whom she greatly admired and devoted much attention to in her writings. She also lauded the Oneidas for their exquisite renditions of Christian hymns, which she believed added to the overall beauty and effectiveness of the Episcopal mission at Duck Creek.[26]

In 1816, Episcopal Bishop John Henry Hobart visited the Oneidas in central New York. Hobart soon sent a catechist, Eleazer Williams, a Mohawk, to proselytize among the Oneidas. Williams' presence occurred at the exact time when the Oneidas in New York were feeling the effects of canal and land pressures from private, local, state, and federal officials who advocated the tribe's removal from the Empire State. Although Williams did convert Oneidas, his religious leadership was ultimately rejected by most of the Indians because of his collaboration with the Ogden Land Company in encouraging tribesmen to leave New York State for Michigan Territory, his marriage to a thirteen-year old Menominee, and his acquisitiveness in seeking tribal lands.[27] A quarter of a century later, Cooper met Williams in Washington, DC, and heard him deliver a sermon there. In her writings on the Oneidas after the Civil War, Cooper devoted significant attention to Williams. Although Cooper never challenged the veracity of his bizarre claim to be the "Lost Dauphin" of France, her chance meeting brought her back to Oneidas and their history.[28]

Despite Williams' self-interest and eccentric behavior, the Episcopal faith took hold because of the work of a series of more respected missionaries that followed the controversial Mohawk cleric after his departure from the scene by 1830. No overriding theological concept brought the majority of Wisconsin Oneidas to the Episcopal religion; however, their Christian faith was real. As James Treat has observed, "to disregard Indian Christians, either as Indians or Christians, is to deny their human agency, their religious independence, and—ultimately—their very lives."[29] The success of the Hobart Indian mission and its acceptance among the Oneidas was largely based on how the Indians viewed their Episcopal clerics after the departure of Williams from the 1830s onward. Bishop Jackson Kemper and Ellen Goodnough were especially seen as good people who understood the Oneidas and their needs and who provided protection during crises. Although missionaries such as Edward A. Goodnough were viewed by some Oneidas at times as being too strict and as meddlers in tribal political affairs, these clerics did make some contributions that were viewed as beneficial to the Indians. Besides religious instruction, they helped teach tribal members how to write English, required in their petitioning to the Office of Indian Affairs in Washington and filed protests with the commissioner of Indian affairs on behalf of the Oneidas. The missionaries supplied charitable goods in times of want and helped organize community building efforts, including appealing for Episcopal financial backing, building materials, and labor to build a new Hobart Church in the early to mid-1880s. These benevolent actions helped deflect some of the criticisms and contributed to the community's acceptance/tolerance of the Episcopal missionaries.[30]

In his autobiography, Chief Hill attempted to explain why many of his people turned to and stood by the Episcopal faith. Before his ascension to the position of Episcopal priest, Hill served as the church organist, interpreter during services, and warden on the vestry council of the Hobart Church. In his autobiography, he focused on the impact of missionary Edward Goodnough and his wife Ellen. Although some Oneidas resented the missionary, the chief claimed that Goodnough resisted efforts by the Indian agent and by some of the Oneidas to sell tribal lands. According to Hill's account, the chief defended the missionary when the clergyman was threatened with removal from the reservation. He insisted that if it had not been for the missionary, his tribe would probably have been removed to the Indian Territory. Hill referred to the missionary's wife affectionately as "Mother Goodnough" and credited her with initiating the building of a larger and more permanent stone house of worship to replace the wooden one built a half century earlier.[31]

Despite being cast as childlike by Cooper and her contemporaries, the Wisconsin Oneidas were hardly politically naive people in the second half of the nineteenth century. They had savvy leaders such as Chiefs Daniel Bread and Cornelius Hill and had learned many lessons from over two hundred fifty years of contact with Euroamericans. The Oneidas had been displaced from their central New York homeland, but had remarkably re-built their lives in Wisconsin despite their resettlement and significant participation on the Union side in the Civil War. They were also suspicious of outsiders, having experienced dispossession after their alliance with the Americans during the Revolution and having been abandoned by Kirkland and later Williams.[32]

The Wisconsin Oneidas were well aware that their bishop Jackson Kemper had a prominent within the Episcopal Church and hoped he would serve as their protector. In 1835, Kemper was appointed the first missionary bishop of the Episcopal Church in America and placed in charge of founding districts in Indiana, Iowa, Kansas, Minnesota, Missouri, Nebraska, and Wisconsin. Because of his stature in religious circles, Kemper's support of the Hobart Indian Mission, the first one of its kind established by the Episcopal Church in the West, became a special experiment in evangelism for him as well as for the national church.[33] The Oneidas could easily see that Kemper's commitment to the community was a real one since he visited the community on an annual basis. They could appreciate the bishop's struggle to travel over a hundred miles by horseback or buggy to Duck Creek from his residence outside of Milwaukee. It was this commitment to the Oneidas and the bishop's sensitivity to and respect for aspects of their culture, not his Anglo-Catholic theology that won acceptance by these Native peoples. It was also no coincidence that Kemper was instrumental in bringing Susan Fenimore Cooper into the mix in a concerted effort to help the Oneidas deal with several crises they faced after the Civil War.

The prominent anthropologist William N. Fenton once observed, "Whoever came to the Iroquois [Mohawk, Oneida, Onondaga, Cayuga, Seneca, and Tuscarora] came on their terms."[34] Outsiders that followed the controversial Williams did not just show up at the reservation. In carefully examining Bishop Kemper's first two visits to Duck Creek in 1838 and 1839, there were clear elements of the ritual paradigm of the Condolence Council, the most sacred of all Iroquoian ceremonies.[35] The bishop, as an invited guest, was welcomed in the traditional manner at the Wood's Edge and incorporated symbolically into the Oneida community. On August 7th, 1838, Kemper laid the cornerstone of the new Hobart Church, which was to replace the log church, the first Protestant house of worship in Michigan Territory that had been constructed by the Oneidas in the mid-1820s. Recognizing, respecting, and working effectively with the tribal leadership, the bishop invited four of the Oneida chiefs, to help him lay the cornerstone of the Hobart Church. In his service, Kemper set the ritual pattern that was used throughout his tenure as bishop, namely the employment of the Oneida language in the service. At the ceremony, the Episcopal service began by the chanting of the *Te Deum* in the Oneida language, an important step in getting tribal support for the mission.[36] Kemper and his missionaries, as Cooper points out in her later writings, encouraged hymn singing in the Oneida language and organ music, a much valued community tradition that began with Kirkland's Presbyterian mission in the 1760s.[37]

On his second visit in September 1839, the bishop consecrated the completed house of worship, the first non-Roman Catholic Church in the Upper Midwest. Now no longer a guest but an accepted part of the community, the bishop performed the consecration ceremony, followed by the formal Oneida response by Daniel Bread, the Wisconsin Oneidas' principal chief. The chief, in the Iroquoian traditional manner, used the metaphor often used in the past at treaty renewals. He insisted: "A chain of friendship is to be formed which we trust will never be broken."[38] Thus, a unique Oneida form of High Church Episcopalianism was born, one that was not just Christian, but was very much Iroquoian. In 1842, Kemper founded the Nashotah House, the Episcopal seminary west of Milwaukee, and trained and ordained its first clerics, including missionary Goodnough. Kemper also mentored Cornelius Hill. As a ten-year-old, Hill, a future chief, attended Nashotah House for five years; in 1903, Chief Hill became the first Wisconsin Oneida Episcopal priest.

In addition to allowing the chanting of the *Te Deum* in the Oneida language, the Episcopal Church's employment of music was attractive to the Duck Creek community and became an important part of Oneida Christianity. Michael D. McNally, in his outstanding work on the Ojibwes, has noted that hymn singing was both an example of colonization and a form of tribal resistance. On one hand, Christian missionaries saw music as a medium for evangelization and acculturation, substituting hymn singing and organ music for the traditional use of the drum and dance; on the other hand, "native people changed the performance style and social constellation of the music to make it their own."[39] Starting in New York a century before that of the Ojibwes, the Oneida hymn singing tradition also had this dual purpose. But today it represents the later, serving as an important touchstone of Oneida identity. In services of both at the Episcopal and Methodist churches, at wakes and funerals, and at community events and meetings, including at the Oneida Longhouse, the presence of these hymn singers and their renditions in the Oneida language provide comfort. The singers bring their tradition outward to other non-Indian churches and venues and to other Native communities throughout Wisconsin. Their performances transcend politics, unifying diverse groups within the Duck Creek community and among other Oneida communities in Canada and New York that had become separated over time.[40] In September 2008, the National Endowment for the Arts awarded the Oneida Hymn Singers the National Heritage Fellowship Award, the highest honor the federal government bestows on folk and traditional artists.[41]

From the 1830s the personal rectitude and charisma of particular clerics, the aid they gave to community causes, their liturgical innovations, and their incorporation of Oneidas into the life of the church all enhanced the practice of the Episcopal faith at Duck Creek. Right after the end of the Civil War, Kemper encouraged

Cooper to start a full-scale history project about the Oneidas.[42] Her connection to Kemper, who became the Bishop of Wisconsin until his death in 1870, was through her maternal uncle, Bishop James DeLancey, whom she frequently visited at his residence in Geneva, New York. Beginning in 1828 and continuing until 1863, DeLancey frequently corresponded with Bishop Kemper about church matters, especially about candidates for missionary service in the American West. Kemper visited DeLancey in Geneva. Moreover, the western New York bishop would refer to his Wisconsin counterpart as his "friend and brother."[43]

In other ways, the Wisconsin Episcopal Diocese was strongly tied to the church's hierarchy in New York State. Bishop DeLancey and Susan's own Episcopal Bishop, William Croswell Doane of the Diocese of Albany, were connected to Bishop Kemper. Both had been shaped by the Oxford Movement and Kemper's theology of Anglo-Catholicism. Both were high churchmen in their ritualistic practices, but each had an evangelical bent with a strong commitment to missionary work. Bishop Doane's father, George Washington Doane, had been the Bishop of New Jersey, and importantly, had been a mentor to Kemper, consecrating him as the Bishop of Wisconsin, then Michigan Territory, in 1835. Bishop William Croswell Doane would view Kemper as his own mentor: "All my life long, I have been looking up to you as being [the] illustration of the great principles of missionary work, which my father [George Washington Doane] originated and loved as well."[44] Moreover, Kemper's successor in 1870 was John Henry Hobart Brown, the first Bishop of the Diocese of Fond du Lac in the mid-1870s, who had formerly served as a priest at St. John's Episcopal Church in Cohoes, Bishop William Croswell Doane's Albany Diocese.[45]

Kemper was increasingly disturbed by events happening at Oneida during and immediately after the American Civil War. The Oneidas faced a series of crises that soon led Cooper to come to their aid. Kemper was increasingly disturbed by events happening at Oneida during and immediately after the American Civil War. The writer was contacted by Bishop Kemper and by missionary Goodnough about events transpiring at the time. The 1,100-member Oneida Indian community in the environs of Green Bay had suffered significantly during the late war. Ten percent of the reservation population had volunteered to serve in the Union Army, and at least forty-six were killed, missing in action, or died of disease while at war. Moreover, at the same time, a severe drought produced crop failures, and smallpox ravaged the reservation community.[46]

In 1866, Morgan L. Martin, a long-time foe of the Oneidas, was appointed federal Indian agent. Starting in the 1840s, Martin had been a strong proponent of removing the Oneidas once again, this time from Wisconsin to the Indian Territory. Morgan had also been heavily involved in land and canal speculation in the Fox River Valley and in other areas of the state. His varied interests included the promotion of the dairy industry in Wisconsin and the founding of the City of

Milwaukee. Hoping to recover from major financial setbacks, he became a proponent of railroad development and, at the same time, he sought political sinecures, holding the office of Civil War paymaster in Green Bay before his appointment as federal Indian agent. Thus, much to the Oneidas' chagrin, by the late 1860s Martin was put in charge of the communications link to the "Great Father" President Grant and to the federal commissioner of Indian affairs in Washington, DC.[47]

Ellen Goodnough, the missionary's wife, wrote in her diary that the federal Indian agent was a "very harsh and arbitrary man and determined to get at these lands from the Indians and drive them West."[48] Martin attempted to take advantage of the internal political divisions within the Oneidas to open up the 65,400-acre reservation for white settlement. In his official report to Washington, Martin argued that *only* 4,000 of over 60,000 acres were being cultivated. "Even if you cut the reservation to 20 percent of the site," the agent continued, "there would still be abundant room for the coming generations of this tribe, until they shall have entirely disappeared or become incorporated with the white race which now surrounds them."[49] Later, Ellen Goodnough wrote that Martin hoped to frighten the Oneidas off. This would allow him to carry out the agenda of Green Bay mill owners who lusted after the timber on the reservation's lands.[50] Consequently, until 1869, when he was replaced, Martin fomented tribal divisions and constantly lied about the Oneidas in correspondence to his superiors.[51]

In 1870, both Ellen Goodnough and Bishop Kemper died. Missionary Goodnough sent Cooper a copy of the eulogy presented at his wife's funeral.[52] Later, in 1878, he answered Cooper's questions about the Oneidas and sent her his wife's journal. Goodnough explained that he allowed Cooper to use his wife's diary as a tribute to her and to her sacrifice during "her long isolation amongst the Indians." He also sent Cooper his notes from the parish's register, journals of the Episcopal Church conventions, and the writings of Albert G. Ellis of Stevens Point on these Native Americans' resettlement in Michigan Territory as well as on Eleazer Williams.[53] Missionary Goodnough had another powerful motivation to reach out to Cooper. Realizing her family's prominence and connections to the Eastern establishment and the Episcopal hierarchy, Goodnough saw Cooper as an asset to help him and the Oneidas raise funding to build a new church. The small wooden frame Hobart Mission Church, then in a decrepit state, was inadequate for the growing number of Oneidas who had been drawn to the Episcopal faith.

Goodnough's mission in the 1870s became part of the Niobrara Mission—Episcopal efforts among the Lakotas, Ojibwes, and Oneidas. Headed by Bishop William Hare, the Niobrara Mission's funding came largely from a group of prominent wives of New York's great financiers, including its president Mrs. John Jacob Astor.[54] It is interesting to note that later Episcopal missionary efforts to promote Oneida lace work came from some of the same New York City women. It was also no coincidence that the Oneida lace—extraordinary altarpieces—were displayed at the opening of the great Episcopal Cathedral of St. John the Divine in New York City in 1911.[55]

By examining Cooper's Oneida manuscript now on deposit in the Beinecke Rare Book and Manuscript Library at Yale University, it is clear she intended to write a full history of the Oneidas, their life in central New York, and the migration to and resettlement of many of their tribesmen in Wisconsin and Canada. She apparently had collected numerous materials starting with Jesuit documents and tracing the Oneidas' Episcopal tradition back to Anglican missionaries in the first years of the eighteenth century and carrying it forward to the 1880s. She drew materials from Ellen Goodnough's diary as well.[56]

By 1873, a committee of the Niobrara Mission, under Bishop William Hare's direction, recognized the Oneidas and their success in promoting the Gospel: "We commend to the Church in the diocese, and in the United States, the efforts of these Indians, and of their devoted missionary, the Rev. E. A. Goodnough, and pray that God may stir us all up to deal truly and faithfully with these wards of the nation." The committee then endorsed that the General Convention of the Episcopal Church "be authorized to receive the gifts of churchmen for the erection of the new church among the Oneidas." Within a year, the Oneidas had secured over one thousand dollars for their church building fund.[57]

With the resulting economic downturn after the Panic of 1873, contributions slowed down. By the time Cooper and Goodnough corresponded again in 1878, the old church was about to crumble. *The Spirit of Missions*, the Episcopal Church's missionary report, observed that the "little old chapel is in a very unsteady condition; the ringing of the bell makes it shake and tremble so that we fear it will tumble down upon us before long."[58] After other moneys were collected, the Wisconsin Oneidas faced another setback. They had deposited their money in the Strong Bank of Green Bay. When the bank failed in 1883, the church building fund was lost.[59]

In June 1883, the Oneidas, led by Cornelius Hill, "Sachem of the Tribe and Senior Warden of Hobart Church," appealed first to the newly created diocese of Fond du Lac and subsequently to the Episcopal missionary society for donations to further their efforts to build a new church. The memorial was signed by other members of the church committee—John Archiquette, the Chief of the United States Indian Police at Oneida, Daniel A. Nimham, junior warden of the church, Peter Bread, Justice of the Peace, well as several vestrymen. They described the old church as "rapidly going to decay; it is too small, and cannot well be repaired or enlarged." They proudly pointed out that for eleven years, they had planned and worked on building a new church, quarried and hauled "a large quantity of stone," and, despite their poverty, had "raised and collected $2,600 in cash." Unfortunately, building costs had risen to $6,500. They described their dilemma: "We are poor, and can do but little in the way of raising money, but we are determined to do all that we can do and if our dear Christian friends will help us in our great work, we shall always be truly grateful."[60] Later, they revised their estimate needed to complete the building project almost doubling the amount.[61]

Cooper responded to this crisis, turning back to her earlier research on the Oneidas. She decided to excerpt her writings in a series of articles, fourteen in number, for a major Episcopal magazine in Chicago, Illinois. These articles appeared in *The Living Church* and were specifically designed to show how the Oneidas, good hardworking Indians, had persevered in the face of numerous struggles. To her, the Wisconsin Oneidas had become good devout Christians, models for other Indians. Thus, Cooper's work in effect was designed to fulfill a promise made to Bishop Kemper, namely to reinforce further Episcopal missionary efforts among American Indians.[62] Whether it was the result of Cooper's articles or not, the church fund was restored. As a result of contributions to the missionary society, the Oneidas began construction of the new Oneida stone Hobart Church. Bishop John Henry Hobart Brown was to lay the church's cornerstone on July 13, 1886. The church was later consecrated in 1897, three years after Cooper's death.[63]

Cooper's series of articles in *The Living Church* began on April 11, 1885. She described the visit to the Oneidas and Mohawks made in 1704 and after by missionaries from the Society for the Propagation of the Gospel—missionaries that included Thoroughgood Moor, William Andrews, Thomas Barclay, and others.[64] Eight days later, she focused on the Oneidas in the American Revolution with discussions of Kirkland's mission and Chief Skenando.[65] On April 25, 1885, Cooper once again discussed Kirkland and his efforts in initiating his Hamilton-Oneida Academy and treated the Oneida belief in the powers of the Standing Stone, the mystical boulder that appeared in central New York every time the tribe established a new village.[66]

After an unexplainable gap of ten months, she resumed the series, indicating her debt to Bishop Kemper and to Ellen Goodnough. She told of the Oneida decision to relocate to Wisconsin and the establishment of the Second Christian Party and the influences of Bishop Hobart and Eleazer Williams.[67] In the fourth, fifth, and sixth installments, Cooper noted the importance of ginseng in Oneida Territory in central New York and how it was marketed as far away as China. She also continued to describe the evolution of the Episcopal tradition among the Oneidas.[68] By the seventh article in the series, on March 13, 1886, she described the Oneidas' Duck Creek Reservation and the mid-1830s arrival of Methodist Oneidas from central New York. In this article, she once again gave high praise to Bishop Kemper, who was honored by the Oneidas with the name "He who has power over all words." She told of his first visit to Duck Creek in 1837, where he confirmed thirty-seven Oneidas.[69] Cooper described Kemper's special connections to this parish.[70] The Bishop "held these visitations among the red people almost yearly and entirely won their sympathy and fatherly interest in them. . . . The church was consecrated by him. He was in constant communication with their missionary

[Edward. A. Goodnough], and on many occasions his kind hand was stretched out to help them." Importantly, she observed: "For the Oneidas he [Kemper] had a peculiar feeling, from the fact that they were already Christian brethren, although surely in need of fostering care."[71]

Cooper was clearly an advocate for both the Oneidas and missionary efforts on their behalf. Like her more famous contemporary, the reformer Helen Hunt Jackson, the author of the classic *A Century of Dishonor*, Cooper brought the vast unscrupulous efforts to take Indian lands to the public's attention.[72] In several installments of her series for *The Living Church*, Cooper wrote sympathetically about the Oneidas' struggle to fight off evil-minded white traders and land speculators, presumably including Martin, who were lusting after reservation lands and trying to drive them further into the wilderness.[73] She noted that the unfortunate Oneida experience of being forced out of their New York homeland was being repeated in the "Badger State." On May 1, 1886, Cooper wrote:

> While the Oneidas were thus improving in Christian civilization, dark clouds were gathering over the tribe. The people were threatened with utter ruin. With every year the lands of the Oneidas improved in value through their own labors. At the same time the adjoining country was filling up closely with a white population. As a natural consequence of this state of things, the greed of speculators increased.[74]

Cooper hailed Chief Cornelius Hill's efforts in foiling these removal pressures in Wisconsin. Hill had received Episcopal religious training at Nashotah House. She reprinted one of Hill's letters that had appeared in the *Green Bay Advocate* in which the chief countered the slanderous remarks about his people made by Agent Martin:

> There is not a jail, a grog-shop, or a house of ill-fame amongst my [Oneida] people; all of them exist where Mr. Martin lives at Green Bay, whose civilized progress must not be arrested by the presence of the Oneidas in its vicinity. Mr. Martin ought to view his own people, they have for more than a thousand years been under the influence of civilization, yet how many reckless, thriftless white people there are. Look at Green Bay whose progress must not be impeded by the presence of Indians; how many drunkards, gamblers, adulterers, shameless women, liars, thieves, cheats, idlers, consumers, slanderers there are there.[75]

In reprinting this article, Cooper clearly saw herself as a reformer. Although she did not question the paternalistic nature of the Indian reform movement of the Gilded Age or its misguided assumptions on allotment, she hailed Bishops Whipple and Hare as well as Herbert Welsh, a founder of the Indian Rights Association, in their commitment to help Native Americans purge the Office of Indian Affairs of all corrupt personnel.[76] She questioned the national policy set forth by the United States Supreme Court in *United States v. Cook* (1873) that forbade Indians from cutting standing trees on reservations, a decision that led to a greater impoverishment in the Wisconsin Oneida community.[77]

Cooper also had high praise for the Goodnoughs. Edward A. Goodnough, known to the Oneidas as "Bright Blue Sky," and Ellen, known as "She Is Planting," were pictured as a perfect missionary team in carrying Christ's message to the Indians. She especially admired the work of Ellen Saxton Goodnough who had come to Oneida as a seventeen-year-old newlywed wife of the missionary in April 1854.[78] For the next sixteen years, "through self-denial and many hardships," she "scarcely left the reservation even for a few hours." She "labored faithfully on behalf of the Indian women," teaching home economics and partnering with her husband in spreading the Christian faith.[79]

Despite Cooper's overall assumption that Native Americans should be and would be assimilated, some of her articles often praise the traditional work of Oneida women and reveal the ability of the Oneidas to retain their culture in the framework of the Episcopal mission. A reader of her articles in *The Living Church* could easily see how the Oneidas had successfully integrated Christianity with long-held traditions. On April 10, 1886, she noted:

> When a Baptism took place all the addresses to the congregation, to the candidates, or the sponsors were given in Oneida; the prayers were in English, the people being familiar with them from their Prayer Book. At marriages portions of the service were given in Oneida, the prayers in English, and they were instructed that solemnly joining the hands as in the presence of God and before witnesses was a binding pledge. At funerals the services were held partly in English, partly in Oneida; the opening sentences and the lessons were given in Oneida, the psalm was generally read responsively in English, the younger people soon learning enough to follow the American Prayer Book in this way. They have however the whole service in their language.[80]

Besides language retention in church rituals, Cooper also pointed out other areas in which Oneidas had maintained their separation from the non-Indian world. She described how Oneidas had retained control in punishing tribal members who committed offenses on the reservation. Their chiefs served as the jury and "some men of character and intelligence" were chosen as judges. Since right through the 1880s many of the Oneidas were monolingual and could not communicate in English, an interpreter was always present at these trials.[81] She also noted that despite church efforts to change traditional gender roles, Oneida women remained attached to the field and would not give up "harvesting the maize" which they considered their *kononshioni* (Iroquoian) birthright.[82]

On June 5, 1886, in her last article for *The Living Church*, Cooper revealed the very reason she had excerpted her extensive research on the Oneidas. She described the Oneida efforts to build a new church. Praising these Indians for their industriousness, she indicated that they now faced a major crisis caused by a bank failure in Green Bay. These honest, hard-working farmers had volunteered their labor and saved their money to build a church for 800 people, but their money had vanished when the bank holding the money went bankrupt. She noted that the Oneidas had no saloons on their reservation and once again praised their women folk for being "modest in manner and chaste in character," values she had first witnessed in central New York in the late 1840s.[83] Thus, her efforts had had a clear purpose, namely to help these good Christian Indians with long roots to the Episcopal faith build and consecrate a new house of worship.

Although Cooper had prepared a draft of a history of the Oneidas, in the last decade of her life she turned to writing about missionary work. Her last major writing was on the life of William West Skiles and his proselytizing in western North Carolina, completing it before her death on December 31, 1894.[84] However, Cooper's outline history and notes lived on and were used by Julia Keen Bloomfield of Oswego, New York.[85]

Julia Keen Bloomfield was the grand niece of Joseph Bloomfield, the fourth governor of New Jersey who had been a military officer and had observed and written an extraordinarily sympathetic account about the Oneidas in the American Revolution.[86] A physically challenged "shut in" all her life, Julia Keen Bloomfield had been loaned Susan Fenimore Cooper's writings and Ellen Goodnough's diary by Frank Wesley Merrill, the missionary to the Wisconsin Oneidas from 1897 to 1906.[87] Undoubtedly Bloomfield, in her seventies at the time, was also drawn to the subject because Susan Fenimore Cooper's family, her great uncle and his descendants, lived in Oswego, and their residence was of historical importance in the community.[88] Cooper's writings were clearly evident in Bloomfield's classic, *The Oneidas*, published in two separate editions in 1907 and 1909, and in the work of the Episcopal Church's Oneida Indian Mission, later renamed the Church of the Holy Apostles, that has been an important part of Wisconsin Oneida history. Although Bloomfield frequently acknowledged Cooper, much of her book appears to be word-for-word out of articles in *The Living Church*, and the Cooper's longer unpublished historical draft.

To Cooper, the Oneidas were heroic, good Episcopalians fighting off bloodsuckers intent on destroying them. Although her writings contained mid- and late-nineteenth century views about the role of missionaries and racial assumptions seen today as offensive, she was also an advocate who recognized and praised certain Oneida qualities, especially the self-reliance of women in central New York or in central Wisconsin. Hence, it was no coincidence that the national Episcopal Church, built upon Cooper's writings by initiating a project working directly with some of these very same Oneida women. At the urging of Bishop Henry Whipple of Minnesota, church leaders in the 1890s sponsored Sybil Carter as an Episcopal missionary who established a self-help project, lace-making for Oneida women.

By the end of the first decade of the twentieth century, approximately 150 women were involved in this enterprise. They served as lace-making artists, packers, and saleswomen, displayed their work at county, state, and regional fairs, and distributed their lace to a sales office in New York City. The project received national acclaim. Twenty-five of their altar lace pieces were featured at the opening of the Cathedral of St. John's the Divine in 1911.[89]

Susan Fenimore Cooper's version of the Leatherstocking Tale was based on real concerns, not the romantic imagery so evident in her father's works. Consequently, she should be recognized not only as James Fenimore Cooper's daughter and for her own writings on nature, but also as an important voice within the Episcopal Church in America. Although reflecting the overbearing missionary zeal of the age, Cooper was intent on protecting the Oneidas and making life better for them as well as for so many of the residents of her own community of Cooperstown, New York.

Notes

1. James Fenimore Cooper's Leatherstocking Tales was a series of five novels that followed the life of Natty Bumppo, later called Hawkeye, on the eighteenth-century New York frontier: *The Pioneers* (1823), *The Last of the Mohicans* (1826), *The Prairie* (1827), *The Pathfinder* (1840), and *The Deerslayer* (1841).

2. By a Lady [Susan Fenimore Cooper], *Rural Hours* (New York: G. P. Putnam, 1850). For excellent studies of Cooper's writings on nature and her contributions to environmental literature, see Susan Fenimore Cooper, *Essays on Nature and Landscape*, ed. Rochelle L. Johnson and David Patterson (Athens: University of Georgia Press, 2002); Rochelle L. Johnson, *Passions for Nature: Nineteenth-Century America's Aesthetics of Alienation* (Athens: University of Georgia Press, 2009), 90–110; and Tina Gianquitto, *"Good Observers of Nature": American Women and the Scientific Study of the Natural World, 1820–1885* (Athens: University of Georgia Press, 2007), 100–36.

3. John Elder, foreword to Susan Fenimore Cooper, *Essays on Nature and Landscape*, ed. Rochelle L. Johnson and David Patterson (Athens: University of Georgia Press, 2009), viii; Michael P. Branch, ed., *Reading the Roots: American Nature Writing Before Walden* (Athens: University of Georgia Press, 2004), 358, 365. For a comparative analysis of Cooper's and Thoreau's writings, see Rochelle L. Johnson, "Walden, Rural Hours, and the Dilemma of Representation," in *Thoreau's Sense of Place: Essays in American Environmental Writing*, ed. Richard L. Schneider (Iowa City: University of Iowa Press, 2000).

4. For a biographical treatment, see Rosaly Torna Kurth, "Susan Fenimore Cooper: A Study of Her Life and Work" (PhD diss., Fordham University, 1974). Susan Fenimore Cooper's contemporary, the noted author Sarah Orne Jewett, wrote a positive portrayal of Episcopal Church services among the Wisconsin Oneidas, but made unflattering comments about these Native Americans. Unlike Cooper, Jewett never became their advocate. "Tame Indians," *Independent*, April 1, 1875, 26.

5. For an earlier but incomplete attempt to write about Susan Fenimore Cooper and the Oneida Indians, see the confusing article by Stephen Germic, "Land Claims, Natives, and Nativism: Susan Fenimore Cooper's Fealty to Place," *American Literature* 79 (September 2007): 475–500.

6. See Julia K. Bloomfield, *The Oneidas* (New York: Alden, 1907, 1909).

7. For this early Anglican mission to the Mohawks and Oneidas, see Society for the Propagation of the Gospel, *Classified Digest of the Records of the Society for the Propagation of the Gospel in Foreign Parts, 1701–1802,* 5th ed. (London: Society for the Propagation of the Gospel in Foreign Parts, 1805), 57–79. Although the diocese of Fond du Lac was established in the 1870s, there is useful information about the founding of the first Oneida Episcopal Church in Alonzo Parker Curtis, *History of the Diocese of Fond du Lac and Its Several Congregations* (Fond du Lac, WI: P. B. Haber, 1925), chap. 1.

8. For more on Daniel Bread, see Laurence M. Hauptman and L. Gordon McLester III, *Chief Daniel Bread and the Oneida Nation of Indians of Wisconsin* (Norman: University of Oklahoma Press, 2005). For Chief Hill, see his autobiography in Hauptman and McLester, eds., *The Oneida Indians in the Age of Allotment, 1860–1920* (Norman: University of Oklahoma Press, 2006), 101–4, as well as Oneida Works Progress Administration (WPA) stories about him. Ibid., 105–8. For his obituary, see "Onon-gwat-go: A Chief of the Oneidas," *Southern Workman* 36 (March 1907): 133–34.

9. Kurth, "Susan Fenimore Cooper," 1–13.

10. "For the Ladies," *Daily Inter Ocean* (Chicago), September 11, 1875; Ralph Birdsall, *The Story of Cooperstown* (New York: Charles Scribner's Sons, 1925), 324–27; Sue Leslie Kimball, "Cooper, Susan Augusta Fenimore," in *American National Biography,* ed. John A. Garraty and Mark Carnes (Cary, NC: Oxford University Press, 1999), 5.

11. Quoted in "Obituary: Susan Fenimore Cooper," *Otsego Republican,* January 2, 1895. See also "Obituary: Death of Susan Fenimore Cooper," *Freeman's Journal,* January 3, 1895.

12. See the masterful Pulitzer Prize–winning book, Alan Taylor, *William Cooper's Town* (New York: Knopf, 1995). For the history of Oneida Indian dispossession from their central New York homelands, see Laurence M. Hauptman, *Conspiracy of Interest: Iroquois Dispossession and the Rise of New York State* (Syracuse, NY: Syracuse University Press, 1999); Karim M. Tiro, *People of the Standing Stone: The Oneida Nation from the Revolution Through the Era of Removal* (Amherst: University of Massachusetts Press, 2011). For the Oneida Indian migration and resettlement in Wisconsin, see Laurence M. Hauptman and L. Gordon McLester III, eds., *The Oneida Journey: From New York to Wisconsin, 1784–1860* (Madison: University of Wisconsin Press, 1999).

13. Lida Penfield, "Three Generations of Coopers in Oswego," *Oswego County Historical Society Journal* (1941): 1–7; and Lida Penfield, "Last of the Coopers of Cooperstown at Oswego," *Oswego County Historical Society Journal* (1948): 59–64.

14. Kurth, "Susan Fenimore Cooper," 1–73.

15. By a Lady [Susan Fenimore Cooper], *Rural Hours* (New York: G. P. Putnam, 1850; reprint ed., Syracuse, NY: Syracuse University Press, 1968).

16. Susan Fenimore Cooper, *Rural Hours,* reprint ed. with introduction by Rochelle L. Johnson and Daniel Patterson (Athens: University of Georgia Press, 1998), ix.

17. Cooper, *Rural Hours* (1968 reprint ed.), 117–20.

18. Ibid., 118–20.

19. Ibid., 123–24.

20. Susan Fenimore Cooper, "Mission to the Oneidas," *The Living Church*, March 27, 1886, 784.

21. Ibid., April 24, 1886, 60–61.

22. Her lengthy manuscript is in Yale University's (YU) Beinecke Library (BL): Susan Fenimore Cooper, "Oneida: A Sketch," in James Fenimore Cooper (JFC) Manuscript Collection (MSS), YCAL MSS, 415, Series II: Writings, box 22, folder 472. In this work, she credits Bishop Jackson Kemper for recommending the undertaking of an "authentic record of the [Wisconsin Episcopal] Oneida mission." Later, in an article, she once again acknowledges Bishop Kemper's influence: Susan Fenimore Cooper, "Missions to the Oneidas," *The Living Church*, April 10, 1885, 14–15. Available at http://anglicanhistory.org/indigenous/oneida /cooper/.

23. For these reformers, see especially William T. Hagan, *The Indian Rights Association* (Tucson: University of Arizona Press, 1985); Francis Paul Prucha, S. J., *American Indian Policy in Crisis: Christian Reformers and the American Indian, 1865–1900* (Norman: University of Oklahoma Press, 1976); and Fred Hoxie, *A Final Promise: The Campaign to Assimilate the Indians* (Lincoln: University of Nebraska Press, 1984).

24. Cooper, "Missions to the Oneidas," *The Living Church*, June 5, 1886, 155.

25. Ibid., April 10, 1886, 28.

26. Ibid., March 6, 1886, 736–37; March 20, 1886, 786–87; April 10, 1886, 28.

27. For the most up-to-date published appraisal of Williams, see Michael Leroy Oberg, *Professional Indian: The American Odyssey of Eleazer Williams* (Philadelphia: University of Pennsylvania Press, 2015).

28. For Cooper's impressions and assessment of Eleazer Williams, see her series of articles, "Missions to the Oneidas," in *The Living Church*, February 20, 1886, 708–10; February 27, 1886, 720–21; March 6, 1886, 736–37.

29. James Treat, ed., *Native and Christian: Indigenous Voices on Religious Identity in the United States and Canada* (New York: Routledge, 1996), 10; Cooper, "Missions to the Oneidas," *The Living Church*, March 27, 1886, 784; April 24, 1886, 60–61; May 15, 1886, 107–8; May 22, 1886, 123–24; June 5, 1886, 155.

30. The work of the missionaries is covered in Bloomfield, *The Oneidas*, 226–325. The vestry council records of the Hobart Church are filled with examples of projects initiated by these missionaries from 1881 to 1906. See John Archiquette MSS, Series III, Vestry Council Records of the Holy Apostles Episcopal Church, box 2, folder 74, Beinecke Rare Book and Manuscript Library, Yale University. For Goodnough, see "Obituary of Edward A. Goodnough," *Wisconsin Daily State Gazette*, February 1, 1890. Goodnough meddled in tribal politics and was seen as too strict by some in his teachings of Oneida children. For a less favorable view of missionary Goodnough, see Hauptman and McLester, *Chief Daniel Bread*, 135–47; and Herbert S. Lewis, ed. *Oneida Lives: Long-Lost Voices of the Wisconsin Oneidas* (Lincoln: University of Nebraska Press, 2005), 203, 276.

31. Cornelius Hill, "The Autobiography of Chief Cornelius Hill," in *The Oneidas in the Age of Allotment*, ed. Laurence M. Hauptman and L. Gordon McLester III (Norman: University of Oklahoma Press, 1999), 101–4.

32. David Hein and Gardiner H. Shattuck Jr., *The Episcopalians* (New York: Oxford University Press, 2004), 237–38; James Thayer Addison, *The Episcopal Church in the United States, 1789–1931* (New York: Charles Scribner's Sons, 1951), chap. 9.

33. Bloomfield, *The Oneidas*, 232–33.

34. William N. Fenton, *The Great Law and Longhouse: A Political History of the Iroquois Confederacy* (Norman: University of Oklahoma Press, 1998), 6.

35. Ibid., 3–18, 135–40; and William N. Fenton, "Structure, Continuity and Change in the Process of Treaty-making," in *The History and Culture of Iroquois Diplomacy: An Interdisciplinary Guide of the Treaties of the Six Nations and Their League*, ed. Francis Jennings, et al. (Syracuse, NY: Syracuse University Press, 1985), 3–36.

36. Bloomfield, *The Oneidas*, 218–223; Frank W. Merrill, *The Church's Mission to the Oneidas* (Wisconsin Oneida Reservation: Oneida Episcopal Mission 1899), 15–16.

37. On July 28, 1776, Major Joseph Bloomfield, after the Revolutionary War the fourth governor of New Jersey, wrote in his diary about the Oneidas' hymn singing at Kirkland's Sabbath service: "The great attention serious, solemn, and devout Behaviour of those poor Savages, with the sweetest, best and harmonious singing I have ever heard, excited the steady admiration of all present, and was an example to whites. . . . The Oneydoes excel in singing. They carried all the parts of the Music with the greatest Exactness and harmony [*sic*]." Joseph Bloomfield, *Citizen Soldier: The Revolutionary War Journal of Joseph Bloomfield*, ed. Mark Leader and James Kirby Smith (Newark: New Jersey Historical Society, 1982), 90.

38. Chief Bread quoted in Merrill, *The Church's Mission*, 17.

39. Michael D. McNally, *Ojibwe Singers: Hymns, Grief, and a Native Culture in Motion* (New York: Oxford University Press, 2000). To McNally, Christianity was "part of the equation of domination of native peoples," while it was at the same time, "an important resource in native struggles to act as agents in a history conditioned by that very domination." Ibid., 6.

40. Terence J. O'Grady, "The Singing Societies of Oneida," *American Music* (Spring 1991): 67–91.

41. Jacqueline L. Salmon, "Oneida Tribe's Hymns Keeping Heritage Alive," *Washington Post*, September 20, 2008.

42. Susan Fenimore Cooper, "Oneida: A Sketch."

43. For discussion of missionary work in the "West, Texas, and Africa," see James DeLancey to Jackson Kemper, 26 March 1840; for certification of missionaries, see James DeLancey to Jackson Kemper, 15 September 1854, 4 April 1856; for transfer of a missionary, see DeLancey to Kemper, 5 March 1860; for censure of a missionary, see DeLancey to Kemper, 10 August 1854; for references by DeLancey to Kemper as his "brother," see DeLancey to Kemper, 9 February 1828, 24 May 1849, 27 March, 18 and 28 May 1860, 21 March 1861, D. Jackson Kemper MSS, Wisconsin Historical Society (WHS).

44. William Crosswell Doane to Jackson Kemper, 18 December 1858, D. Jackson Kemper MSS, WHS. Bishop George Washington Doane formally consecrated Kemper as bishop. George Washington Crosswell, *The Sermon at the Consecration of the Right Reverend Jackson Kemper, D.D., Missionary Bishop for Missouri and Indiana in St. Peter's Church, Philadelphia, September 25, 1835* (Burlington, NJ: J. L. Powell, 1835).

45. For Bishop John Henry Hobart Brown, see Curtis, *History of the Diocese of Fond du Lac*, chap. 2.

46. Robert Smith and Loretta Metoxen, "Oneida Traditions," in *The Oneida Indian Experience: Two Perspectives*, ed. Jack Campisi and Laurence M. Hauptman (Syracuse, NY: Syracuse University Press, 1988) 150–51; Laurence M. Hauptman, *The Iroquois in the Civil War: From Battlefield to Reservation* (Syracuse, NY: Syracuse University Press, 1993), 67–84.

47. For Morgan L. Martin's schemes to force the Wisconsin Oneidas off their lands, see Hauptman and McLester, *Chief Daniel Bread*, 150–54. Morgan's early life and influence are treated well in Alice E. Smith, *History of Wisconsin, Volume I: Exploration to Statehood* (Madison: Wisconsin Historical Society, 1973), 194–95, 232–33, 278–90, 365–66, 419–22, 455–63, 661–62.

48. Ellen Goodnough quoted in Bloomfield, *The Oneidas*, 280–81.

49. Quoted in U.S. Commissioner of Indian Affairs, *Annual Report for 1867* (Washington, DC: n.p., 1867), 294–95.

50. Bloomfield, *The Oneidas*, 246–47.

51. Morgan L. Martin to Dennis N. Cooley, 27 and 28 July, 8 August, 1866; Martin to N. A. Taylor, 25 June, 9 July, 1867, Office of Indian Affairs (OIA), M234, OIA, Green Bay Agency Records (GBAR), Microfilm Reel (MR) 325, Record Group (RG) 75, National Archives (NA); Martin to N. A. Taylor, 28 January 1868; Martin to Ely S. Parker, 5 June 1869, OIA, M234, GBAR, MR 326, RG75, NA.

52. Eulogy at Ellen Goodnough's funeral, Susan Fenimore Cooper materials found in Cooper Family MSS, Fenimore House, New York State Historical Association Library, Cooperstown. The authors would like to thank Dr. Rochelle L. Johnson of the College of Idaho for sharing this eulogy.

53. E. A. Goodnough to Susan Fenimore Cooper, 23 April 1878, YCAL MSS, 415, James Fenimore Cooper MSS, box 15, folder 369, BL, YU. Besides writing historical accounts, Albert G. Ellis, an early associate of Eleazer Williams, was a former federal Indian agent, newspaper editor, historian, and land speculator who like Morgan L. Martin was strongly resented by the Oneidas. See Hauptman and McLester, *Chief Daniel Bread*, 10–12, 88–90, 112–15. For Ellis's writings, see "Fifty-Four Years' Recollections of Men and Events in Wisconsin," *Wisconsin Historical Collections* 7 (1876): 207–68; and "Recollections of Rev. Eleazer Williams," *Wisconsin Historical Collections* 8 (1879): 322–52.

54. Niobrara League of New York, *Second Annual Report of the Niobrara League of New York: A Branch of the Women's Auxiliary to the Board of Missions, 1873–1874* (New York: American Church Press, 1874), 1–6, 12, 14–15.

55. For this lace project, see Patricia Matteson, "Sybil Carter and Her Legacy," in *A Nation Within a Nation: Voices of the Oneidas in Wisconsin*, ed. L. Gordon McLester III and Laurence M. Hauptman (Madison: Wisconsin Historical Society Press, 2010), 67–80. For recent efforts to revive lace making, see Betty McLester and Debra Jenny, "Reviving Oneida Lace-making," in *A Nation Within a Nation: Voices of the Oneidas in Wisconsin*, ed. L. Gordon McLester III and Laurence M. Hauptman (Madison: Wisconsin Historical Society Press, 2010), 81–82.

56. Susan Fenimore Cooper notes in "Oneida: A Sketch," in James Fenimore Cooper MSS, Series II: Writings, box 22, folder 472, BL, YU. The item is marked "title page" and is the preface of the planned work. Cooper also credits Bishop Kemper for suggesting this undertaking of an "authentic use of the Ellen Goodnough Diary," Cooper, "Missions to the Oneidas," *The Living Church*, April 11, 1885.

57. William E. Wright, James Jenkins, and C. A. Galloway, "Fond du Lac Report," *The Spirit of Missions* 48 (1873).

58. *The Spirit of Missions*, 43 (1878): 239.

59. Cooper, "Missions to the Oneidas," *The Living Church*, June 5, 1886, 155.

60. Cornelius Hill et al., Memorial of the wardens and vestrymen of the Hobart Church Indian Mission, Oneida, Wisconsin, June 11, 1883, reprinted in *The Spirit of the Missions* 48 (1883): 435–36.

61. "State News," *Wisconsin State Journal*, July 24, 1883.

62. The articles in *The Living Church* ran from April 11, 1885, to June 5, 1886.

63. The cornerstone was dedicated by Bishop John Henry Hobart Brown on July 13, 1886. Bloomfield, *The Oneidas*, 293.

64. Cooper, "Missions to the Oneidas," *The Living Church*, April 11, 1885, 14–15.

65. Ibid. April 18, 1885, 26–27.

66. Ibid., April 25, 1885, 38–39.

67. Ibid., February 20, 1886, 708–10.

68. Ibid., February 27, 1886, 720–21; March 13, 1886, 753.

69. Ibid., March 13, 1886, 753.

70. Ibid.

71. Ibid., May 1, 1886, 75–76; May 15, 1886, 107–8; May 22, 1886, 123–24.

72. Helen Hunt Jackson, *A Century of Dishonor: A Sketch of the United States Government's Dealing with Some of the Indian's Tribes* (New York: Harper and Brothers, 1881).

73. Cooper, "Missions to the Oneidas," *The Living Church*, March 13, 1886, 753.

74. Ibid., May 1, 1886, 75–76. See also, May 15, 1886, 107–8; May 22, 1886, 123–24.

75. Ibid., May 15, 1886, 107–8.

76. Ibid., May 1, 1886, 75–76.

77. Ibid., May 22, 1886, 123–24; United States v. Cook, 86 U.S. 591 (1873).

78. Cooper, "Missions to the Oneidas," *The Living Church*, March 27, 1886, 784; April 10, 1886, 28; April 24, 1886, 60–61.

79. Ibid., April 24, 1886, 60–61.

80. Ibid., April 10, 1886, 28.

81. Ibid. As late as 1889, John Archiquette, a prominent Oneida Episcopal churchman and chief of the federal police force on the reservation, reported that only 900 Oneidas out of a total population of 1,713 could use English on a daily basis. John Archiquette, "Annual Statistical Report," May 2, 1889, John Archiquette MSS, box 1, folder 3, BL, YU.

82. Cooper, "Missions to the Oneidas," *The Living Church*, April 24, 1886, 60–61.

83. Ibid., June 5, 1886. See also Bloomfield, *The Oneidas*, 290–94.

84. Susan Fenimore Cooper, ed., *William West Skiles: A Sketch of Missionary Life at Valley Crucis in Western Carolina* (New York: J. Pott, 1890).

85. "Miss Julia K. Bloomfield Has Historic Letter Written by Gen. Pike," *Oswego Daily Times*, November 28, 1906; "Funeral of Miss Bloomfield," *Oswego Daily Times*, January 13, 1916; "Obituary of Julia Keen Bloomfield," *Oswego Daily Times*, January 12, 1916. The obituary of January 12, 1916, misidentifies her as the daughter of Joseph Bloomfield, whereas she was actually his grandniece.

86. "Obituary of Julia Keen Bloomfield," *Oswego Daily Times*, January 12, 1916; Joseph Bloomfield, *Citizen Soldier: The Revolutionary War Journal of Joseph Bloomfield*, ed. Mark E. Lender and James Kirby Smith (Newark: New Jersey Historical Society, 1982), 66, 90–93, 107–8.

87. Bloomfield, *The Oneidas*, preface.

88. Penfield, "Last of the Coopers of Cooperstown at Oswego," 59–64.

89. For the Oneida altar lace featured at the cathedral opening, see "News and Notes," *The Indian Friend* (National Indian Association, June 1911): 4; "Set of Altar Linen Made by Indian Women for Cathedral," *New York Herald*, April 9, 1911.

5

A MISSION OF MUTUALITY

The Relationship between the Oneidas and the Nashotah House Theological Seminary

Very Rev. Steven A. Peay

Iᴺ ᴀ ᴄᴏᴍᴍᴇᴍᴏʀᴀᴛɪᴠᴇ ʙᴏᴏᴋʟᴇᴛ ᴘᴜʙʟɪsʜᴇᴅ ʙʏ ᴛʜᴇ Oɴᴇɪᴅᴀs' Church of the Holy Apostles in 1942, an anonymous author wrote, "Oneida is historic ground, and has been justly called 'The cradle of the church in the Northwest.' Twelve years before Bishop Kemper, eighteen years before Nashotah was thought of, Christian Indians under a clergyman of their own blood [actually the Mohawk Eleazer Williams], were using the ancient liturgy and prayers under the trees and in the old log church."[1] This passage sets the tone when we begin to look at the connection between Nashotah House Theological Seminary (originally called the Nashotah mission) and the Oneida mission. What becomes readily apparent is that this was a mission of mutuality, a shared service, if you will. To understand this mutual mission involves our first looking at what set the stage for this mission and then how it unfolded.

The dawn of the nineteenth century did not reveal a robust Episcopal Church. The identification with the Church of England exacted a toll during the Revolutionary War. In the colonies and states where the church had been established, its status had been lost, along with its financial backing. The development of the first offshoot of the Church of England did not come easily. To be an Episcopal Church, one needed a bishop, and even that proved difficult, though Samuel Seabury managed to get the Scottish nonjurors to consecrate him in 1784. Three years later, William White and Samuel Provoost were consecrated by the archbishops of Canterbury and York, along with the bishops of Peterborough, Bath, and Wells. Even with bishops and a church organization, the situation did not look promising.[2]

The religious climate of the new nation was rapidly evolving as it began to look westward. The almost meteoric rise of the Baptist and Methodist movements among the settlers did not bode well for the Episcopal Church. If it could not get itself to move forward in the states where it had formerly been established, how could it possibly undertake the task of sending a mission to the expanding frontier? Indeed, this was true not just for the Episcopal Church but also for other churches holding to the necessity of an educated clergy, like the Congregationalists and the Presbyterians.[3]

Eleven years into the new century, a series of events set the stage for the recovery of the Episcopal Church and the beginning of its domestic missionary enterprise. Four names are tied to those events. John Henry Hobart is the first, consecrated as the assistant bishop of New York in 1811 and ordinary in 1816. For the purpose of this study, two of his significant actions were undertaking the mission to the Oneidas in New York in January 1815 and the founding of the General Theological Seminary in 1817.[4] Alexander Viets Griswold was the second clergyman who changed the direction of the church figure. He was consecrated as the bishop of the eastern diocese (encompassing all of New England, except Connecticut) in 1811. Griswold was a scholar, writing a significant work on the office of the bishop, and an evangelist. He served as the chancellor of Brown University for eight years and as presiding bishop from 1836 until his death. The third figure was William Meade. After studying at Princeton, he felt called to the ministry so began to read for orders in his native Virginia. He was ordained deacon in 1811. He would aid in the founding of the second Episcopal seminary in the United States, the Virginia Theological Seminary, in 1823. Consecrated as the assistant bishop of Virginia in 1829, he would become ordinary and also serve as the president of the seminary.

The last clergyman, and the most directly tied to the establishment of Nashotah House, was Jackson Kemper, who was also ordained deacon in 1811. It was Kemper who answered the call of the church to serve as its first missionary bishop, consecrated in 1835. He was the second such missionary bishop in the still-forming Anglican Communion, the first being Charles Inglis, the missionary bishop of Nova Scotia in 1786. However, the Church of England would not undertake a systematic and formalized approach to mission work until Colonial Bishopric Council was formed in 1841. By then, Kemper had been at work for six years in his territory, which spanned Indiana, Wisconsin, Minnesota, Iowa, Missouri, Kansas, and Nebraska.

Kemper made his first visit to Duck Creek in 1838. He held a special regard for the Oneida mission and was greatly concerned that it succeed. His residence "outside of Milwaukee" was Bishop's Stead, near the Nashotah House campus.[5] Kemper quickly discovered that he needed good clergy who could tend to his far-flung flock, including the Oneidas. His vision was to establish a mission house that could serve as a hub for ministry and a school for a frontier-oriented clergy. Kemper was looking for, in his words, "self-denying men" who would be willing to take up the hard life of a missioner. His idea was to organize following the ideal of the colleges in English universities, with the group of fellows following a rule and even observing celibacy for a time.[6] He was not interested in "misfits from the East" but sought those who would be willing to provide an adequate ministry for the West.

The bishop then turned to the General Theological Seminary for recruits. There Kemper discovered a number of young men who had been captivated by the Catholic views promoted by Professor William R. Whittingham (who would become the fourth bishop of Maryland in 1840). Whittingham introduced them to the work and self-denying lives of great monastic missionary saints: St. Augustine of Canterbury; St. Boniface, "apostle to the Germans"; and St. Anskar, missionary to the Danes. Kemper spoke at General Theological Seminary in May 1840. Several of the students recorded that his words had left a deep impression on many. What he presented to the students was the need for priests willing to deny themselves and do the work of missionaries in the expanding West. One of the young men who heard him, William Adams, a young Irishman, wrote to his father that he was about to "take part in a missionary and educational enterprize [*sic*] our Church is going to establish in the far-west in the Territory of Ioway [*sic*] or Wisconsin. This will be an enterprize of some hardship and abundance of self denial."[7]

Seven students who heard Kemper speak considered the mission. Only three would actually follow through with the work. James Lloyd Breck, from Pennsylvania, had come under the influence of William Augustus Muhlenberg. From his teenage years he had felt the call to become a missionary. Kemper's words fit Breck's vision for the ministry. William Adams, the young Irish correspondent, a graduate of Trinity College–Dublin, also accepted the challenge of the "associated mission," as they would call themselves for a time. The final one was John Henry Hobart Jr., son of the New York bishop and founder of the General Theological Seminary. The three were ordained deacons, commissioned as missionaries, and told to make their way west.

Adams's and Breck's journey involved taking various steamers, railway trains, canal barges, and a stage coach, which eventually brought them to Milwaukee. They obtained lodgings in the town and established an academy, the beginning of their educational work. Hobart would arrive later. Their initial mission work was in the town of Prairieville (now Waukesha). From Prairieville they set out to care for the people in various nearby communities. The first quarterly report they sent to the Board of Missions, which was dated December 30, 1841, noted 101 divine services held in seventeen places, nineteen baptisms, and two marriages. They had traveled over an area fifty by forty miles, walking 736 miles and covering 1,851 miles on horseback. They had 150 church members, 52 confirmed, and 32 communicants. They had managed to form a parish at Prairieville (Saint Mathias) and in Elkhorn (Saint John in the Wilderness) and revived an earlier parish (Saint Luke's) in Racine.[8]

Realizing the need to expand the work, Breck and Adams went looking for land. They found a fine tract for sale on the shores of Upper Nashotah Lake. Hobart remained "back East" to work on fund-raising. His efforts allowed the clergymen to purchase land for their planned seminary in 1842. They took possession of the land and held services there for the first time on August 30, 1842. They soon found three young men who were interested in pursuing studies, and now the work of the mission was ready to begin. However, before they could start their training of seminarians, the time had come for the missionaries to be ordained to the priesthood. Now all they needed was a properly consecrated church building for the ordination service, and there were only two in Wisconsin, both well to the north. One of these was at the Oneida mission in Duck Creek.

The journey to Duck Creek took four days on foot and riding in a wagon filled with lumber. They arrived on Saturday, October 8, 1842, and prepared themselves for the next day's services. Breck described the day:

> Early in the morning the solemn tones of the Church bell fell strangely solemn on the ear. . . . At the hour appointed for worship, we accompanied the Bishop to the Church. By this time groups of Indians had arrived, and were sitting, some on the Church steps, some on this log and others on that,—a sight so full of interest to a Churchman that we can never forget it. The bell at length ceased its tolling, and the Indians were all within the consecrated walls. . . . So soon as we had risen, a single voice commenced chanting the first sentence of the *Te Deum*, in the Oneida language, at the close of which the whole congregation sung aloud *Hallelujah* three times, and so they continued doing at the end of each sentence. . . .We were then ordained, after which was administered the Holy Eucharist. The sight was now in the highest degree interesting. There are 110 communicants amongst the Indians. Their humility is striking, and well worth the white man's imitation.[9]

Breck was clearly affected by the demeanor and the piety of the people. His experience with them led him to later express a desire to develop a whole chain of missions, extending to the Pacific. To some extent, he attempted this work when he left Nashotah House in 1850 and moved to Faribault, Minnesota. Eventually he would continue the journey to California, where he died in 1876.

Adams and Breck returned to the Nashotah mission bearing gifts from the Oneida people. Some of the items were pertinent to the setting up of a school—books, globes, and a bell. The bell, christened "Michael," was hung in an oak tree and called the community to prayers, to meals, and to classes. Susan Fenimore Cooper, in her articles, recounts how one local boy heard the bell through the thick woods and was drawn to it. Eventually this young man presented himself and became a student. His name was Edward Augustus Goodnough, the missionary sent to minister to the Oneidas by Bishop Kemper in 1853. "Little Michael" continues to call the community to prayer—the "little" is used since the large bell, given by the Delafield family in 1884, was also christened "Michael."[10]

Three young members of the Oneida tribe—John Cornelius, Cornelius Hill, and Daniel Nimham—accompanied Breck and Adams back to Nashotah House. According to a letter from Breck, "There are three of this tribe with us (respectively of the ages of twenty, sixteen, and thirteen years), who are preparing for the Ministry, or to become teachers."[11] Hill, later chief of the Wisconsin Oneidas, spent five years at Nashotah House, but there is no evidence of his having taken a degree. He was not ordained as a deacon until 1895, and Bishop Charles Chapman Grafton priested him in 1903. The young Edward Augustus Goodnough would finish his work at Nashotah House and begin a distinguished career as the beloved missionary to the Oneida. He served thirty-seven years, from 1853 until his death in 1890. It is clear that Father Goodnough, and his wife Ellen, had a fruitful ministry among the Oneida.

The relationship between the two missions—Nashotah and Oneida—has continued to be one of mutuality, a chain linking two traditions. Mutuality implies a sharing of sentiments and intimacy. Reading the literature assembled over time, a shared sentiment is evident in the concern for the spread of the Gospel, for the building up of the church, and for the care of the people—body as well as soul. It has also been one of intimacy, because it has been achieved through personal relationships. Both of these missions were launched in accordance with Kemper's vision and concern for the spread of the church on the frontier and among the Native peoples. While it may no longer be quite as close, there is still much to be shared in this mission of mutuality; the chain still holds.

Editor's Note: Excerpts from three clergyman's memoirs, describing the early links between the Oneida Episcopal mission at Duck Creek and Nashotah House, follow.

Schetky Excerpt 1

G. P. Schetky was an Episcopal priest who attended Nashotah House from 1845 to 1851. The following excerpt is from *Recollections of Nashotah and Its Vicinity Being Extracts from the Diary of One of the Alumni* by Rev. G. P. Schetky, D.D. Class of 1851.

Friday—April 25, 1845 St. Mark's Day. The following is the routine of the daily system:—Bell rings at 4 1/2 o'clock a.m. for all to rise. Ten minutes later the bell again rings for Roll-call, when all go to the front of the Recitation-room, and answer to their names. From this time until 6 1/2 o'clock, each student is occupied in his room in devotions and studies. The bell tolls for Chapel Service:—Morning

Prayer by the Rev. J. L. Breck. After Chapel Service, a number of the students recite antiphonally a number of Psalms from the Psalter.

At 7 o'clock the Bell rings for breakfast, at which, as, also at all the meals, a book is read aloud by a member of the mission, appointed weekly. After breakfast, at 7 1/2 o'clock, the Bell rings for the recitations of the Divinity class—Rev. W. Adams. Prof.: These recitations are followed by those of the Latin, Greek, and Hebrew classes taught by the same Prof. At 9 o'clock, a Litany service is said by the Rev. Mr. Breck in the Chapel. The Litany of the Church is read on the proper days, and a special Litany approved by Bishop Kemper, is read on the intermediate days—At 11 1/2 o'clock the recitations are concluded, and at 12 o'clock noon, the Holy Eucharist is administered, to all who are willing to partake. At 12 1/2 o'clock the Bell is rung for Dinner, and at 1 1/2 o'clock the different committees proceed to their duties which last till 5 1/2 o'clock. The Bell summons them back to the Mission to prepare for Evening Prayer in the chapel at 6 1/2 o'c. The whole body of the students with the exception of cooks and one or two others, form a line in front of "the Blue House"; the roll is called, and they march in regular order to the Chapel.

At 7 o'clock the Bell rings for Supper, after which each one retires to his room for study; or may employ his time as he sees fit until 9 o'clock when all absentees from the Mission are summoned to return by the Bell, and those who desire attend Family Evening Prayer in the Chapel. At 10 o'clock the Bell rings for the last time at night, when all lights must be extinguished, and all must go to bed. A watchman is appointed each week to go the rounds, to see that this rule is complied with, and that each student has his pail filled with water to be ready in the event of a fire. Before this watchman retires he makes his report to the Rev. Mr. Breck. On Monday there are no recitations, and on Saturday but two hours work. The Rev. James Lloyd Breck is the Superior, and was with Bishop Kemper, Rev. William Adams, & Rev. John Henry Hobart in founding this missionary Institution. He is a true follower of the Cross, and exhibits that spirit of self-denial, which becomes a true Christian. He is both dignified as becomes his position, and kind and affectionate to all. His age is about twenty-eight, and in height he is above six feet.

Rev. William Adams is the Professor of Divinity and the Languages, and a remarkably talented man. The students describe him as an eccentric person, as continually doing or saying something to make a pleasant joke, and cause an incessant merriment—. In this he is quite the opposite of the Rev. Mr. Breck who is grave and sedate, and illustrates the subjects recited in his classes by some pleasant anecdote. He familiarly styles the Rev. Mr. Breck, to whom he is very sincerely attached, "Brother Lloyd"— He is a man of earnest piety, and deep thought as may also be seen from his articles which appear in "The Churchman," signed "W. A." He is about thirty years of age and in height not quite six feet.

At the present time there are twenty four members, as follows: Brother Wm. Leach, Steward Brother Wm. G. Armstrong, Gardener Brother John

Johnstone—M.D., Physician Brother Lucius Taft, Farm Brother Edw[ar]d A. Goodnough, Brother Franklin R. Haff, Washing Committee Brother Geo. R. Bartlett. Brother Jno [John] P. T Ingraham, Brother Leverett D. Brainard[,] Brother Albert Bingham, Tailor Brother David Keene, Tailor Brother Augustus Ellis, Chapel Brother John A. Wheelock, Brother Nicholas Bibby[,] Brother Wm. H. Irish, Baker. Brother Henry E. Montgomery Daniel Nimham, Carpenter. John Cornelius Glaenis [Cornelius] Hill[.] These last three are Oneida Indians—the first named eighteen years, and a communicant, the last two, boys of sixteen and ten years— Reginald Heber Weller, son of the late Rev. Geo. Weller, D. D. Samuel R. Kemper, son of Bishop Kemper–[,] Knud Petterson, a Swedish boy[,] Jens Jergensen, a Norwegian boy, and myself. Besides these there is a Swedish gentleman[,] a graduate of the University of Up[p]sal[a], who resides with his family at Pine Lake about four miles north east of the Missions, and is pursuing a course of study preparatory to taking orders—His name is Gustaf Unonius. He will shortly be ordained.

Schetky Excerpt 2

Monday. May 19, 1845: Worked in the field, planting corn and beans, with [Edward A.] Goodnough, Dr. Johnstone, Malcolm Breck, (a younger brother of Rev. Mr. Breck, residing with his brother Samuel, at the north end of the Lake.) and John Cornelius and Glaenis [Cornelius] Hill, the [Oneida] Indian boys.

Schetky Excerpt 3

Fourth Sunday after Trinity. June 15, 1845. Ottawa Schoolhouse, Sunday School, 9 o'clock. Seven scholars. At the Service eight adults. Read sermon by Rev. Edwd. Berens "On a future judgment." Returning, at Dousman's met Mr. and Miss Paddock, with whom I rode to Waterville, where dined at Dr. Meigs. Service at 3 o'clock. Read sermon "On Prayer," by Rev. B. Berens. Dr. Wolcott from Milwaukee present. Left Waterville at 4 o'clock, and stopped at Sadd's for a few minutes, and from thence through Delafield, arriving at Nashotah at 7 1/2 o'clock. John Cornelius and Gloenis [Cornelius] Hill sang a Hymn in Oneida-language. A very sultry night, and mosquitoes very annoying.

Schetky Excerpt 4

Tuesday, Jan. 1, 1850 I walked out to Duck Creek, giving Bro. Haff and his family a pleasant surprise. Attended services at Hobart Church, where I met John Cornelius and Daniel Nimham . . . The response, the chants, the singing, the close attention to the entire services, and the short sermon might well be imitated by many congregations in our church. Of this interesting service, including the celebration of the Holy Communion, than which I have never witnessed one more filled with solemnity, I wrote a lengthy account which I sent East for publication. After the services, the whole tribe were sumptuously entertained at the neat and commodious residence of Daniel Bread, one of the Chiefs—an annual custom among them. He had presented the Church with a Bell some years before, and was liberal in his offerings, and largely contributed in the erection of the Church, which was built by the Indians themselves without any foreign aid—I remained that night at Duck Creek and returned to Green Bay the next day.

Diary of James Lloyd Breck

The Life of the Reverend James Lloyd Breck, D.D. Chiefly from Letters Written by Himself, comp. Charles Breck, D.D. (New York: E. & J. B. Young, 1883).

July, 1847: It may be interesting for you to know that the Primary Convention of Wisconsin has been held in Milwaukee, at which above twenty clergymen belonging to Wisconsin alone were present. The Rt. Rev. Missionary Bishop [Jackson Kemper] was unanimously elected Bishop of Wisconsin. All was harmonious, and the promise of great good to Wisconsin was the result in the organization of a Diocese. Two Norwegian parishes were represented by lay-delegates; and one Indian. At the close of the Convention, late at night, the head chief (one of the four delegates present) arose [Chief Daniel Bread] and in the Oneida tongue made a speech to the Convention, which was anglicized by the Indian Interpreter of the Tribe. During the speech, the white delegates drew near and sat upon the chancel kneeling-board before him, in order to hear the more distinctly. The Indians were appointed to the most honored pew in the Church. The effect was highly beneficial, and all closed with the blessing of our Rt Rev. Father.

November 1847: Here, therefore, I must close, after making a few remarks on the Indians, amongst whom another of our graduates, the Rev. F. R. Haff, has gone, purposing to devote himself for life to their spiritual good. These Red men occupy the Oneida Reserve, one hundred miles to the north of us, and are for the most part Christianized. They have a commodious frame church built, surmounted by a cupola that holds a bell, which, at the cost of sixty dollars, was presented by the head chief. The Church Service is said in their own tongue, which is the Mohawk, and scarcely anything can exceed the beauty and the devotion of their native chants. It was here that the Rev. William Adams and myself were admitted to Priests' Orders in 1842. The women retain the Indian attire, which at the time of public worship gives an air of great simplicity and earnestness to the service. Most especially are they devout at the celebration of the Holy Communion. These people are very anxious to hold those who serve at their Altar in just esteem, particularly the Bishop, whom they escort into their settlement with great joy, sometimes sixty of their warriors going forth on horseback to meet him. One of the three Indian youths, whom we received from this tribe into our house to educate, after remaining with us four years, has returned to aid the Missionary the Indian parish school, where the Mohawk alone is taught.

November, 1849: On Tuesday the Rev. Mr. [Solomon] Davis and his wife went with me to his old Mission at Duck Creek, where the Rev. Mr. Haff (one of our graduates) is stationed in charge of the Oneidas. I find him in good health, and with the extended charge of 160 communicants, besides the much other work arising from a large number of souls yet to be brought to a sense of their duty. It was here that I was ordained to the Priesthood; and now, borrowing the keys of the church, and withdrawing from my brethren, I retired to the same, and there before the Altar went through the Ordinal for the Priesthood, and again, before GOD and his Holy Angels, renewed the vows that I had before made there at.

Rt. Rev. William Ingraham Kip

Later Bishop of California, Rev. Kip visited Nashotah House in 1847, and mentions, as did Breck, his attendance at the same Episcopal Convocation held in Milwaukee. (From "A Few Days at Nashotah." Albany: J. Munsell, 1849.)

1847: These Indians [at Nashotah House] are Oneidas from the Mission of Mr. [Solomon] Davis on Duck Creek, where a flourishing Church has been formed, and a system of discipline adopted as strict, as that introduced by the Jesuits, and far more efficient. The Indians, in their own figurative language, have bestowed upon Bishop [Jackson] Kemper a name signifying The Keeper of the Word, and on Mr. Davis that of The Clear Sky. When the late Convention of our Church was held at Milwaukie [*sic*], four Lay Delegates from the Oneidas appeared and took their seats. They walked the whole distance from the Mission [about 90 miles], the last day travelling forty-five miles. On the evening that the convention closed, a resolution was passed expressing the gratification of its members at the presence of their Indian brethren; which being explained to the Chief, he rose with the interpreter, and replied in his own tongue in a short speech, which even when heard as a translation, showed the point and sense which has always marked the addresses of our Indians. We believe, however, that it is the first time the voice of one of our aborigines has been heard in the Councils of the Church.

Notes

1. "A History of the Oneida Indian Mission," in *Our Anniversary Book: The Oneida Mission 1822–1942* [n.p./n.d.]. Booklet, Nashotah House Theological Seminary Library, Nashotah, Wisconsin.

2. See David L. Holmes, *A Brief History of the Episcopal Church* (Valley Forge, PA: Trinity, 1993), chap. 2; and Robert Prichard, *A History of the Episcopal Church* (Harrisburg, PA: Morehouse, 1999), chaps. 4 and 5.

3. Roger Finke and Rodney Stark, *The Churching of America 1776–1990: Winners and Losers in Our Religious Economy* (New Brunswick, NJ: Rutgers University Press, 1990), chap. 3.

4. Susan Fenimore Cooper, "Missions to the Oneidas," in *The Living Church* (April 1885 to June 1886). Available at http://anglicanhistory.org/indigenous/oneida/cooper/. See also chapter 4 of this book.

5. Ibid., 22.

6. See Imri Blackburn, *Nashotah House: A History of Seventy-Five Years*, chap. 1, MSS Nashotah House Theological Seminary Library, Nashotah, Wisconsin. On the issue of celibacy and the quasi-monastic orientation of Nashotah House, also see Clarence E. Walworth, *The Oxford Movement in America*. Reprinted from the edition of 1895 with an Introduction by David N. O'Brien and a Commentary by James H. Smylie. United States Catholic Historical Society Monograph Series XXX (New York: 1974), chap. 8, "A Protestant Citeaux in America."

7. Ibid.

8. Blackburn, *Nashotah House*, chap. 1.

9. James Lloyd Breck, *James Lloyd Breck: Apostle of the Wilderness as Excerpted from the Life of the Reverend James Lloyd Breck*, comp. Charles Breck and ed. Thomas Reeves (Nashotah, WI: Nashotah House Theological Seminary, 1992), 53.

10. Ibid., 54.

11. Ibid., 88.

6

WEARING TWO HATS

Cornelius Hill and John Archiquette, Oneida Nation and Episcopal Church Leaders

L. Gordon McLester III and Laurence M. Hauptman

O NEIDA LEADERS IN THE LATE NINETEENTH AND FIRST years of the twentieth century were almost always members of the Episcopal Church. Two of the most prominent were Cornelius Hill and John Archiquette. In this important era in Oneida history, Hill symbolically wore two hats—an Iroquoian *kastöwe* as chief and, by 1903, an Episcopal biretta as the first ordained Oneida priest. From 1880 to 1901, Archiquette also had two roles—as head of the Oneidas' federal constabulary and tribal council member and as recording secretary of the vestry council of the Episcopal Church.

Both Hill's and Archiquette's lives clearly illustrate the interconnecting links that existed between the Wisconsin Oneida leadership and the church. Their stories also reveal the Oneida side of the chain. At a crisis time in Oneida history, these devout Episcopalian Christians sacrificed much for both their community's and their church's survival.

Born on the Wisconsin Oneida reservation in 1834, Cornelius Hill was baptized by Rt. Rev. Jackson Kemper, who later became his mentor. In 1844, the ten-year-old Hill was one of three Oneidas who went off to study at Nashotah House, where he was to spend five years. There Hill and the two other Oneidas worked part of the day to support the institution; the rest of the day was spent learning English, being instructed in Episcopal teachings, learning to play the church organ, or in solemn prayer. Importantly, while at Nashotah House, he also became acquainted with Edward A. Goodnough, a seminarian there. Hill and Goodnough, whom Bishop Kemper later appointed as missionary to the Oneidas, were to become lifelong friends and political allies, further cementing the bonds between church and community.[1]

On Hill's return from his education at Nashotah House, the Oneidas gave a feast in his honor. He was made a chief and given the name Onan-gwat-go, which has usually been translated as "Big Medicine." According to the chief's nephew, Chauncey Baird, Hill's Oneida name was Onuhgwatgo' and it didn't mean "Big Medicine," but rather it referred to a pine tree, possibly a princess pine, that had sprung up just prior to the chief's birth. He claimed that the elders interpreted this as indicating that Hill was destined to do great things and be the protector of the Oneida lands, since the pine tree is a symbol of leadership in Hodinöhsö:ni' communities.[2]

By the age of eighteen, Hill took his place on the chiefs' council. In the mid-1850s, he was appointed to the position of distributing the federal annuities under treaties with the United States and was put in charge of taking the federal census. While his political career was on the rise, he served as a delegate to Episcopal Church councils held in Milwaukee.[3]

Until the Civil War era, Chief Hill remained largely in the shadow of Daniel Bread, his political rival, the principal chief of the Oneidas in Wisconsin. Ironically, Hill's wife was Chief Bread's granddaughter.[4] For more than four decades, from the late 1820s onward, Bread was the dominant voice within both the tribal council and among the Oneida membership in the Episcopal Church. Much of the tension between the two Oneidas was caused by generational factors. Bread represented the first generation of Oneidas who had been born in New York and resettled in Wisconsin. The much younger Hill was to represent the voice of the second generation of Oneidas, those born in Wisconsin.[5] An Oneida leader who once debated with President Andrew Jackson about the evils of Indian removal, Bread had become less adversarial and more of an accommodationist in his old age.[6] Until his death in 1873, Bread's strategy was to do everything to remain in Wisconsin and prevent the Oneidas from being forced out of their new home as they had been in New York. He was even willing to accept the dividing up of the reservation and awarding individuals fee simple title.[7] Supported by missionary Goodnough, Hill challenged Bread and called for a change in the structure of the Oneida government.[8] Hill, now a justice of the peace, and these second-generation Oneidas, such as his friend and political ally John Archiquette, were more outspoken and clearly less willing to accept the dictates of federal Indian agents or the actions of local whites impinging on Oneida sovereignty. Hill and his allies also advocated reforming the ruling structure of Oneida governance and pushed for the establishment of an elected system to replace the chiefs' council. This change occurred only after Bread's death. In the first and second popular votes in 1878 and 1879, Hill was elected sachem.[9]

For much of Hill's adult life, the Oneidas faced pressure from non-Indian outsiders who threatened these Native peoples' continued existence in Wisconsin. These included lumber companies from Green Bay, a center of wood processing, and those pushing for railroad development in the region. Lumber companies sent their employees to trespass on Indian lands to strip trees and carry off valuable lumber; they also were involved in bribing individual Oneidas to go against tribal and federal regulations to do their dirty work and carry off timber from the reservation. These schemers, allied to local, state, and federal officials, perpetuated "fake news" and spread false images about the Oneidas. One of these individuals was Morgan L. Martin, the federal Indian agent. Martin, a major land speculator and canal and railroad developer in Wisconsin, was one of the founders of the city of Milwaukee.[10] He not only wrote his negative assessments of the Oneidas in newspaper accounts but also communicated his outwardly held racist opinions to the Office of Indian Affairs in Washington while serving as federal Indian agent.[11] Hill responded to Martin's damaging and slanderous misrepresentations of the Oneidas in letters to the editor, the first appearing in the *Green Bay Advocate* in 1868.[12]

Besides his career as a political leader, Hill served the Episcopal Church and its interests in numerous ways. As a member of the vestry council and senior warden in the church, he led the tribal effort to raise funds and secure volunteer labor for the building of the third Episcopal Church at Oneida, usually referred to as Stone Church, which was finally completed in 1886. Working with his former seminarian and friend Daniel Nimham and John Archiquette, the Oneidas' chief of police, he helped raise funds for the building of a new church, recruited volunteers from the community to quarry stone and provide teams to transport building materials, and defended church interests, including those of the Methodists, before the Oneida council to limit the activities of other religious sects from missionizing on the reservation.[13] He also performed multiple roles even during church services. As an accomplished musician, he was the church organist for thirty-seven years. At the same time, he acted as the official translator every Sunday at church services. His role in this regard was later described by Julia Bloomfield: "He interprets the lessons from the English Bible into the Oneida language, with a remarkable fluency." Bloomfield added: "It is said to be deeply interesting to see *Onan-gwat-go* standing by the Missionary, his face turned toward the speaker as he listens attentively, and then turning to the people speaks to them of the things of God." On some occasions, as Bloomfield noted, the chief interspersed certain English words since there was "no Oneida equivalent." She concluded about Hill: "Nothing is so bracing, so inspiring, so gladdening . . . as hearing a real message, words, that come straight from God and go straight to the hearts of the listeners."[14]

After Hill's half century of service to the church, Bishop Charles Grafton ordained Chief Hill as deacon of the Episcopal Church on June 27, 1895. Just prior to the ceremony, Hill's youngest child had died. At the ceremony, Cornelius Hill once again served as translator of the Gospel in his longtime role as Episcopal Church translator. Afterward, in his new position as deacon, he assisted missionaries Solomon S. Burleson and later Frank Merrill in parish work and frequently made visits to the sick and aged.[15]

Eight years later, on June 24, 1903, on Saint John the Baptist Day, Bishop Grafton, acknowledging Hill's valuable service as deacon, ordained the sixty-nine-year-old chief as an Episcopal priest. In a High Church ceremony, Hill wore his Episcopal vestments, and on his head he wore his biretta. In a ceremony well attended by Oneidas and non-Indian churchmen from all over Wisconsin, the bishop, in his elaborate vestments, conducted the ordination by laying on the hands and celebrating the Holy Eucharist. At the ceremony, Oneidas solemnly sang the *Gloria in Excelsis* and the *Te Deum* in their native language. Rev. William Thorn from Saint Paul's Church in Marinette delivered the sermon while Joel Archiquette, one of John Archiquette's sons, acted as translator. After recognizing the chief's revered position as a temporal leader among his Oneida people, Thorn described Hill's new role as that of "spiritual chief." He insisted that his duty now was "to rally the people around you, raise the war-cry of the Prince of Peace, and lead them, men, women, and children against the enemies of their souls. You are to show them how to fight these enemies, and this you will do by your teaching."[16]

In the same year as Hill's ordination as an Episcopal priest, the Oneidas found themselves at the beginning of a new crisis, one coming from the state capital in Madison. The Wisconsin state legislature formally established the town of Hobart in Brown County and the town of Oneida in Outagamie County. These municipalities, which quickly established town governments and came under county and state regulations, were carved out of the original Oneida reservation established by federal treaty in 1838. Initially, the Oneidas outnumbered the non-Indian population of the two towns and controlled the major government offices in both towns.[17]

In 1906, Congress passed the Burke Act, federal legislation that modified the Dawes General Allotment Act. The Burke Act led to the rapid conversion of Oneida trust patents into fee simple patents.[18] Once the Oneidas had fee simple title, their lands became taxable, and many acres were lost to the two towns for nonpayment, leading to foreclosure. Local real estate companies from Green Bay and its environs, with the support of local politicians and even the federal agent, also encouraged Oneidas to take out mortgages, using their land as collateral. When they couldn't pay back their mortgages, the Oneidas lost their lands. Subsequently, these same lands were sold off by the companies to non-Indians who were rapidly settling in Brown and Outagamie Counties, and soon the Indians lost political control of the two towns. Moreover, some Oneidas themselves, products of boarding schools, inculcated with the idea that reservations were not suitable for modern Indians and that private property and American citizenship were requisites for success, sold off their lands once they were converted from trust allotments.[19] Chief Hill died on January 26, 1907, before the full extent of federal allotment policies were felt at Oneida. These policies led to the loss of most of the 65,400 acres of the Oneida reservation guaranteed by federal treaty in 1838. By 1920, over 50,000 acres were already out of Oneida hands.[20]

Unlike Hill, John Archiquette lived to see the disaster that affected the Oneidas under federal allotment policies. Although John Archiquette was slightly younger than Chief Hill, their careers overlapped both as leaders within the Wisconsin Oneida Nation and within the Episcopal Church. Archiquette served as a federal lawman at the Wisconsin Oneida reservation from 1877 to 1901 and was officially appointed to the post of chief of police in 1881. He was a member of the first elected tribal council elected in 1878 and also served on the tribal court.[21] He was the leader of the Oneida National Brass Band, headed by Chief Hill, and, as a proud veteran of the Civil War, he was an active member of the Grand Army of the Republic, organizing events and commemorative ceremonies.[22]

Archiquette was baptized in the Episcopal Church by missionary Solomon Davis in March 1847.[23] Later, in 1868, Episcopal missionary Edward A. Goodnough performed his marriage to Elizabeth Smith in the same church. After her death in 1888, he married Christine Hill Summers in a church ceremony performed by missionary Solomon S. Burleson in 1894. When he became incapacitated toward the end of his life, Jonathan D. Goodnough, the missionary's son, became his legal guardian.[24] Further evidence of his commitment to his community's welfare and to the Episcopal Church was his appointment to the board of trustees of the mission hospital.

John's son Oscar noted that, after his father's Civil War service, John turned back to the deep religious Episcopalian beliefs of his parents.[25] Importantly, Archiquette's approach to his official duties as an Indian agency lawman was shaped by his Protestant faith and his service as an Episcopal Church leader. Indeed, at times as a lawman, he saw himself in the role of an elder in the church carrying out its moral codes and defending its interests more than merely being a policeman carrying out federal laws.

While reminiscing about decades past, Tom Hill, an Oneida elder, in a WPA Oneida Language and Folklore Project interview, described another major role of members of the vestry council—namely, as enforcer of a code of morality. He stated that it "looked after the church, and they used to look after the congregation too. Sometimes if a man or person would go to a dance he or she would be banned from taking their communion for three month, and if someone got drunk he or she would be barred from taking communion for one year. And if anyone does worse than that—like if they commit adultery—they would be barred for a longer time. This is where the vestryman looked after their congregation."[26]

As a deeply religious person who had abandoned his own drinking for a life of temperance, Archiquette cautioned his men against the "demon rum" and punished them when they went astray if he had proof of their misconduct.[27] When one of his most trusted policemen was charged with public intoxication in 1883, Archiquette defended him until the charge was corroborated by his colleague on the vestry council, Chief Hill. Subsequently, the policeman was fired.[28] A similar incident happened in 1896 when two of his officers were forced to resign for public intoxication.[29] He also warned his men about how they should present themselves and what they said in public meetings. On August 1883, one of his policemen attended a tribal meeting and indiscreetly spoke out against the sachem and tribal council. In response, Archiquette wrote D. P. Andrews, the federal Indian agent at Keshena, criticizing the policeman and distancing himself from the lawman's statements.[30]

Captain Archiquette's major duties as required by Washington and Keshena were largely focused on two areas: (1) stamping out the liquor traffic and its resulting effects and (2) the protection of federal property as defined by the Green Bay Indian agent, Washington officials, and judges in the federal courts. From the late 1870s onward, Archiquette's police force disproportionately dealt with these two matters. Since it was against the federal law until 1953 for alcohol to be sold or distributed to Native Americans on a reservation, he was obligated to carry out its enforcement. The brisk whiskey trade dispensed from Green Bay and its environs onto the reservation was frequently a focus of Archiquette's reports.[31]

On many occasions, Archiquette's deep religious faith intersected with his many duties as an Oneida tribal councilor and chief of police. His sense of morality led him to make reports listing Oneida adulterers to both the tribal council and to Washington officials.[32] On May 27, 1882, he reported to the commissioner of pensions about a widow cohabiting with her lover who had applied for her dead husband's Civil War pension. On another occasion, he brought a couple accused of adultery before a tribal court, which subsequently decided to allow the "wanton woman" to return to her husband but ostracized her lover from the reservation.[33] In a third instance, Archiquette brought an adulterer before the tribal court; after the man admitted to his infidelity, and "promised to do better," he was exonerated.[34]

Despite the sordid nature of his work, the Oneida police captain, nevertheless, could be a man of compassion. He sought peaceful resolutions of disputes between Oneidas and their white neighbors and between tribal members.[35] He frequently tried to keep Oneida bullies in check and kept tabs on reservation troublemakers.[36] Importantly, throughout his service as a policeman, he saw himself as a defender of Oneida women, especially young girls, widows, the elderly, and the infirm. Time and time again, he intervened on their behalf to provide them with protection and assistance.[37] When a "respectable peaceful woman" was attacked in a maliciously ugly incident, he apprehended the Oneida assailant and recommended that he be severely punished. He investigated various incidents and made arrests, including in a case of rape, a husband's abandonment of his family, and damage to property owned by women.[38] In 1887, he came to the aid of Margaret Schuyler, a widow who had been charged a usurious rate—73 percent—on a loan and was being threatened with eviction from her residence.[39] In another instance in the same year, Archiquette intervened to help Hannah Scanandore, another widow, when her prized bull was stolen and sold off; the policeman was able to get partial financial restitution for the widow and recommended that the offender be punished and made an example of in the community.[40]

By the 1890s, Archiquette was dealing with problems women faced after the passage and application of the Dawes Act. Right to the end of his police career in 1900, he attempted to help women who had no land rights to inherit their deceased husband's allotment under the act.[41] The chief of police was also concerned about the needs of infirm women who required special care. In 1899, he recommended confinement of a mentally ill woman "for her own safety."[42]

At times, the police captain was critical of the actions and nonactions of the tribal council; however, throughout his career as a policeman, he was a fervent defender of the Episcopal and Methodist Churches on the reservation. When an Oneida attempted to close the access road to the Episcopal Church after getting permission from the tribal council, Archiquette and Chief Hill helped mediate the dispute, a solution that favored his church.[43] Moreover, he opposed the expansion of competing churches and their influences on the reservation. In the late 1880s and early 1890s, both the Mormon and Catholic Churches attempted to establish a presence on the reservation. In late 1887, Archiquette wrote that he had driven out the Mormon missionaries, whom he viewed as trespassers.[44] In 1890, the policeman opposed the effort by a priest at Shawano to secure a political appointment as the census taker, a position held by Archiquette and Chief Hill.[45]

After the passage of the Dawes Act, the Catholic archdiocese attempted to secure an allotment at Oneida. The controversy infuriated the policeman and led him into a bitter battle with Thomas Jennings, the federal Indian agent, who supported the efforts of the Catholic Church. On March 29, 1890, the policeman personally appealed to Commissioner Morgan, condemning the actions of Jennings. He questioned Jennings's actions in securing a favorable vote in an Oneida tribal meeting that only one hundred people attended. Openly condemning Jennings at a second meeting, he lambasted the federal agent for limiting discussion. He claimed that there was only one baptized Catholic on the reservation and argued that it was unfair to give the Catholics an allotment equal in size to "that allowed the congregations [Episcopal and Methodist] which have remained here more than 50 years."[46]

When the Catholic diocese began construction without formal permission, its actions were temporarily suspended when the commissioner of Indian Affairs,

Morgan, ordered them to stop. However, after Morgan, an uncompromising opponent of the Bureau of Catholic Missions, left office, the Catholic Church succeeded in its efforts to establish a parish on the reservation; by 1909, the diocese had completed the building of Saint Joseph's Church at Oneida.[47]

Even after Jennings's dismissal from office, he and his supporters sniped at Archiquette. The former agent retaliated against what he viewed as Archiquette's insolence in challenging his authority and claimed that reservation police were receiving kickbacks and making false arrests. Archiquette was forced to counter these false charges and defend his constabulary. On April 20, 1894, Archiquette responded to these accusations: "We have not demanded from any person special pay for our work—We have rec'd what the law allows when liquor cases were examined in the U.S. Court." He added that he and his men had faithfully carried out the official directives related to reporting alcohol dispensing to and by the Indians and protected the United States' property, meaning the standing trees on the reservation. "We have forbidden the Oneidas to cut green timber unless for agricultural purposes, we have reported timber cases."[48]

In the aftermath, the clergymen of the two Protestant churches on the reservation, fearing Archiquette's dismissal from his post, came to the constabulary's defense. Because of this escalating conflict, Solomon Burleson, the Episcopal missionary at Oneida, wrote a letter of recommendation supporting Archiquette's retention as captain of the constabulary. On April 21, 1894, Burleson noted that the policeman's enemies were notorious lawbreakers "who were selling and dispensing alcohol to the Oneidas and were also involved with stealing timber from the reservation." Burleson added that Archiquette had carried out the duties of his office "as an honorable man and Christian gentleman."[49] Nine days later, R. R. Pike, the Methodist clergyman on the east side of the reservation, repeated Burleson's assessment. He indicated that during his six-year tenure at his church on the reservation, "no cases were brought without foundation" by Archiquette's constabulary, and there had been "no immoral conduct" on the part of the police under his command.[50]

Despite being a law-abiding, churchgoing man of temperance, Archiquette had to deal with accusations leveled against his character, brought against him apparently by malcontents on and off the reservation. He was resented because he had to follow the federal law restricting individuals from clearing and logging standing trees on reservation lands. Another divisive issue was tribal eligibility for trust allotments under the Dawes Act; Archiquette was seen as being quite conservative in deciding these matters. His enemies accused him and his men, among other things, of taking bribes and not doing his job well enough to stop the liquor trade.[51]

In 1900, the Office of Indian Affairs appointed Joseph C. Hart, superintendent of the Oneida Government School on the reservation, as the interim federal

Indian agent. Hated by most Oneidas because of his meddling in internal tribal affairs, Hart pushed for the buyout of federal treaty obligations to the Oneidas and the rapid conversion of trust patents to fee simple title. Hart accused Archiquette of neglecting his duties by not getting his men to testify against community members on liquor violations.[52] In 1901, Archiquette's service as the captain of the Oneida tribal police came to an end. His position had increasingly become untenable because of Hart and because the police chief's political opponents on the reservation were now criticizing him and reporting his alleged misconduct. Suffering from severe rheumatism in his arms and shoulders that sapped his strength, the police chief was forced out of his post in 1901.[53]

After Archiquette's dismissal from his post as lawman, he turned to farming but remained active in Oneida community and church affairs.[54] From the Burke Act of 1906 onward, he challenged the conversion of allotments to fee simple title for fear that the imposition of taxes would be too great to prevent foreclosures. He continued to make that argument right through his testimony before the federal Competency Commission in 1917.[55] His appeals were to no avail.

At his death in 1924, Archiquette was buried atop the hill in the Holy Apostles Episcopal Church cemetery, quite appropriately next to missionary Burleson's grave and in the section devoted to veterans of the Civil War. The vestryman had successfully balanced his tribal and federal governmental responsibilities for a quarter of a century. He was largely able to do so because of his standing within the Episcopal Church and through his good works of Christian Indian charity.

Both Chief Hill and Captain Archiquette left more than the legacy of Christian good works that inspired many in their community. The two men, as vestry council members, had organized the effort to quarry and build the Episcopal Church in the 1870s and 1880s. Its stone walls survived the destructive fire of 1920, and the church stands as an imposing structure even to this day. In addition, the extensive papers that John Archiquette wrote and collected, now at Yale University's Beinecke Rare Book and Manuscript Library, are one of the best primary sources we have about the Wisconsin Oneidas. They provide insights about nearly every aspect of Wisconsin Oneida life in the late nineteenth and first two decades of the twentieth century. The collection is composed of church records; correspondence to the Office of Indian Affairs in Washington and to the Indian Agency headquarters at Keshena, Wisconsin; diary notations in both Oneida and English about community events; tribal censuses and account books; and police reports for nearly a quarter of a century.

Hill's and Archiquette's children became major voices in the community well into the twentieth century. Hill's daughter Josephine Webster was the leader of the church-sponsored lace makers. Although the official Sybil Carter Indian mission lace-making program ended in 1926 at Oneida, Hill continued to promote this new traditional form of art until her death in 1953. In the 1930s, Archiquette's son Oscar was one of the most vocal supporters of the Indian New Deal, which reorganized the Oneida tribal governing structure. Importantly, Oscar Archiquette deserves much credit for the success of the WPA's Oneida Language and Folklore Project, which amassed the largest collection of Oneida tribal history, culture, and language materials, because of his linguistic abilities and his close working relationship with anthropologist Floyd Lounsbury.[56]

Notes

1. Cornelius Hill, "The Autobiography of Chief Cornelius Hill," September 7, 1899, MSS, Oneida Indian Historical Society, Oneida, Wisconsin.

2. Chauncey Baird, "Chief Cornelius Hill," MSS, WPA Oneida Language and Folklore Project Stories and Interviews, Oneida Nation of Indians of Wisconsin.

3. Albert Hill Interview, "Chief Cornelius Hill," MSS, WPA Oneida Language and Folklore Project Stories and Interviews, Oneida Nation of Indians of Wisconsin.

4. Herbert S. Lewis, ed. *Oneida Lives: Long-Lost Voices of the Wisconsin Oneidas* (Lincoln: University of Nebraska Press, 2005), 409n1.

5. We have discussed this rivalry more extensively before. See Laurence M. Hauptman and L. Gordon McLester III, *Chief Daniel Bread and the Oneida Nation of Indians of Wisconsin* (Norman: University of Oklahoma Press, 2002), 153–59.

6. For Chief Bread's debate with President Jackson, see ibid., 69–73.

7. See Hauptman and McLester, *Chief Daniel Bread*.

8. Cornelius Hill to Charles Mix, 27 March 1867, Office of Indian Affairs (OIA), M234, Green Bay Agency Records (GBAR), Microfilm Reel (MR) 325, Record Group (RG) 75, National Archives (NA); Cornelius Hill et al. to President of the United States, 28 June 1867, OIA, M234, GBAR, MR 325, RG 75, NA; Cornelius Hill, Henry Powless, et al. to President of the United States, 23 March 1870, OIA, M234, GBAR, MR 327, RG 75, NA. See also Lewis, *Oneida Lives*.

9. Petition of Cornelius Hill et al. to J. C. Bridgman, 24 September, 30 November 1878, OIA, M234, GBAR, MR 234, RG 75, NA; Hill to Commissioner of Indian Affairs, 20 January, 25 and 27 October 1879, OIA, M235, GBAR, MR 235, RG 75, NA; Sachem Cornelius Hill, Councillors [sic] and Headmen Petition to Commissioner of Indian Affairs, 30 March 1880, OIA, M235, GBAR, MR 236, RG 75, NA WPA. See also Hill interview, "Chief Cornelius Hill."

10. Morgan L. Martin, "Sketch and Narrative of Morgan L. Martin," in *Wisconsin Historical Collections (WHC)* 13 (1895): 163–246, ed. Reuben G. Thwaites. Martin is treated extensively in his daughter's book, Deborah B. Martin, *History of Brown County, Wisconsin: Past and Present* (Chicago, IL: S. J.Clarke,1913), vol. 1, 100, 174–76, 200; vol. 2, 28–31; and in Richard Current, *The History of Wisconsin; The Civil War Era, 1848–1873* (Madison: State Historical Society of Wisconsin, 1976), vol. 2, 19–23, 448, 581–84.

11. Morgan L. Martin to Dennis N. Cooley, 27 and 28 July, 8 August 1866; Martin to N. A. Taylor, 25 June, 9 July 1867, OIA, M234, GBAR, MR 325, RG 75, NA; Martin to Taylor, 28 January 1868, OIA, M234, GBAR, MR 327, RG 75, NA. U.S. Interior Department, Commissioner of Indian Affairs, *Annual Report 1867–1868* (Washington, DC, 1867), 294–95, 331–33.

12. Cornelius Hill, letter to the editor, *Green Bay Advocate*, June 18, 1868. Hill's letter to the editor was reprinted as far away as Chicago. See chapter 4.

13. Cornelius Hill, "The Autobiography of Chief Cornelius Hill." Chief Hill along with John Archiquette led the effort to raise funds and quarry stone to build the new Episcopal church. Cornelius Hill, John Archiquette, et al., "Memorial of the Wardens and Vestrymen of the Hobart Church Indian Mission, Oneida, Wisconsin, June 11, 1883," reprinted in *The Spirit of Missions* 48 (1883): 435–36. For the names of volunteers for this project, see lists of May 1882, 6 November 1882; 18 October, 1 November 1883, JA MSS, Records of the Vestry Council, box 3, folder 3, Beinecke Library (BL), Yale University (YU).

14. Julia K. Bloomfield, *The Oneidas* (New York: Alden, 1907), 330.

15. Ibid., 328–29. Bloomfield, however, gives the wrong year. She states Hill became a deacon in 1905. It was really 1895.

16. Ibid., 330–34. "Red Man Becomes Priest," *New York Times*, May 6, 1903.

17. For a more extensive treatment, see Laurence M. Hauptman and L. Gordon McLester, eds., *The Oneida Indians in the Age of Allotment, 1860–1920* (Norman: University of Oklahoma Press, 2006), 179–240.

18. The Dawes General Allotment Act, 24 *Stat.*, 388–91 (February 8, 1887). The Burke Act, 34 *Stat.*, 182–83 (May 8, 1906).

19. Four WPA Oneida Language and Folklore Project interviews tell much of the story of how the land was lost: Filmore Cooper, "[Dawes] General Allotment Act"; Rachel Swamp, "Before They Started to Pay Taxes"; Levi Baird, "In Deceit"; and Guy Elm, "Property and Land Loss.'"

20. Caroline Andruss, "Changing Indian Conditions," *Southern Workman* 51 (January 1922): 26.

21. List of newly elected tribal council, John Archiquette Journal entry (JAJ), 9 November 1878, John Archiquette MSS, box 1, folder 1, JA MSS, BL, YU.

22. For his role as director of the Oneida National Brass Band, see for example, John Archiquette to Col. C. K. Pier, 6 May 1887, box 1, folder 3; JAJ, 5 July 1889, box 1, folder 3; 20 September 1997, JA MSS, box 1, folder 5; Archiquette to George Knowlton, 24 May 1899, JA MSS, box 1, folder 6; JAJ, 4 July 1898, JA MSS, box 2, folder 7; Program of the 16th Reunion of the 14th Wisconsin, 16–18 June 1903, New London, Wisconsin, JA MSS, box 2, folder 57, BL, YU.

23. W. B. Thorn [rector of Hobart Church] Deposition about John Archiquette's date and place of birth and date of baptism, 19 April 1913; John Archiquet [*sic*] to J. L. Davenport [commissioner of pensions], 23 April 1913, John Archiquette's Declaration for Bureau of Pensions, 26 March 1915; State of Wisconsin, Outagamie County Judge's Order, Letter of Guardianship to Minors [of John Archiquette] for Jonathan D. Goodnough, Town of Hobart, Brown County, 23 July 1919; Goodnough's Declaration for [four Archiquette] Children Under Sixteen Years of Age, to Bureau of Pensions, 2 October 1920. All found in John Archiquet[te]'s Civil War Pension, Co. D, 14th Wisconsin Volunteer Infantry, Certificate # 678911, RG 94, NA.

24. Nearly every other page of Archiquette's extensive journals deal with church matters. For his specific work as junior warden and vestryman of the Hobart Church for a quarter of a century, see Hobart Church Vestry Council Records, 18 April 1881, 16 April 1906, JA MSS, box 3, folder 75, BL, YU; JAJ, 7 December 1898, JA MSS, box 1, folder 6, BL, YU.

25. Oscar Archiquette, "Autobiography," in Lewis, *Oneida Lives*, 140–41.

26. Tom Elm quoted in Lewis, *Oneida Lives*, 31.

27. Oscar Archiquette, "An Important Man" [John Archiquette], WPA Oneida Language and Folklore Project, Oscar Archiquette, folder 7, Oneida Nation of Indians of Wisconsin, Cultural Heritage Department, Oneida, Wisconsin.

28. Ebenezer Stephens [federal agent, Green Bay Indian Agency] letter of appointment of John Archiquette as Lieutenant Police in the place of Joseph F. Scanadere [Scanandore], 31 May 1881, JA MSS box 1, folder 1, BL, YU. The appointment also indicated that Archiquette was thirty-three years of age, 6'1½" tall, and had a family of nine.

29. John Archiquette Police Reports (JAPR), July 1883, JA MSS, box 1, folder 2; Archiquette to Thomas Savage [federal agent, Green Bay Indian Agency], 2 October 1896, JA MSS, box 1, folder 5, BL, YU.

30. John Archiquette to D. P. Andrews [federal agent, Green Bay Agency], 13 August 1883, JA MSS, box 1, folder 2, BL, YU.

31. For the repeal of this restriction on the sale and/or distribution of alcohol to American Indians, see 67 Stat. 586, "An Act to Eliminate Certain Discriminatory Regulations against Indians of the United States," Public Law 83-277 (August 15, 1953). Attempts to restrict liquor and its distribution were frequently cited in Archiquette's police reports. See JAPR, August 1880, February 1882, JA MSS, box 1, folder 1; May 1885, box 1, folder 2; January and March 1886, box 1, folder 3; October and August 1893, box 1, folder 4, BL, YU. For problems of enforcement, see Archiquette to M. C. Phillips, 27 July 1897, JA MSS, box 1, folder 5, BL, YU.

32. John Archiquette to Ebenezer Stephens, JA MSS, July, 20,1882, Box 1, Folder 2, BL, YU.

33. "John Archiquette to William Dudley (U.S. Commissioner of Pensions, May 27, 1882 JA MSS, Box 1, Folder 4; Archiquette to Edward Ferguson [U.S. Pension agent], April 12, 1882, JA MSS, Box 2, Folder 19, BL.YU. JAPR for August 1886, JA MSS, Box 1, Folder 2, BL, YU.

34. JAPR for January 1882, JA MSS, Box 1, Folder 1, BL, YU.

35. JAPR [theft—white-owned, full jar of butter stolen by an Oneida], 25 October 1880, JA MSS, box 1, folder 1; Police Report to agent Stephens [damage done by an Oneida's runaway ponies to another tribal member's fields], October 1881; JAPR [Oneida-owned colt went astray and now held by a white man in De Pere], June 1882, JA MSS, box1, folder 1, BL, YU.

36. For example, on May 2, 1883, Archiquette wrote that he was monitoring the activities of "a troublesome man, lawless, and an abusive and a leader of others into drunkenness." JAJ, JA MSS, box 1, folder 2, BL, YU.

37. John Archiquette to Ebenezer Stephens ["troublesome" Oneida man], 12 December 1881, JA MSS, box 1, folder 1, BL, YU. See also JAJ ["troublesome" Oneida women who attacked "Ida Baird walking innocently"], 30 June 1897, JA MSS, box 1, folder 6, BL, YU.

38. JAPR [alleged rape], 31 July 1880, JA MSS, box 1, folder 1, BL, YU; JAPR [family abandonment and a case of property damage—field of hay], October 1881, JA MSS, box 1, folder 1, BL, YU.

39. John Archiquette to Thomas Jennings, 28 September 1887, JA MSS, box 1, folder 3, BL, YU.

40. JAPR, February 1887, JA MS, box 1, folder 3, BL, YU.

41. John Archiquette to D. H. George, 30 November, 6 and 27 December 1898, JA MSS, box 1, folder 5; Archiquette to George, 1 May, 3 October 1899, 19 February 1900; Archiquette to M. C. Phillips [US attorney], 6 October 1899, box 1, folder 6, BL, YU.

42. John Archiquette to D. H. George, 12 February 1900, JA MSS, box 1, folder 6, BL, YU; JAPR, November 1885, box 1, folder 2; February 1888, box 1, folder 3, BL, YU.

43. JAPR, May 1885, JA MSS, box 1, folder 2, BL, YU. The tribal council had previously given the assigned parcel to an Oneida who blocked the road.

44. JAJ [Mormons], 27 August 1888, JA MSS, box 1, folder 4, BL, YU.

45. JAJ, 15 October 1890, JA MSS, box 1, folder 4, BL, YU.

46. John Archiquette to Commissioner of Indian Affairs, 29 March 1890, JA MSS, box 1, folder 4, BL, YU. Archiquette also wrote to the US attorney: Archiquette to Elihu Colman, 17 August 1891, JA MSS, box 1, folder 4, BL, YU. By 1891, the Catholic diocese had already started construction on the church. JAPR, July 1891, JA MSS, box 1, folder 4, BL, YU. For Commissioner Morgan, see Francis Paul Prucha, *The Churches and the Indian Schools, 1888–1912* (Lincoln: University of Nebraska Press, 1979).

47. The church was finally completed on the reservation in 1909. JAJ, JA MSS, box 2, folder 7, BL, YU.

48. John Archiquette to Thomas Savage [federal agent, Green Bay Indian Agency], 20 April 1894, JA MSS, box 1, folder 4, BL, YU.

49. Rev. Solomon S. Burleson to John Archiquette, 21 April 1894, JA MSS, box 1, folder 5, BL, YU.

50. Rev. R. Pike to John Archiquette, 30 April 1894, JA MSS, box 1, folder 5, BL, YU.

51. Frank Roma to Secretary of the Interior, 24 June 1898; John Archiquette to D. H. George), 17 January 1898, JA MSS, box 1, folder 5, BL, YU. Well into the twentieth century, the eligibility issue simmered. JAJ [meeting with F. M. Conser, BIA Inspector], JA MSS, 13–16 April 1906, box 2, folder 7, BL, YU. Archiquette's journal entries increasingly dealt with tribal enrollment problems in the decade before his service ended.

52. John Archiquette to Joseph Hart, 7 November 1900, JA MSS, box 1, folder 6, BL, YU; J. Archiquette to Charles Anderson [US attorney], 16 January 1901, JA MSS, box 1, folder 6, BL, YU. Previously, Archiquette fully described his problem of getting Oneidas to testify in these liquor violation cases. Archiquette to M. C. Phillips [US attorney], 6 October 1899, JA MSS, box 1, folder 6, BL, YU. For more on Agent Hart, see Hauptman and McLester, *The Oneida Indians in the Age of Allotment*, 65–66, 209–16.

53. Cornelius Hill's deposition on the health and character of John Archiquette for the Bureau of Pensions, March 4, 1901, John Archiquette Civil War pension record, Co. D, 14th Wisconsin Volunteer Infantry, Certificate # 678911, RG 94. NA.

54. JAJ, 19 June 1905, JA MSS, box 2, folder 29; 13–16 and 18 April 1906; 30 January, 10 February, 14 March, 4 June, 31 December 1908; 31 January 1909, box 2, folder 7, BL, YU.

55. Minutes of the First Meeting of the Federal Competency Commission at Oneida, Wisconsin, 7 August 1917, James McLaughlin MSS, box 1, Wisconsin Historical Society [WHS]; Minutes of the Second Meeting of the Federal Competency Commission at Oneida, Wisconsin, 14 August 1917, James McLaughlin MSS, box 1, WHS.

56. Thelma Cornelius McLester, "Oneida Women Leaders," in *The Oneida Indian Experience*, ed. Jack Campisi and Laurence M. Hauptman (Syracuse, NY: Syracuse University Press, 1988) 116–18. For Oscar Archiquette, see Laurence M. Hauptman, *The Iroquois and the New Deal* (Syracuse, NY: Syracuse University Press, 1981), 70–87, 170–76; L. Gordon McLester III and Laurence Hauptman, eds., *A Nation Within a Nation: Voices of the Oneidas in Wisconsin* (Madison: Wisconsin Historical Society Press, 2010), 5, 8–9, 41–45, 184–89, 225; Lewis, *Oneida Lives*, xxxv.

7

THE EPISCOPAL MISSION
1853–1909

Three Church Accounts

Ellen Saxton Goodnough

"Christmastime at the Mission, 1869." From Julian K. Bloomfield, *The Oneidas* (New York: Alden, 1907).

We had a glorious Christmas, The Church is beautifully dressed with ever-greens; cedar, pine and ground-pine are used for wreaths, Flowers were made of fancy papers and fastened among the wreaths very tastefully. The chancel is simply decorated with ground-pine. [At] Christmas Eve the Church was brilliantly illuminated for the . . . children's festival . . . The music was perfectly grand. In the Christmas hymns all joined, old and young in the Oneida tongue. It was so affecting I had to wipe my eyes several times during the singing . . . When it came to the children's part of the festival, their delight and excitement was more than words can tell. They had never before known anything so grand as this Christmas Eve. After the prayers and singing were over, Cornelius Hill, the young chief, made a speech in Oneida; then we gave out the toys sent by Miss B [Julia Keen Bloomfield] from Oswego. The dolls we gave the little girls, pictures and other toys to the older ones. I went among the boys with a little box of toy watches, holding one up for them to see. Instantly all order was overthrown. Such a scrambling I never saw; the excitement was tremendous. John Baird, the head warrior, called to them angrily to be quiet, but there was little order until the last watch was gone. The clothes were next shown, and the drawing began. The girls who had been to school most steadily had the first choice, then the next, and so on. It was quite dark when all was over, but it was a happy day, one never to be forgotten by the Oneidas . . . I had another surprise that Christmas Eve. The women of the parish gave me a fruit-dish, silver-plated. It is very pretty indeed. Was it not kind of them? Christmas Day itself, was a blessed, holy, and joyous Festival, as it must always be. The Church was crowded to its utmost capacity. And the Holy Communion service was very solemn with a large number of our Oneidas kneeling at the chancel. Oh, it has indeed been a glorious Christmas!

Rev. Solomon S. Burleson

Burleson's account is of his providing medical care to the Oneidas and his desire to build an Episcopal mission hospital. Quoted in H. L. Burleson et al., *An Officer of the Line in the Conquest of the Continent* (Hartford: Church Missions, 1911).

From Christmas to Epiphany I slept in a bed only six times; the rest of the nights were spent by the side of sick-beds. Pity it is that my sixty years are beginning to unfit me in some ways for the work which I would willingly do. The hard part is that I cannot trust any of them to do the nursing, but must attend to it myself. Churchmen, Methodists, and Romanists I attend alike. Some of them manifest gratitude, some do not. Perhaps it matters little, but when one gives all that is in him to help another's suffering a little gratitude goes a long way. . . . And yet, there comes to me the memory of the words of a brave little woman, who, after a fearful operation, laid her hand upon my shoulder and said, "Dear father, do you think the good Father in Heaven will let me live?" When I told her that I trusted He would, she said: "Then you will thank Him now in *my* house, and tell Him when I am well enough I go thank Him in *His*."

Or again, just after Christmas, I was attending Z—, who was suffering from congestion of the lungs and erysipelas (the fact that he had been in a saloon fight only makes it all the more certain that it was Z—). I had taken care of him all night, and just as it was getting daylight he passed his hand under his pillow and drew out a prayer book, which he held suggestively. I asked him if he would like me to have prayers with him. Conceive my surprise at receiving in answer an emphatic "You bet!" After prayers he looked up and said: "Your medicine, that is good; but your pray [*sic*], that is better."

The thermometer registered 20 degrees below zero this morning when I was called to go and see a child sick with pneumonia. It is a desperate case. Eight in the family; one room; cooking, washing, etc., done there; doors and walls reeking with moisture; ice on the bottom of the window-panes an inch thick; the air of the room suffocating,—partly from the foulness, partly from vapor; and a case of pneumonia which they expected that "the doctor" was going to cure at once. This is a sample case of many, and you will not wonder that I sigh from the depth of my heart for a decent place where the suffering can have a fair chance for life. I am well aware that hospitals cannot be erected and sustained without money, a commodity which missionaries never have in excess, but if any one desires to enjoy an honest heart-ache I can furnish him an opportunity in the homes of these poor Indians at any time when it is too cold for them to sleep out of doors.

Rev. Frank Wesley Merrill

Merrill describes the beginnings of the Sybil Carter Indian mission's lace-making project at Oneida sponsored by the Episcopal Church. From Frank

Wesley Merrill, *The Church's Mission to the Oneidas* (Wisconsin Oneida Indian Reservation: Oneida Episcopal Mission, 1899).

Miss Sybil Carter, who has done the splendid work of establishing this helpful industry among the Indian women of the country, kindly sent a representative to spend some days on the reservation in August who helped at the start when about a dozen women undertook the new work. Later on Miss Carter sent a lace teacher who remained through the winter helping the women in their work. As soon as the first lot of lace had been dispatched to Miss Carter at New York, and there were tangible results in the shape of half dollars and larger sums for the workers, the interest speedily grew, and by degrees the band of lace workers increased until at the close of the first year, i.e. September, 1899, the class numbered seventy-five women who made over 500 pieces of lace, including 600 yards of lace edging, in strips of two and three yards each, and many dollies. This brought them in a cash return of $425. Ordinarily, a lace school attempts but one kind of lace; either the braid lace, which is of needle-work, or the pillow or bobbin lace, as it is called. At Oneida we are doing both kinds of work. As this is an art entirely new to the women, it must necessarily grow gradually . . . The work is, of course, open to all, and many of the older women are glad of the opportunity to earn money, and as glad, too, to be able to "make pretty things." It is to the women's credit that their work is all done in their homes . . . In some schools this would not be possible, and the teachers even baste the work; but our pupils prepare their own work and return it ready to be sent to New York [for sale], except for the pressing . . . One never ceases to marvel at the delicate dainty work accomplished by hands that would seem better fitted for out-door work, and it is always a pleasure to see the women's delight in this fascinating art. The coming year should bring greater returns as it opens with as many practical workers, and we have hope of even sending some good specimens to the Paris Exposition [World's Fair of 1900].

Oneida Church of the Holy Apostles, Oneida, Wisconsin, February 21, 2017. Photograph by Dan Hawk. Courtesy of the Oneida Church of the Holy Apostles.

Rev. Samuel Kirkland, Presbyterian missionary to the Oneidas, 1767–1808. Painting by Augustus Rockwell, ca. 1870s, at Hamilton College.

Good Peter, Oneida chief (ca. 1717–1793). Painting by John Trumbull, 1792. Yale University Gallery. Good Peter was a devout Christian who served as an assistant cleric to Rev. Samuel Kirkland's Presbyterian mission from the late 1760s to the chief's death in 1793. He opposed sales of Oneida lands to land speculators who were colluding with New York State officials to get at the Oneidas' vast estate.

Rt. Rev. John Henry Hobart, third bishop of the Episcopal diocese of New York. Bishop Hobart first established the Oneida mission in 1816. This engraved image by J. W. Paradise was first published in *The Evergreen* in 1844.

Rev. Eleazer Williams, Episcopal missionary to the Oneidas. Daguerreotype, 1854. Image #93231, Wisconsin Historical Society. Williams, a Mohawk Indian, had initial success in converting Oneidas; however, his subsequent nefarious actions and bizarre behavior brought him disrepute, and consequently he was dismissed as their missionary. Courtesy of the Wisconsin Historical Society.

Rt. Rev. Jackson Kemper, the first frontier missionary of the Protestant Episcopal Church in the United States and later bishop of Wisconsin. Bishop Kemper helped establish the bonds between the church and the Oneidas by working with chiefs Daniel Bread and Cornelius Hill. He was a protector and defender of Oneida interests from 1834 until his death in 1870. Courtesy of the archives of the diocese of Fond du Lac.

Chief Daniel Bread (1800–1873). Painting by Samuel Brookes, ca. 1859. Image #2550, Wisconsin Historical Society. Bread was the principal chief of the Oneidas in Wisconsin from the late 1820s until his death in 1873. As a leader within the Oneidas, he helped establish the link with Bishop Kemper and the Protestant Episcopal Church. Courtesy of the Wisconsin Historical Society.

Susan Fenimore Cooper, ca. 1855. The daughter of
James Fenimore Cooper was a noted author in her own
right. She was the first woman to be viewed as a major
nature writer in the United States. Her *Rural Hours*
(1850) preceded Thoreau's *Walden* by four years. She
was a devout Episcopalian and the niece of the bishop
of western New York. Influenced by Bishop Kemper to
write on the Oneida, she later became their advocate
in a series of fourteen articles published in *The Living
Church*. Photograph by W. G. Smith.

Hobart Church, also known as Stone Church, Oneida Indian reservation, Oneida, Wisconsin, 1900. Photograph by Thomas D. Bowring. Image #43659, Wisconsin Historical Society. After years of quarrying stone and fund-raising, the church was completed in 1886 and consecrated in 1897 by Bishop Charles Chapman Grafton. Except for its magnificent stone walls, its interior was destroyed by a fire in the summer of 1920. The restored structure was rebuilt and reconsecrated in 1922. Courtesy of the Wisconsin Historical Society.

Rev. Edward Augustus Goodnough, Episcopal missionary to the Wisconsin Oneidas, 1853–1890. A graduate of Nashotah House Seminary, he was mentored by Bishop Kemper and became a confidante and close adviser to Oneida chief Cornelius Hill. Image reproduced from Julia Keen Bloomfield, *The Oneidas* (New York: Alden, 1907).

Rev. Solomon S. Burleson, Episcopal missionary to Wisconsin Oneidas, 1891–1897. A son of a physician and practicing dentist, Burleson became a major advocate for the establishment of an Episcopal mission hospital at Oneida. Image reproduced from Sons of Rev. H. L. Burleson, et al. *An Officer of the Line in the Conquest of the Continent* (Hartford, CT: Church Missions, 1911).

Rev. Frank Wesley Merrill, Episcopal missionary at Oneida, 1898–1907, shown in his church vestments and biretta. Merrill frequently made trips to the east to fund-raise for the Oneida mission. During Rev. Merrill's time, the Episcopal missionary Sybil Carter established a major lace-making project at Oneida. Image reproduced from Julia Keen Bloomfield, *The Oneidas* (New York: Alden, 1907).

Rt. Rev. John Henry Hobart Brown, first bishop of the diocese of Fond du Lac, 1875–1888. In his years as bishop, the Oneidas volunteered their labor, raised money for building materials, and constructed their new house of worship, the Hobart Church, also known as the Stone Church, which opened in 1886. Courtesy of the archives of the Episcopal diocese of Fond du Lac.

Rt. Rev. Charles Chapman Grafton, bishop of the diocese of Fond du Lac, 1889–1912. The bishop supported efforts at improving medical care delivery to the Wisconsin Oneidas, consecrated the Hobart Church in 1897, and ordained Chief Cornelius Hill as a deacon in 1895 and as an Episcopal priest in 1903. The Oneidas' Parish Hall was named in his honor. Image reproduced from Julia Keen Bloomfield, *The Oneidas* (New York: Alden, 1907).

Chief Cornelius Hill, Oneida Episcopal priest in his church vestments and biretta, ca.1903. Chief Hill was the most prominent Oneida political leader in the last three decades of the nineteenth century and first years of the twentieth century. He was ordained an Episcopal deacon in 1895 and a priest in 1903. Courtesy of Chief Hill's great-granddaughter Geraldine Villalobos.

Sybil Carter, ca. 1895. Carter, made a deacon of the Episcopal Church in 1893, was an extraordinary missionary who established a lace-making effort among the Wisconsin Oneidas and nine other Native American communities. At Oneida, Wisconsin, as many as 150 tribal members, mostly women, participated from 1898 to 1926. Twenty-five pieces of their magnificent altar lace was featured at the opening of the Cathedral of Saint John the Divine in April 1911. The Wisconsin Oneidas are reviving lace making today. Laurence M. Hauptman Collection.

Oneida lace makers, ca. 1910, showing a tablecloth and lace-making tools. From *left to right*: Mrs. Jonas Skenandore, Mary James, Josephine Hill Webster, Tillie Baird, Angeline Hill, Levinia John. Courtesy of the Oneida Church of the Holy Apostles.

One of the twenty-five pieces of altar lace made by Oneida women working for the Sybil Carter Lace Association under the auspices of the National Episcopal Church, which were presented to the Cathedral of Saint John the Divine on its opening in April 1911. The association's efforts formally lasted at Oneida from 1898 to 1926, but women there still continued to do lace making for decades. In recent days, this artistic tradition has been revived. Courtesy of the Cathedral of Saint John the Divine.

Sister Augusta and Oneida youngster, ca. 1950s. The widely admired Episcopal nun was teaching lace making here to an Oneida youngster. Before her residence as a teacher at Oneida, Sister Augusta survived the hardships of being incarcerated by the Japanese as a prisoner of war in China during World War II. Courtesy of the Oneida Church of the Holy Apostles.

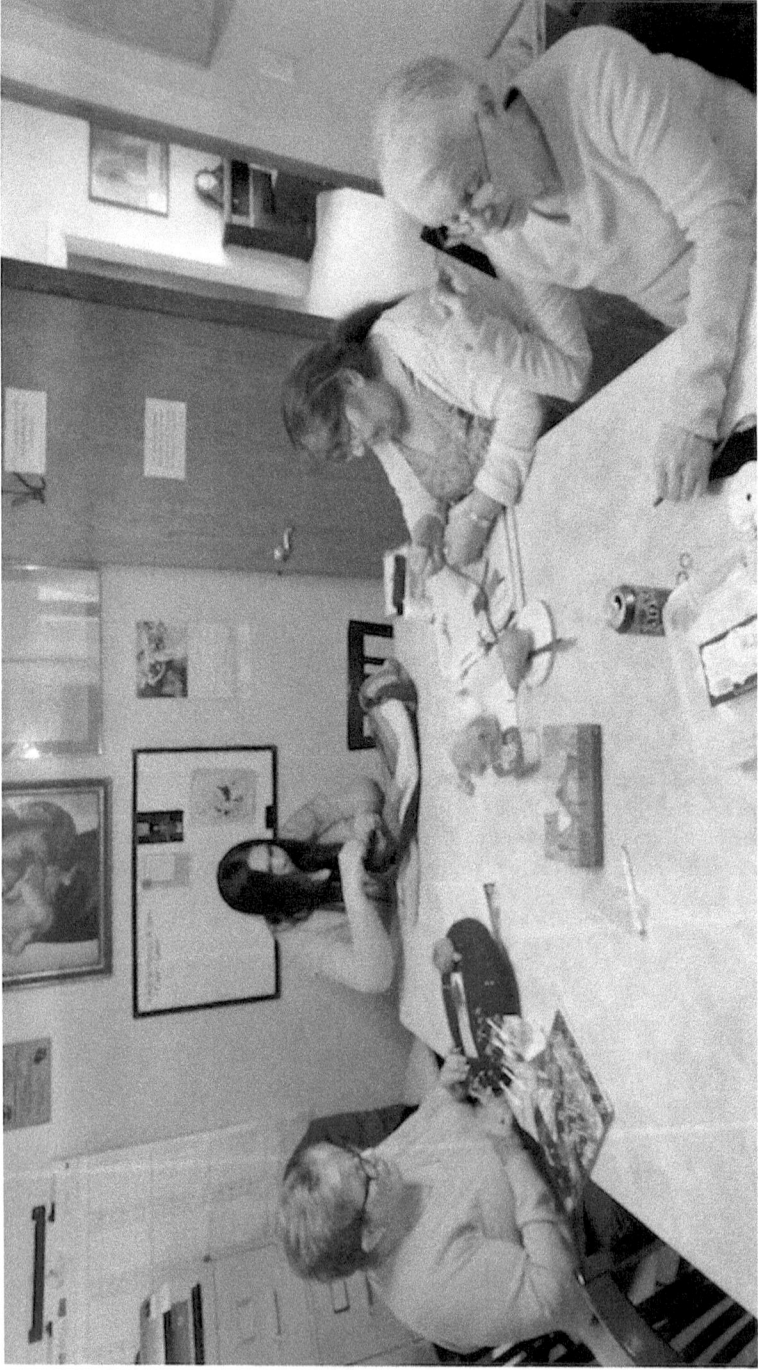

Oneida Craft/Lace-Making Group, 2016. *Left to right*: Victoria Jicha, Jennifer Skenandore, Judy Skenandore, Betty McLester. Courtesy of Oneida Church of the Holy Apostles.

Episcopal Mission Hospital at Oneida, Wisconsin. Planned by missionary Solomon S. Burleson in 1893, the hospital opened in 1898, a year after the missionary's death. It preceded federal efforts there to fight trachoma, tuberculosis, and influenza by a decade. Among the prominent Oneidas who provided health care there were Dr. Josiah Powless, the first Oneida graduated from an American medical college (Milwaukee Medical College, now Marquette University Medical School, in 1904) and two of the earliest trained American Indian nurses—Lavinia Cornelius and Nancy Cornelius (Skenandore). Courtesy of the archives of the Episcopal diocese of Fond du Lac.

Nancy Cornelius (Skenandore), Oneida nurse. After attending Carlisle Indian School, she entered the Hartford Training School for Nurses. On graduation, she served in various American Indian communities, eventually returning to Oneida. She, along with Lavinia Cornelius, was a nurse at the Oneida Episcopal Mission Hospital. Courtesy of the Oneida Church of the Holy Apostles.

Dr. Josiah Powless, First Lieutenant, Medical Branch, American Expeditionary Force, World War I. Dr. Powless was killed trying to save three of his comrades during fighting in the Ardennes in the fall of 1918. He had been encouraged by missionary Solomon Burleson and Bishop Charles Grafton to seek a career in medicine. In 1904, he graduated from the Milwaukee Medical College. He was the first Oneida to become a licensed physician in the United States. After that, he served as the resident physician at the Episcopal Mission Hospital at Oneida. Courtesy of the Oneida Church of the Holy Apostles.

The Sisters of the Order of the Holy Nativity's residence at Oneida, ca. early 1920s. Image reproduced from A. Parker Curtiss, *History of the Diocese of Fond du Lac and Its Several Congregations* (Fond du Lac, WI: P. B. Haber, 1925). Courtesy of the archives of the Episcopal diocese of Fond du Lac.

Women's Altar Guild, February 21, 1939. *Left to right*: Lavinia Cornelius, Pearl House, Rosetta House, Melvinia "Molly" Smith. Lavinia Cornelius (along with Nancy Cornelius) was a nurse who worked at the Oneida Episcopal Mission Hospital and later at the infirmary. Pearl House was the leader of the Oneida Hymn Singers. Courtesy of the Oneida Church of the Holy Apostles.

Rev. William F. Christian, Episcopal priest, who served from 1937 to 1956. A beloved clergyman, he fostered connections with other congregations, including ones in the Iroquois homeland in New York. He took a personal interest in the welfare of the children, seniors, and infirm in his parish. Courtesy of the Oneida Church of the Holy Apostles.

Rev. Dewey Silas, Oneida Indian and Episcopal priest. Courtesy of the Oneida Church of the Holy Apostles.

Left to right: Oneida elder Blanche Powless; Rt. Rev. Russell Edward Jacobus, bishop of Fond du Lac; Oneida deacon Edmund Powless, at the ceremony in which Blanche Powless received the Bishop's Cross for service to the Episcopal Church, 2007. Photograph by Matthew Payne. Courtesy of the archives of the Episcopal diocese of Fond du Lac.

Rt. Rev. Katherine Jefferts Schori, the presiding bishop of the National Episcopal Church, on her visit to the Oneidas' Church of the Holy Apostles in 2011. *Left to right*: Rt. Rev. Russell Edward Jacobus, bishop of the diocese of Fond du Lac; Bishop Katherine Jefferts Schori; Deacon Deborah Heckel of the Oneida Church of the Holy Apostles. Photograph by Matthew Payne. Courtesy of the archives of the Episcopal diocese of Fond du Lac.

Oneida Hymn Singers receiving award from the National Endowment for the Arts, 2008. Back row, *left to right*: Betty Dennison, Eleanor Bailey, Harry Cornelius, Bruce Danforth, Earl Smith, Neal Cornelius, Kenneth House, L. Gordon McLester III; middle row, *left to right*: NEA director of Folk and Traditional Arts Berry Bergey, Betty McLester, Mercy Danforth, Arlene Elm, Opal Skenandore, Rose Johnson, Doug Skenandore, Norma Skenandore, Beverly Skenandore, Lois Powless; front row, *left to right*: Frank Cornelius, LouAnn Summers, Bev Anderson, Noel Cleven, Brucie Benson, Josie Daebler, Carol Cornelius, Patti Skenandore. L. Gordon McLester III Collection.

Rt. Rev. Matthew Gunter, bishop of the diocese of Fond du Lac with Oneida elder Pearl Schuyler McLester at the Oneida Veterans of Foreign Wars building in August 2014 at a conference commemorating the 175th anniversary of the consecration of the Episcopal Church by Bishop Jackson Kemper. Courtesy of the Oneida Church of the Holy Apostles.

Celebration of new ministry at Church of the Holy Apostles on Sunday, March 26, 2017. *Left to right*: Very Rev. Steven Peay, former dean and president, Nashotah House Theological Seminary; Rev. Deborah Heckel, deacon; Rt. Rev. Matthew A. Gunter VIII, bishop of Fond du Lac; Rev. Rodger Patience, vicar. Courtesy of L. Gordon McLester III.

PART III

ONEIDA FIRST-PERSON ACCOUNTS OF THE EPISCOPAL CHURCH AND ITS CLERGY

Editors' Introduction to Part III

Part III of this book contains two chapters that include seventeen first-person accounts by Wisconsin Oneidas—eight collected by Oneidas working in the WPA Oneida Language and Folklore Project between 1938 and 1942, and nine other first-person accounts delivered at two recent conferences on the history of the Oneidas' Episcopal Church and its mission. The excerpts from WPA interviews and testimony from current church members clearly show the importance of Episcopal clerics, men and women, and their work on behalf of the Oneida community. Indeed, for much of Wisconsin history, the Episcopal Church was an anchor for the Wisconsin Oneidas when these Native Americans faced one crisis after another—local, state, and federal pressures to allot and sell off their reservation; the Great Depression; overseas wars from World War I to the First Gulf War; termination policies aimed to end federal treaty status; Wisconsin's efforts to extend its jurisdiction; and finally county and municipality efforts to levy taxes on tribal lands. By 1933, almost all the Wisconsin Oneidas' federal treaty lands of 65,400 acres had been alienated out of their hands. Much of their remaining lands at Duck Creek were those reserved for churches, cemeteries, and schools. Even at this time, when Oneidas were forced to move away to seek employment in Chicago, Detroit, Milwaukee, and Minneapolis, they still returned to Duck Creek, often to attend church services at Christmas and Easter and major events sponsored by the church. Importantly, Oneidas also came back to the cemetery on the hill at the Episcopal Church to bury their dead or to attend funerals of important tribal and church friends and leaders. Thus, while serving as a magnet drawing people back to the community, the church actually reinforced Oneida identity.

In the first excerpt from a WPA interview, Sarah Cornelius provides information about the Episcopal clergy in the last decades of the nineteenth century and first decades of the twentieth century. She describes the charitable efforts of Edward A. Goodnough as well as Chief Hill's important role as organist and interpreter during church services. She also reveals a split over the nuns' roles at the mission during missionary Solomon S. Burleson's tenure and comments on the High Church ritual employed by missionary Frank Wesley Merrill.

Guy Elm, a member of the vestry council, then describes the overall importance of the Church of the Holy Apostles and its sponsorship of programs and community events. At the end of his interview, he comments about the False Face Medicine Society. His skepticism about the efficacy and nature of traditional healing and beliefs is revealed in the excerpt, indicating a wide gulf that developed in the century after the Oneidas' migration out of New York. Despite Elm's disparagement of the False Face Society, Lena Silas, in her interview, does not dismiss long-held traditions. She reflects on how the Trinity actually fit into Iroquoian beliefs.

In his first of two WPA interviews, Oscar Archiquette, the prominent son of John Archiquette, describes how the Church of the Holy Apostles was organized and functioned in the late 1930s. In his second interview, he describes the practice of collecting holy water at Eastertime, a practice that the Oneidas brought from New York. Archiquette's accounts are followed by one by Pearl House, the head of the Oneida Hymn Singers and member of the church Altar Guild. She recounts the important work of the Episcopal nuns who served the mission. Although they faced gender bias during Burleson's priesthood, the nuns served the Oneida mission as catechists, as assistants to priests, as teachers including in lace-making instruction, as health care workers, and in the collection of clothing donations for the Indians. In two excerpts from WPA interviews, David Skenandore presents a description of the festivities in June 1922 at the reopening and reconsecration of the Episcopal Church after the disastrous fire that gutted the inner structure of the building in the summer of 1920. His second interview describes an Episcopal Church–sponsored trip by the church choir to Philadelphia; Washington, DC; New York City; and to the Iroquois homeland. Led by Episcopal priest Rev. William F. Christian, the trip renewed ties to other Iroquois and their congregations.

In chapter 10, the second section of Part III, contemporary Oneidas provide the reader with more detail about the nature of the relationship between the Oneida and the church since the 1930s. Kenneth Hoyan House focuses on Rev. Christian, who first arrived at the Church of the Holy Apostles in 1937, and who influenced so many of the Oneida youth until his retirement in 1956. House's description of this remarkable priest and his total commitment to the community is followed by accounts of the Oneida mission school by Blanche Hill Powless, a descendant of Chief Cornelius Hill, who was awarded the Bishop's Cross for lifetime service in 2007. The remarkable story of Powless's late husband, "Deacon Ed," is then presented by their daughter Kathy Powless Hughes, the former vice-chair of the Oneida Nation of Indians of Wisconsin. Hughes tells of Deacon Ed, a hero of World War II who was awarded the French Legion of Honor, its highest military honor, and his long road to becoming deacon in the Church of the Holy Apostles in August 1990. Blanche Powless's daughter, Sister Theresa Rose, is also represented in Part III, along with Mother Superior Alicia Torres, both Oneidas in the Sisters of the Teachers of the Children of God, who describe the influence of clergy at the Church of the Holy Apostles in their decision to become Episcopal nuns. After the two nuns' accounts, Pearl Schuyler McLester, an Oneida elder and contemporary of Blanche Powless who became a church member after her marriage, reminisces about the Episcopal mission's impact on the community's welfare from the 1940s onward.

Rev. Deborah Heckel, the present deacon in the Church of the Holy Apostles, then tells how another Oneida churchman, Rev. Dewey Silas, inspired her to serve Christ. The deacon's account is followed by Judy Cornelius-Hawk's account of the importance of women church members and nuns in personally influencing her; she also makes reference to some of the problems facing the church today. Then Betty McLester and Judy Skenandore describe Oneida lace making, first introduced at the Episcopal mission in the 1890s, and its revival in recent days. Part III concludes with a brief essay by L. Gordon McLester III on the famous Oneida Hymn Singers, an interdenominational group of Christian hymn singers who have performed in the Oneida language for at least the past 240 years. Besides touring Europe, they frequently perform today at churches of different denominations, at wakes, at community events, and at many other venues throughout the Midwest. In 2008, the National Endowment for the Arts awarded the Oneida Hymn Singers its National Heritage Fellowship Award.

8

SIX ONEIDAS RECOUNT EIGHT WPA ORAL HISTORIES, 1938–1942, ABOUT THE EPISCOPAL MISSION

Sarah Cornelius

Remembrances of the Oneida Episcopal Mission, from the 1880s through 1907, and evaluation of the work of its missionaries. From WPA Oneida Language and Folklore Project Stories and Interviews (OLFP) Oneida Nation of Indians of Wisconsin (ONIW).

My father and mother were not very active members, but they helped when they had their church dinners. My father and mother lived near Seymour and the roads used to be so rough and muddy that it was hard to travel at certain times of the season and that was one reason they did not come to church often. I used to stay with my grandparents when I was school age, and attended the Episcopal mission school under Father Goodnough. My grandparents lived about two miles from the mission. In those days it was quite different. The schoolhouse was a big frame building, across the road form the church, and there was about at lease one hundred pupils attended at that time. Father Goodnough taught the higher grades, and his second wife Miss Berry taught the lower grades. There used to be students about eighteen years old going to school. About that time some started to go to Wittenberg, and Keshena, Wisc. They were Indian boarding schools. It was partly run by the government. Father Goodnough used to issue clothing for the day school students, and they were new things. May be the government used to send the clothing but wherever it came from it was all new. At Christmas time then every body got a bundle, that was both new, and old clothes, quilts, sheets, pillow cases, and toys for the children. They used to make the Christmas eve service the most wonderful service. The choir sang Christmas carols and the Christmas tree in front of the church used to be elaborately trimmed and a few lighted candles on the tree. As a child I was very much impressed the first time I attended the Christmas eve services and may be I only attended once or twice in my childhood, yet after I was away to school in Pennsylvania[,] whenever I hear the old Christmas carols and hymns[,] my thoughts always take me back to the first Christmas eve service, and I was always anxious to be present at this particular service, as well as the Christmas day service. Most all the old Oneida church members like the way the services were officiated at that time even though the services used to last at least two hours. The sermons were interpreted by Cornelius Hill, and the Gospel and the Epistle, but the prayers . . . were in English. The old Indians were very strict in regards to their belief. They hardly ever missed the services and the means of conveying was not as handy as today. Most of the Oneidas had only horse and buggy, and others used their lumber wagon, and some walked 2 or 3 miles, and they did not thinking [*sic*] nothing of it. The church had large attendance every Sunday. I used to enjoy the sermons that Father Goodnough preached because he made it very simple, so that it was easily interpreted. He used to tell them mostly Old Testament stories. Most of the old Oneidas were well posted on the Old Testament stories, and also the New Testament. I was too small to realize what sort of sermons Father Goodnough preached but I know he made a good strict teacher.

I was about ten years old when I went to Martensburg [Martinsburg], Pa. The school was partly supported by the government and partly by rich Episcopal people. There were only about 200 students altogether. At that time Carlisle Indian school was in force. Our school was abolished and we were all transferred to Carlisle School and that is how I entered Carlisle Indian School. I stayed there five years then I returned home. I was away from home six years and when I came home[,] Father Burleson . . . [was] the priest and even then the services had changed to some extent. It was after Father Burleson's death that the church became a high church. The bishop had the high church doctrine and he placed a priest here that had the same belief. Father Goodnough and Father Burleson did not dress so gaudy, and elaborately when they officiated church services. Their ceremonies at the alter [*sic*] were plainer, not so showy.

The new priest was Father [Frank Wesley] Merrill, and he was the priest that had all the regalia of a high priest. The people did not know just what it meant. They had a chance to accept one of the Burleson brothers [Solomon S. Burleson's sons] as their priest, but the majority of the vestry men had rejected the young priest, because the Sisters of the Holy Nativity and Father Burleson had some misunderstanding [over nuns' service in the hospital] regarding the hospitals, and the few vestry men headed by Cornelius Hill wanted the Sisters to return and they thought that if the Burlesons remained[,] the Sister[s] would not want to come back. The Oneidas were not used to the elaborate service, but the new priest had a good personality and he soon made lots of friends. He instituted the vested choir[;] he was quite musical so he and the sister taught the choir the church music. Father Merrill had two boys about twelve and fourteen years old, and a daughter about sixteen years old. They were all good singers and they were in the choir. Father Merrill also started the acolytes. The choir use to go from the church basement and came in through the front door of the church in the summer time. The choir was accompanied by the pipe organ and two cornet players. There were some women [who] helped the choir, but they were not vested. They stayed up in the chancel but they took the rear seats. I think Father Merrill had a better choir then they have now. These were more male voices, and all the different parts were well represented. The leader of the choir was a man and he had a very good clear voice. They did not sing very much in Oneida, but they had one that they used to sing pretty near every Sunday, and before long the whole congregation learned it and when every body sang it sounded good. The old Indians were good singers, and they sang by notes. There was a man from New York named Luther Jack that came here in 1875 and he was the man that taught the Oneidas to sing by notes of the church hymns. He tested their voices and told them what part . . . [to] sing according to their voices. In that way some sang tenor, some bass, and the women had such high pitch voices that many of them sang tenor instead of alto. Most of them sang soprano. Luther Jack was a Seneca and was well educated man. Some Oneida man who had been to New York brought this man to Oneida and he stayed a year or so[;] then returned to New York. It was at this [time] that the first band [was] organized.

While Father Merrill was here the addition to the church that Father Burleson started was completed (the addition was the chancel with the full basement). . . . It was furnished and used as a hospital. Father Merrill was a very active missionary. He was the first priest to go east, and ask for donations from the rich people for the Oneidas, and he was given a good support. Money, clothing, and cattle was sent to Oneida by [the] wealthy class. He did so well as a lecturer and solicitor that the Bishop sent Father Sheldon a retired clergyman to take charge of the services whenever Father Merrill was away. The Parish Hall was built while Father Merrill was the missionary but it was never fully completed. The basement was to have had bathrooms, and there was going to be a room fixed up for the band to be used for practicing their parts. Father Merrill was a good preacher although I can't recall now just what sort of sermons he delivered, but any way he always had [a] good congregation, whenever I attended the services. His sermons were interpreted by Cornelius Hill who was deacon at the time. Father Merrill had a fiery temper and he would scold the acolytes at the alter [sic] if they made a mistake and one Sunday he was very much provoked at the leader of the choir, and had a paralytic stroke at the alter [sic] while celebrating the high Mass. He was taken out of the church during the service. Father Merrill never recovered. He went to Florida in the winter time[;] then he rented a log house near the Mission and stayed there.

Guy Elm

A member of the vestry council, Elm describes the importance of the Oneidas' Church of the Holy Apostles, its sponsorship of programs and community events, and Iroquoian traditional practices and beliefs that survived in Wisconsin. From WPA OLFP ONIW.

The Oneidas here on the reservation that are looked upon as leaders . . . are most[ly] all church members. I have observed for the last twenty [-] five years that the Oneidas that hold any kind of office such as town office, tribal, church organization and benefit societies are all good church members and their families are like wise members of different churches here on the reservation. And it has been like that as far as I can remember. You just can't get away from this religion stuff if you want the people to back you up to the limit. It seems that it [is true] with the Oneidas, that if you are a good church member, you stand more of a chance in getting to hold an office, [and] it doesn't make any difference what kind of office. The Oneidas for some reason prefer man with some kind of religion, than [a] man that don't believe in God at all. For one thing they have more respect for him . . . [;] they will trust him and they will do all they can to help him more than the other fellow that they know hasn't any religion at all. Of course now [a]days it isn't quite like that[;] once in a while they will get a man in a office that they don't know what church he belongs to. . . .

The churches now [a]days sponsor more social activities than they did years ago. There is some difference in the kind of social events sponsored now then formerly. The present day social activities changes with the seasons of the year. . . . [I]n the summer time . . . [the] churches sponsor picnics, dances, dinners, and moving picture shows. . . . [T]he picnics are held several time[s] during the summer months and the church usually make[s] about $100.00 or more at these doings. . . . Confirmation Day or as the old Oneidas call it the Bishop's Day, [is] the date usually held on around the early part of June. This is one of the biggest day[s] on [the] Church's calendar. The visitors come from all over the state on that day to visit . . . [the] old stone church. The program for the day starts with service at High Mass at 10 o-clock in the morning. During this service the [bishop holds] confirmation classes. . . . Shortly after the service a dinner or lunches are served by the women of the different women's organization and the vestry [council]. These organizations usually have stands selling different kinds of things to eat and drinks . . . [They also sell] their lace, blankets, dresses, aprons, and other Oneida made articles.

The old Oneida [Nation] band . . . [was] always on hand to furnish the music, but now [a]days they have much difficulty in rounding up enough Oneida musician to form a band. At 2 o'clock in the afternoon[,] they have a program . . . [in] . . . both Oneida and English singing in the Parish Hall. And at this time the bishop usually talks to all the people of the congregation, and some time[s] they have some other outside speaker to climax the program. In the evening they have a dance, which used to draw big crowds, but in recent years the crowd hasn't been so large. When its over every one that help[s] with the work are glad to rest up for the rest of the night, because [on] the next day [there] is another big job [namely] to clean up the hall and the grounds. . . . [At] these church picnics [it] doesn't make any difference whether . . . [it is sponsored by] the Methodist, Church of Christ, Lutheran, Roman Catholic or the Episcopal Church[;] they get big crowds . . . [and they get] from the outside. . . . [T]hey all put on good dinners or supper, [and] usually its chicken. The biggest picnic that is put on here in Oneida is sponsored by the Catholics[,] which is held in August. They draw . . . over two thousand people . . . [at this annual affair]. A baseball game is played in the morning, between the home team and some outside team. They have concession stands such as beer stands, game of chance of all kinds, [as well as] a dance in the evening and amateur shows. One year they raffle[d] a brand new automobile. A governor of [this] state was a speaker. They had two airoplanes [*sic*] for the public to ride [in] for one dollar per person. They had these two planes going all afternoon. The governor came in the airoplane [*sic*] and he made quite [a] hit with the people.

The Episcopal Church hold[s the] Fourth of July celebration[s] that usually is [*sic*] a big time affair because some times it lasts two days. The program is some thing like the Bishop's Day. [The o]nly thing is they have more attraction[s]. In the afternoon they have [a] ball game, [and] foot races both for men and women, boys and girls. They have prizes for the winners in all the events. A boxing show is also held during the after noon . . . [and] Indian war dancing, music by the [Oneida Nation] band, and a dance [are held] in the evening in the Parish Hall. A few years ago, they put on a minstrel show, which was some thing different . . . [;] it sure was a success.

Labor Day is another day that usually draws big crowd[s] of people back to Oneida. Our church some times have [*sic*] their picnic on Sunday, [the] day before Labor Day[,] for the Oneidas that come back to visit. The church activities during the summer months comes to a close the last of October. They hold [the] annual Bazzar [*sic*] in the Parish Hall. The bazzar that they had last fall was the best that they ever had so far. All the different organizations of the church had a stand of some kind in the parish hall. All . . . [the] proceeds taken in by the organizations were turn[ed] over to the vestry [council] for the church to . . . [use] for paying bills that has been carried [over] from last year. The total was $169.00[, a] nice stake for two day's [*sic*] doings. This bazzar started on Saturday afternoon . . . [;] they served supper and that evening they put on a good program and free dance. . . . The next day on Sunday they continued with their bazzar [*sic*]. After church services they served chicken diner [*sic*] for about one hundred and fifty people. We had visitors from Green Bay, Sturgeon Bay, Shawano, Ocnto, Manitowac, and Sheboygan. The Holer sisters were also with the visitors and brought along a . . . [puppet] show with them. They put on the show that Sunday afternoon. We charge[d] a small admission fee of $.10 to all. This show won a prize at the Wisconsin State Fair last fall. Everybody enjoyed the show very much. . . . [W]e certainly appreciated to have these people help us with out [*sic*] no cost to us to put on the show, and all the proceeds [were] given to the church. After it was all over, we started to tear . . . [the] stands down. . . . We counted the money several times to make sure that there were no mistakes[;] then we turned the money over to our treasurer. . . . The vestry [council] this year with the full . . . [cooperation] of the congregation . . . made the most money for the church in its history. . . .

During the winter months, the vestry [council] . . . from time to time sponsor[s] church dinners on Sundays, when the weather is favorable to do so. Last winter we used to have moving pictures show[n] every Monday evening, but due to the fact that there are so many of the young boys have gone [off] to C.C.C. [Civilian Conservation Corps] camps and the army camps we have discontinued the shows for the time being at least. The shows were mostly attended by the young people of the reservation. The church received $10.00 per month for rental for the hall for these shows.

The church choir is a[n] organization that has done much good work . . . [The church has] donated much of their time and money towards its support. Some time during the winter [the] vestry [council] sponsors a play either [in] Indian . . . [or] in English[;] this usually draws big crowd[s] and every body [*sic*] has a good time. The bingo games[,] card parties and other doings are held during the winter months.

Years ago the church didn't have so much expenses as they do now [a] days. They had church doing[s] but not as often as they do now [a] days . . . [;] in the summer time . . . [it] had few picnics, but [it] . . . made enough to take care of the general expenses of the church, and as a rule had some money on hand. At that time . . . [the church] didn't have to buy coal . . . [and] . . . burn[t] wood[;] in the fall of the year . . . wood cutting bees [were held] for the church. [Church volunteers] . . . would cut enough wood to last over [the] winter.

They usually served suppers and after wards [*sic*] they played games of different kinds . . . [.] The grown ups used to play this game call[ed] the fox and the geese, and others games [included] . . . drop handkerchief and blind man try and catch 'em. Any way[s] it seemed to me they used to have lots of fun[;] more than now days, of course[.] I was a young boy at that time, but the way they used to laugh and yell I think they really have some thing [*sic*] there. About 1907 they started holding dances in the New Parish Hall . . . [;] before that time they used to dance in the homes. . . . [I]t was mostly square dancing at that time, and as far as I know . . . it was private parties. . . . [W]hen the new Parish Hall was completed [in 1906], it was then open for public dancing, and admission was . . . some thing [*sic*] like $.25 per couple. When I came back just before I went to join the army [in World War I], I had to pay $.75 to go in and dance. After the World War . . . I went to . . . dances at the Parish Hall and other dance halls[;] they all charge[d] any where from fifty cents per couple up to one dollar. The church capitalize[d] on these kind[s] of entertainment by sponsoring the dances too. A good music could be had for twenty-five dollars for an orchestra, so that it was easy to clear good profits from the dances that they had. The church got its money through this kind of amusement. It went on for a long time up to the depression time in 1930. From that time on they still had the dances sponsored by the different organizations of the church, but it's not so hot anymore. By that I mean the people for some reason don't like to go in and dance in this hall . . . [;] they prefer to go to the other dance halls with the taverns next door to [them]. . . .

In recent year[s] the observance of Sunday has changed to [a] certain extend [*sic*]. About . . . twenty-five years ago . . . [the church had] three services on Sunday. The first service was at 7:30 a.m. . . . [called the] . . . low mass[;] another service at 11:00 a.m. . . . called high mass . . . [;] and the third service at five o'clock in the evening . . . called service evensong. Well, the people were more interest[ed] in their church at that time than now[a]days, because they used to almost fill the church at the 11:00 mass service. . . . [T]he early service at that time had more people than our 11: a.m. service at this present time. At the evensong during the winter months [, there] . . . used to . . . [be] . . . quite a crowd. They had a choir practice after this service and they used to have a very good choir of mostly [male] . . . voices [of] between 30 and 40 members. . . . [T]he best church choir that they ever had . . . was [in] Father Merril[l]'s time [1898–1909]. He personally directed the choir at their practice.

During the lant [Lent] . . . [church] services [were] on Wednesdays, and Fridays during the week, and on Sunday evenings . . . [H]e had . . . stereopticon pictures [about] the life of Christ and his disciples and many other pictures of the Holy Land. The people were very interested in th[ese] pictures just about like the movies now[a]days. For the last ten year[s] . . . church attendance has fallen way down in almost all the church[es] here in Oneida[,] . . . [s]o much that . . . the Episcopal church . . . [has] done away with the evening service on Sundays. The attendance isn't nothing like it used to be when I was a boy. The choir is small and mostly made up of women and girls and few men; how ever[*sic*] they have [a] pretty good choir at that. Since Father Christian has been here in Oneida as our priest, I have noticed that the attendance has increased considerabbly [*sic*], so that some times [*sic*] it looks like the old times years ago. The main reason for people not observing Sunday like they it used to do, in my opinion is that this depression came on and many of them couldn't afford to support the church . . . [and support their families at the same time]. . . . [T]here is [*sic*] expenses to belong to a church, and a person has to look half way decent to go to church. Another thing is the cars, [since] during the summer months almost every body [*sic*] likes to make a trip . . . [on weekends] to visit some distant relatives. . . . [Consequently,] during the summer . . . months of July and August, we have only one service at 8 o'clock in the morning. Here in Oneida [during] these two months the Oneidas usually go to Sturgeon Bay . . . to harvest the cherry crop, and for that reason the choir . . . [has its] vacation during this time. Of course if there is funeral or a day of . . . [a special] service[,] the choir usually reassemble[s] for that occasion. . . . [During] the winter months when the weather is good[,] . . . church attendance is good and especially during the lant [Lent].

A distinction between the magic and religion is that the magic is only practiced by very few people[;] mostly the old people believe in magic. The young Oneidas now days don't believe in magic in any form. A very few Oneidas that I know still have what is called false face society. These group[s] of Indians believe in curing the sick with ritual ceremonial Indian dancing and other acts in connection with their curing. I might give an example just what goes on at one of these curings[.] I have seen only once in my life so far . . . [and what] I have been able to get the old people to tell me [about] . . . the false face society. As far as I am able to find out[,] the persons that belong to these societies are naturally born with magic powers. They claim that usually the child that doesn't get baptized when they are born are the ones that usually acquire the supernatural powers[.] . . . [T]hose that are born twins, only one of . . . them can have the magic power.

About three years ago, I went to a false face curing of a sick boy about six years old. . . . I went to interview one of the members of this false face society[,] an old man who has since died. . . . [He told me] that . . . maybe . . . [I] wouldn't believe it. He said we are having a cure for a boy tomorrow night. . . . [W]hy not come over to my home and you can go with some of. . . . [I]n that way you can see every thing [*sic*] for yourself. I consented to go. I went to this man's place about 7 o'clock in the evening. When I got there, he said to me, well I'm going to tell few things that you shouldn't do. . . . [W]hile this curing is in progress, one thing you mustn't [do is to] laugh at the dancers and the other acts that goes with it. I promised him that I would do nothing that would displease the members. And so I went to his place at the appointed time.

He finally got his things together, and he said well we have to pick a fellow and two women on our way over. And so we did. When we got there the rest of the false face members and the medicine man were there. They put their old cloths on and some wore false face[s]. When they all got ready they started to growl like a wild animal. . . . They had a sort of club or stick [which] they bang[ed] . . . against the house[;] . . . they never knock[ed] at the door . . . [but] just walked in and left their sticks outside. Everything of course was prearranged with the parents of the sick boy. . . . [T]he man that took me along[and] told me that [a] few days before their visit[,] the medicine man or the doctor, who makes the visit to see the sick person[,] finds out what is . . . [the] ailment. . . . [A]fter fin[d]ing that out he instructs the folks what to prepare for the false face dancers to eat during ritual ceremonials.

In this case it seems that the boy was full all the time and he wouldn't eat anything[,] and he was loosing [*sic*] weight. . . . [T]he medicine man decided that the bear had something to do with his ailment. And so he ordered the folks to prepare food [specifically] what . . . bears like to eat such as fried corn soup with lots of wild meat in it, black berries, [and] nuts of different kinds. Well, I watched them closely [especially at first the] . . . medicine man . . . towards where the sick boy was laying on the bed. They started to chant some kind of lingo that I couldn't quite make out[.] I imagine that this was a prayer. After this was over than he started to chant another song [and then] than the dancers started to dance round and round in the room. All at once [the medicine man] stopped dancing. . . . He went to the stove and took two good handfuls of the wood ashes that were still burning and he threw . . . [them] over the sick boy's body. I didn't see any thing [*sic*] burn[,] either the boy's clothing or the medicine man's hands. After this ritual, the dancers again resumed their dancing for a little . . . [and] then once more they stopped their dance. This time I noticed there was a big paper bag hanging in the middle of the room on the ceiling. Well the doctor took his magic wane [wand] or stick that looked to me like a snake of some kind with spots and crooks all along the stick. He took a good toe hold and [swung]. . . . [H]e miss[ed] it by one inch. He kind of said some thing [*sic*] to himself and danced around in one spot . . . [;] than once more he got himself set and this time his aim was true to the mark . . . [and], peanuts [fell] all over the floor. At this stage of [the ceremony] . . . I almost broke my promise not to laugh, but I did manage to hold everything all though [*sic*] I took plenty punishment [since] my sides were just about [to burst] . . . The next thing I saw was that all the members of this society were crawling on their hand and knees gathering the nuts, and some of them were eating. This soup . . . [was then] eaten by the false face dancers.

The result of this curing was that in few days[,] the boy was on his way to recovery from his sickness or whatever was wrong with him. I can't say that they did . . . [effect] a cure[,] . . . [but] it was just then that he got over . . . his ailment. My mother was really interested in this false face curing societies and other group curing societies. And besides she knew lots of different kind of medicines. My grandmother was the same way. She could go in the woods and pick the herbs, shrubs, . . . and roots of all kinds. The only thing is that I never heard [was] if [my family] were member[s] of the false face society.

Lena Silas

In contrast to Guy Elm's dismissive comments about the False Face Society, Silas discusses the Christian belief in the Trinity and how it fits in with traditional Iroquoian beliefs. From WPA OLFP ONIW.

In our church [Church of the Holy Apostles] we are taught in the Sunday school that God is a spirit . . . that He is Almighty . . . [and] [t]hat He has no beginning. He always was God and always will be. Then we are taught that there are three persons in one God . . . [:] The Father, Son and Holy Ghost or Spirit. That is called the Trinity. God sen[t] his Son into the world as one of us to save the people. That was the Son, Jesus Christ, and the Holy Ghost came and descended on the Apostles and they were given the power to preach the [G]ospel. The Holy Spirit is in the holy communion that we take, and we take that in remembrance that Christ died to save the people. We were taught that God is not in any one place, but all over. That is the only comparison we can make with the Great Spirit the [G]od that the Indians worshipped. The Indian spoke of their [G]od as one that is almighty, and had power to come on earth as a man [the Peacemaker], and again he is in the thunder and in the trees and in nature, but he was not considered to be in three persons.

Oscar Archiquette

Archiquette, the prominent Oneida and son of John Archiquette, describes the Church of the Holy Apostles and its organizations in 1941. From WPS OLFP ONIW.

Church Choir

The Holy Apostle Choir Organization sing in church every Sunday at 10 a.m. and for every funeral. . . . [T]hey also help pay for the up keep of the church and help with the work. . . . [T]hey raise money by giving dinner[s] in Parish

Hall. . . . The officers are Stadler King[,] chairman, Guy Elm[,] vice chairman, Joseph Swamp[,] sec[retary], Father Christian[,] treasurer. . . . [T]here are about 28 members in the choir. The choir director is Mrs. Pearl A. House. The choir always sing couple numbers in Oneida every Sunday. Business meeting[s] [are] once a month [and] election of officers [are held] once a year . . . [O]f the members [who] are active, about half of this group are men . . . [A]ges of members range from 18 years to 55 years old. Choir practice [is held] every Sunday at 1 P.M. A week before Christmas they practice every evening. . . . [C]hoir goes out and sing[s] for [the] sick at their homes. Any members of the Episcopal Church can join the choir by presenting their name to [the] secretary.

Altar Guild

The members of this organization are all young women. . . . [T]heir work is to keep the altar clean and they also help with other church work. . . . [T]hey sew linen for the altar, and help sick people in any way they can. There are 14 members to this organization . . . [The] business meeting [is held the] second Tue[sday] in a month [and an] election of officers [is held] once a year. The officers now are Mrs. Jonathan John[,] president, [and] Sister Phillippa is secretary and treasurer. [C]onfirmed woman can join this organization and can also be a member of the Guild Auxiliary.

The Altar Guild was organized in April of 1938. They raise money . . . [from] dues which . . . are $0.10 per month, and by making and selling altar linens[,] table mates and candle ends. Money is also made by selling soup and postcards, candy bars, pop, and ice cream on Bishop['s] day, and by socials and raffle[s]. . . . [T]hey [also] raise chicks for money . . . [and make] money by selling lunch[es]. . . . They pay for [the laundry of] altar [pieces] . . . and priests['] service linens. . . . [T]hey buy wine [and] candles[,] altar rug[s] and vestments [and] they contribute to [the] kitchen fund and school hot lunch project[s] . . . [and pay] for electric wiring in [the] chapel. They buy medicine for sick Oneida women. They help the church magazine by putting . . . [advertisements] in it and they also help the vestry [council] at the [Church] Bazaar.

Guild Auxiliary

The members of the Guild Auxiliary are mostly married women. . . . [T]heir work is making quilt[s] and clothing, which is sent away to help . . . poor people. . . . [T]hey meet every Thursday at the Parish Hall . . . [;] every first Thursday in a month they serve dinner for $0.15 and they have [a] sale on clothing now and then. . . . [T]hey also help with other church work. . . . [E]lection of officers is held] once a year in Dec[ember]. Business meeting[s] [are held] once a month. There are 30 members of the Guild Auxiliary. . . . [T]he officers for 1941 are Mrs. Rosetta H. House[,] President, Mrs. Virgie Powless[,] vice president, Miss Lavinia Cornelius[,] secretary, Sister Amy[,] treasurer. Money is . . . [raised] from raffles of quilts and [admission to] socials. Any woman who is confirmed in the Episcopal Church is suppose[d] to be a member of the Guild Auxiliary and pay $0.25 a year dues. Dinner is usually given by the Guild Auxiliary when there is a Church Bee.

The members of the Guild Auxiliary can also be a member of the Altar Guild if they wish. The Oneida Indian Guild Auxiliary is perhaps the oldest organization in this part of the country . . . [dating back to] the Oneidas starting [to build] . . . the Episcopal Stone Church [in early 1880s]. . . .

Parent-Teacher Organization

The purpose of this organization is to promote a closer cooperation between parents and teachers. . . . [T]heir business and recreation meetings . . . [are held] once a month, [and the] election of officers is [in] the second meeting in the fall. The president is John A. Skenandore, vice president is Mr. Spalding[,] Oneida Mission School teacher, secretary is Andrew Beechtree, [and] treasurer is Dennison Hill. At the present time there are about 20 members . . . [in] this organization. Dues . . . [are] $0.10 [per] . . . family per month. Any parent of school children can join this organization by paying $0.10 per month dues. [The] Parent Teachers Organization was . . . established in November 1940.

Church School Teachers

The purpose of this organization is to teach the Oneida children religion. The teachers are Father Christian, the three Sisters, Mr. Spalding, Miss Rueiger, Miss Powless, Miss Vera Skenandore . . . , and Miss Lavinia Cornelius. During school months they have church school every Saturday at 9:30 a.m. to 11:30 a.m. Church School enrollment is 127[, but the] average attendance is 74. Church School [was] organized three years ago.

Young People['s] Fellowship

This organization was just reorganized [and the] election of officer[s] will be [held on] Dec[ember] 15, 1940[;] there after [*sic*], election[s] will be once a year. There is going to be 7 new members initiated at that time. The purpose of this organization is mostly for recreation. They make money by having socials. Young people who belong to the Holy Apostles Church can join this organization.

The Holy Apostle Church Choir Sick and Death Benefit Committee

The purpose of this organization is . . . to help each other. . . . The dues . . . [are] $0.10 per month . . .[;] benefits . . . [are] $2.00 for sickness and death is $5.00. The election of officers is every July, and [a] general meeting is held twice a year July and Jan[uary]. At the present time there are about 15 members [in] this organization[.] [M]embership is now open to the congregation. The name of this organization will no doubt be changed to Church Sick and Death Benefit Organization. The officers are Oscar H. Archiquette[,] chairman, Stadler King[,] vice chairman, treasurer Dennison Hill, [and] secretary Mrs. Ruth Baird. The chairman or the executive committee can call for a special meeting at any time. . . . [The] Sick and Death Benefit [committee] was organized in the summer of 1940.

Cemetery Organization

The purpose of this organization is to look after . . . [and care for] the cemetery. . . . [T]he Treasurer . . . collect[s] the cemetery dues . . . [are] $2.00 a year. The officers are elected every three years in Jan[uary] by the congregation of the Episcopal Church. The chairman is Mrs. Eli Cornelius, [the] vice chairman [is] Father Christian, . . . Mrs. Josephine Webster [is the clerk] . . . Miss Grace Powless [is the treasurer] . . . [and] Stadler King and Robert Ruther Hill [are committeemen]. This organization was organized in 1937.

Improvement Committee

The committee [officers are] . . . Guy Elm[,] chairman and Cornelius Baird[,] assistant. Their business is to . . . suggest what improvements [need] to be made on [the] church property and donate their time . . . [to] improving it. They . . . raise money twice [a year] by having socials. The committee . . . [is] elected by the congregation . . . once a year in Jan[uary]. [The] [c]hairman and the Priest can call a meeting any time. . . . [The] Improvement Committee was started in 1937.

Oscar Archiquette

Archiquette discusses the origins of securing holy water at Easter. From WPA OLFP ONIW.

I am 39 years old[,] and ever since I can remember[,] my people always got up before sunrise and go [sic] after spring water on Easter morning before sunrise. I was told by my parents and heard the old Indians talking about Easter and Holy Water. If you want to get Holy Water you must get up early before sunrise an[d] when you get up[,] you must start praying and . . . not talk to any body [sic]. . . . [I]f they talk to you[,] do not answer but keep right on praying . . . [using] whatever prayer you know. The[y] take a pail or a kettle of some kind and go to a spring and get spring water before sunrise[;] then [they] go home[.] [W]hen you get home then you can talk and eat and go on with your business as before[.] [Y]ou might put the Holy Water in a glass jug and put it away[.] [T]his Holy Water is suppose[d] to keep until the next Easter. This water is used for making and mixin[g] Indian medicine. . . . [W]hen an Indian is sick he is given this water for drinking water. It is said when Christ arose from the dead[,] everything was still[,] even the water in creeks and rivers was at a stand still. Just before sunrise on Easter morning . . . [,] the animals were praying on their knees. What I have written here was told to me in [the] Oneida Indian language. To those of my age, it is an old custom or practice with us Oneidas, but the school children of today I doubt whether a person could find one . . . who would know how the Oneidas get Holy Water on Easter. Very few Oneidas get Holy Water on Easter now. About 20 years ago I was told by an old Indian that I could get Holy Water from the creek, river, well or spring[;] it doesn't have to be from the spring [but] only all that is necessary is to get it before sunrise, and . . . pray to [G]od from the time you get up until you come back with the water. It made me very happy when I heard Father [William] Christian asking for Holy Water from us Oneidas which he said will be used in our Holy Apostle's Church. This . . . is one belief we Oneidas believe in, which . . . [is] good and pure.

Pearl House

House, the head of the Oneida Hymn Singers, recounts the work of the Episcopal nuns and the problems they at times faced. From WPA OLFP ONIW.

The Sisters of the Holy Nativity belong to the Episcopal organization of nuns. I think that Bishop [Charles C.] Grafton was the first Bishop to send . . . sisters here to Oneida to help with . . . church work. When the sisters . . . [first] came here[,] their work was to teach the children the catechism . . . and lacemaking . . . [;] they were [also] to operate the Oneida Episcopal [mission] hospital but they were not permitted to . . . [do so] by the missionary [Solomon S. Burleson] in charge. At the present time the sister[s] fix all the things on the altar and the priest outfit and they also keep all the clothing donations for the Oneidas and give [them] out as the people need them . . . [;] their work is to visit the sick[.] [In the past] . . . they didn't . . . [used] to do any visiting, but now that they are provided with a car, may be they will do more traveling amongst . . . church members. They are sent here as missionaries, and they are supposed to help the minister.

David Skenandore

Skenandore recounts the Oneida Nation's 1923 commemoration of its hundred-year residency in Wisconsin, which centered on the Church of the Holy Apostles and the Oneida Episcopal mission. From WPA OLFP ONIW.

The three-day celebration in the year 1923 on June 9–10–11. . . . Hundred years after Oneidas first came and settled in Wisconsin in 1823.
　　On exhibits: (the committees of that day)

Mrs. I. N. Webster—Sewing

Mrs. Solomon Webster—Chairman

Mrs. Cornelius Hill—Guild work

Mrs. Eli Cornelius—Chairman

Mrs. Elijah Skenandore—Hospitality

Mrs. Nicholas Elm—Chairman

Mrs. Isabel Denny—Entertainment and games

Jefferson Baird and Joseph Swamp—Sports

Mrs. Fred House—Reception for congregation

Mrs. Jonas Metoxen—Chairman

Mrs. I. N. Webster [Josephine Hill Webster]

Mrs. Anderson Skenandore

Mrs. Hobart House

Mrs. Chauncey Baird

Anderson Skenandore—chairman on stands

Elijah Skenandore

Nicholas Baird

Thomas Cornelius

Fred Cornelius—1923 Celebration grounds

Baptist King

Solomon Webster

Chauncey Baird

Ludovic Hill—Kitchen helpers

Noah Swamp

Jonas Skenandore—Decorations

Levi Baird

Jonas Metoxen

William Danforth and members of the Vestry

Rev. L. D.—Diocesani

Van E. C. Gear

Messrs Harry Price and Hamilton Roddis

The Right Rev R. H. Weller DD Bishop

Program of Hobart Oneida Mission Centennial . . . —one hundred years ago where [the] first Hobart Oneida Mission was established and . . . [at] this same spot[,] the younger generation . . . [organized a] centennial for three days, Saturday, Sunday and Monday, June 9th, 10th, and 11th[, 1923,] respectively. Everybody was welcome home again[;] invitation[s] were sent to the Oneidas who were away from home[—]by telephone, telegram and by letter; . . . nearly all the Oneidas were present at the centennial of Hobart Mission. An invitation was made to out side[r]s [*sic*] as well.

There wasn't much doing [on the] first day buy at 5 p.m.[;] reception near the Mission House for the Bishop and visitors; the Oneida National Band attending at 6 p.m. Supper on ground[s] near Grafton Parish House at 7:30 p.m.[;] [e]vening prayer and preparation in Holy Apostles Church. First day was fairly [well] attended.

Sunday, June 10th

This being Sunday[,] the day [began] . . . with early service at 7:30 a.m.—Holy Communion which was well attended. 11 a.m.—Holy Communion with sermon by the Bishop [R. H. Weller] of Fond du Lac[,] Wisconsin, and this service was well attended[;] also . . . included visitors . . . [and] friends of the Oneidas[.] [A]t 1 p.m. [d]inner on the grounds. Oneida National Band gave the most enjoyable music through out [*sic*] the after noon [*sic*]. At 3 p.m. out door [*sic*] song service[—]mission hymns, Indians songs, addresses on the history of the Oneida Indians.

1. Mission in New York State

2. Early days in Wisconsin

3. Contemporary events speakers: [d]elegates at the council and others.

At 6 p.m. supper [was held] on the ground, at 7:30 p.m.—Even[ing] song in Hobart Church[;] Sermon by the Rev. Father Hopkins. It was quite a successful day and people from all over were there and stayed as long as their time permitted.

Monday, June 11th St. Barnabas day

This day . . . [began] with [e]arly [church] service at 7:30[;] Holy Communion [at] 10 a.m. [and] Holy Eucharist with sermon by Rev Father Curtis. At . . . [noon] [d]inner [was held] on the [church] grounds. [At] 2 p.m. sports, games and other things were carried on. At 6 p.m. supper [was held on the church] grounds. [At] 7:30 p.m. moving pictures [were shown]; [then the] Oneida National Band benefit concert was held which was well attended.

In connection with these [t]hree days[,] [exhibits] and [a] bazaar [were held] in Grafton Parish House. . . . [Included] were . . . Oneida Indian curios; Lost Dauphin relics from [the] Green Bay museum; . . ; [an] old barrel organ; pictures; [and] Oneida basket[s] . . . [and] bead work. All exhibits or loans were delivered the day before on Friday June 8th. . . . [A]ll contributions of food and other provisions were delivered . . . by 10 o'clock Saturday morning. All other things were set up the day before, . . . [including] tents, stalls and booths. . . . Every possible means was done to make it convenient for travelers to get to this centennial[;] all train schedule[s] . . . were distributed through out [*sic*] the reservation and [in] other places.

* * *

Skenandore describes Episcopal Church–sponsored visits of the church choir to Philadelphia; Washington, DC; New York City; and to the Iroquois homeland, thus renewing ties to other Hodinöhsö:ni'. From WPA OLFP ONIW.

[On] Oct[ober] 5th . . . 1940[,] the Oneida Episcopal Church quartet went to New York where they attended the World's Fair. . . . [T]hey [also] visited Washington[,] D.C. before returning home. They were absent for one month. The quartet were dressed in full Indian costume and entertain[ed] at various churches. The singers are Mrs. Cornelius, Willard Archiquette, Roderick Cornelius, and Mrs. Blanche McLester. The Rev. W[illia]m Christian[,] their pastor, . . . [traveled] with them. . . . [They] returned from their journey on Fri[day], Nov[ember] 8th. . . .

Some of the [other] places they visited [included] . . . the Mohawk Valley, the home of Betsy Ross [in Philadelphia], . . . [the] Statue of Liberty, Oneida Castle, N.Y. [where they] saw the Oneida secret stone [Standing Stone]. . . . [Father] Christian showed the stone to [the quartet and] . . . told them that he . . . [hoped] to place the secret stone in [the] Hobart Church altar here in Oneida[,] which he thought would be a very special place for it.

When the quartet returned home[,] they were given a surprise party by various organizations of the Church of the Holy Apostles. . . . The purpose of this party was mainly to express the appreciation [for undertaking] their great journey. This trip was a benefit to all people who belonged to the congregation. . . . [A] luncheon was served free and each member of the quartet [was] asked to say some thing [*sic*] . . . [about] the trip they made and . . . what interested them the most on their journey. F[athe]r Christian . . . was called last [and] gave the most interesting speech of all the happenings . . . [on the] . . . trip. [He told the church gathering that] [t]hey were invited back . . . next year . . . [to] various congregations which they visited in [the] state of New York.

F[athe]r Christian told . . . that the Mohawk Indian[s] [whom they had met on their journey] . . . [were] planning . . . to visit [the Wisconsin] Oneidas next year] [1941]. . . . [On their visit to New York] the Mohawks and [the

Oneida quartet had] sang together in Indian, and talked and understood one another quite well, even tho[ugh] they spoke . . . a different dialect. They were very friendly people. The quartet were given . . . hymnal books combined with prays [prayers] written in [the] Mohawk language and translated [in]to English which they brought home to Wisconsin.

It is not . . . [determined] as yet what group will go . . . [back to New York] next year. The purpose of this [Oneida Fall 1940] tour was to raise funds for the church here in Oneida which . . . has many depths [debts] . . . —[and needs] a new furnace . . . [and] a new pipe organ . . . [to replace the one] which burned up when the church here in Oneida was completely destroyed by fire about twenty years ago [August 1920]. . . .

Some times [*sic*] as . . . [the Oneida quartet] traveled[,] they collected a little cash donation from . . . programs [which] they gave in various churches. Through these donations . . . they were able to meet their expenses, such as their meals, lodg[ing], gas and oil. . . . There were many questions [that the] quartet and the priest were [asked] by various people in the east, as to what was most needed out here in [the] Oneida church. So the answers were . . . [a] large furnace[,] . . . [a] pipe organ . . . , stage curtain[s] for [the] parish hall, and cash to pay some of the depths [debts] the church has. . . . [The] money which they were able to raise as they went along their journey enable[d] them to pay . . . [off] choir depths [debts] [and purchase] . . . shingles [for the] parish hall roof. . . . [The] quartet and the priest . . . [have a] great deal already to be proud [of] . . . [on] what they have accomplished on their short . . . tour. . . . The greatest hopes of F[athe]r Christian and the quartet [would be] that this trip . . . would bring the Hobart Church of Oneida back to its standards. . . . [T]he Oneidas' [Church] of Holy Apostles should remember and be thankful for . . . what Rev. F[athe]r Christian and the members of the quartet [have] done for the people . . . [by] this trip.

And there is lot more than this that the Oneidas should be thankful [for]. . . . A year ago or so ago, F[athe]r Christian went out east and travel[ed a] great deal to make friends again with [the] people that use[d] to help [the] Oneida[s] [Sybil Carter Indian Mission Association] as well as [members of] their great church [Cathedral of Saint John the Divine] years ago. . . . [On] his tour at different occasions[,] he was given a great honor of celebrating high mass in various . . . Episcopal churches out east. So . . . [on] these occasions it gave him the opportunity to express his main reason for making his tour [namely to] . . . [call attention to] the Oneida Mission['s] needs. . . . [He] was able to meet . . . women in N.Y. who gave him a considerable amount of money to replaster [the] Parish Hall. . . . [T]wo hundred dollars was spend [*sic*] . . . [on] church fixtures in remembrance of Rev Cornelius Hill and [his] wife. . . . [The] children has [*sic*] [a] great deal to be thankful for what Rev Father Christian has done for them.

9

TEN CONTEMPORARY ONEIDAS REMINISCE IN NINE ACCOUNTS ABOUT THE HOLY APOSTLES EPISCOPAL CHURCH AND THE EPISCOPAL MISSION

Kenneth Hoyan House: Father Christian Puts Me on the Right Path

My first day at the Oneida Mission School was in 1946. I rounded the corner on my way there, and, as I drew closer to the convent, I saw a priest walking down the driveway. My first impressions of the man coming in my direction was that he was a tall man with large hands and a stern face. Upon coming up to me, he said: "Good morning young man," and then he asked me my name. My first thought was that I was about to get into big trouble since I stuttered and often remained silent for fear of being mocked. He had no idea at that time that I had a speech impediment. But I was wrong from the first about Father William Christian. As I reflect back to the beginning, I realize now that Father Christian guided me through thick and thin. He always led me down the right path.

When the Oneida Mission School classes began that day, the Sisters of St. Anne spoke to us about rules and regulations. My first teachers were Sisters Augusta and Mabel. After finishing the eighth grade there, I moved on to Washington Junior High School in Green Bay. Four months into the term there, my science teacher took me aside and told me to go to the vice principal's office. After a lengthy discussion about me there, the vice principal bluntly told me that I couldn't attend the school because I needed special help because of my stuttering. They asked me to tell them who they should contact about this decision. I replied that they should telephone Father Christian at the Church of the Holy Apostles at Oneida. Father Christian was called and he immediately came to my aid. First, he enrolled me in a two-hour a week special program at East High School in Green Bay. Then he arranged for me to attend a speech therapy program at the University of Wisconsin. After that, I was sent to the Shady Trail Camp in Ludington, Michigan, that was affiliated with the University of Michigan. Through Father Christian's encouragement and intervention, I conquered my speech impediment.

Father Christian and I had many talks over the years. He told me how he came to the Oneidas' Church of the Holy Apostles in 1937 based on the recommendation provided by Harwood Sturtevant, the Bishop of the Episcopal Diocese of Fond du Lac. Upon his arrival at Oneida, he feared that the people would not trust him and was concerned about how to achieve acceptance in the community[.] He told me that he arrived at a conclusion, namely that he had to approach things one day at a time to succeed in his ministry. In 1940, Father Christian revived the Vestry Council that was quite important at Oneida in the second half of the nineteenth century and first decade of the twentieth century. He worked closely with Oneidas who held posts or headed organizations sponsored by the church—Senior Warden David Skenandore, Stadler King, who headed the church choir, Mrs. Walter House, the leader of the Woman's Auxiliary, and Winifred McLester, who directed the Young People's Fellowship. His advisory group, what he referred to as "his right and left hand," included Dennison and Sadie Hill, Anna and Norman John, Sadie and Jonathan Johns, Virgie and Ernie Smith, Abby and John Skenandore, Nancy and Lambert Metoxen, Sarah King, Bill Webster, Ruth and Elroy Baird, and Blanche McLester[.]

Despite his stern appearance, Father Christian was viewed by the Oneidas as a God-loving, caring man, loyal to mainstream Episcopal traditions. God's teaching taught him well. I would accompany him when he would drive to visit sick Oneidas and take them to doctor's appointments or to obtain groceries for them at Morgan's Store. I would travel with him on his frequent visits to our elders. He would give priority to them and the children in the community who were going through hard times. Each Fall, we would go to various stores and agencies requesting coats for the needy elderly and youngsters who were facing the bitter Wisconsin winter weather. Indeed, his generosity was never ending. He put quite a bit of mileage on his old station wagon.

I learned from him countless things because of his mentoring. These not only included all of the aspects of the Episcopal faith and its required liturgical steps. I also learned to respect every human being and follow the straight and narrow path and be guided by God's teachings.

Blanche Powless: Reminiscences about the Oneida Mission School

I was born and raised on the Oneida Reservation. I attended the one-room Oneida Mission School, that was held in [Grafton] Parish Hall. It was not the first school established on the reservation since an earlier one had been founded by Eleazer Williams after the Oneida migration from New York to Wisconsin. The initial one room at the Parish Hall was not large enough to accommodate the amount of students wanting to attend. Consequently, another room was added and then subsequently a third room was also added. Hot lunch was cooked by Oneida women and provided to all schoolchildren. Initially there were two teaching nuns from the Order of the Holy Nativity who taught grades one through eight. They were assisted by an Oneida teacher by the name of Alice Cornelius, the sister of Oneida activist Laura Minnie Cornelius Kellogg. Alice had previously taught at the Government School at Oneida until it closed at the end of World War I. After the Sisters of St. Anne left the Oneida mission, they were replaced by the Order of the Teachers of the Children of God.

When the local schools began to provide transportation to and from the reservation, the number of students attending the Oneida Mission School began to dwindle and soon it was forced to close. The Oneida Mission School, which had always served as a meeting place for dinners, housed a library, and hosted boys and girl scouts, athletic events and various social and educational activities, fell into disrepair. In the late 1990s the Oneida Nation of Indians of Wisconsin, realizing the historical significance of the Parish Hall, renovated the building and now once again, the building is used for community events.

Kathy Powless Hughes: Reflections on My Father, Deacon Edmund Powless

I am the daughter of Blanche and Deacon Edmund Powless. My father was born, raised, and lived most of his adult life on the Wisconsin Oneida Indian Reservation. When the United States entered World War II, he enlisted as an Army paratrooper. He experienced the horrors of war firsthand at the Battle of the Bulge in December, 1944. After the defeat of Nazi Germany, he returned home to Oneida after his discharge. He worked in the Green Bay area for the next forty years until his retirement at age sixty-two.

My father was a person who was totally committed to everything he did and especially in his work for the Church of the Holy Apostles. He served on the Vestry Council and was its treasurer for many years. He worked tirelessly in helping to maintain the church and organize church activities. Because he was so totally dedicated to all aspects of the needs of the church, he was encouraged by friends and family to think about serving as a deacon. Previously, the Diocese of Fond du Lac had established a three-year diaconate program and subsequently, Edmund, to his credit, signed on to attend this religious training. On August 25, 1990, he was ordained as a deacon by the Diocese of Fond du Lac. He served as a representative of the church as well as the diocese, making house calls to the elderly, to those who suffered family losses, and to patients in hospitals. Much like traditional Oneida faithkeepers, he served his people 24/7, often getting up in the middle of the night to respond. "Deacon Ed," as he was fondly called in the Oneida community, was there to help and provide his caring support for nineteen years before his second retirement at the age of 86 in 2009. Deacon Edmund Powless entered eternal rest on December 30, 2010.

Sister Theresa Rose and Mother Superior Alicia Torres of the Order of the Teachers of the Children of God: Reminiscences of Two Oneida Nuns

Sister Theresa Rose

I am the daughter of Blanche and Edmund Powless, the Deacon of the Church of the Holy Apostles. In my youth, I attended the Oneida Mission School where

I strongly admired the commitment of the Sisters of the Order of St Anne to the Oneida children there. Consequently, I wanted to emulate the good work of the Sisters. In 1946, teaching nuns came from Baltimore, including Mothers Edith, Augusta, Mable and intermittently Mother Harriet. Clara D. Abbott, a missionary from Baltimore, taught seventh and eighth grades. I was motivated and encouraged by these nuns to enter the sisterhood and become a teacher. Both Father Nelson Skinner of the Church of the Holy Apostles and William Hampton Brady, the Bishop of Fond du Lac [1956–1980], supported my desire to teach and enter the ministry. Father Skinner, with the blessing of Bishop Brady, worked in tandem with the Sisters of Saint Anne for the benefit of our youth. With the help of my Wisconsin Oneida Nation, I was fortunate enough to have the opportunity to attend Harvard University in my pursuit of a career in teaching. In 1961, I entered the Order of the Teachers of the Children of God and its convent in Tucson, Arizona. At that time, the order administered approximately thirteen schools in different parts of the United States. I would spend ten years in this order before I decided that I wanted to know what the non-secular world was all about. I came back to the Oneida reservation where I stayed for thirty years helping my own people. I have recently returned to the Teachers of the Children of God's convent in Tucson.

Mother Superior Alicia Torres

During the tenure of Harwood Sturtevant, the Bishop of Fond du Lac [1933 to 1956], I attended the Oneida Mission School. I was heavily influenced by the nuns of the Order of the Holy Nativity, and, through their work and encouragement, I decided to become a nun. Like Sister Theresa Rose, I was also encouraged by Father Nelson Skinner in my religious studies. I subsequently joined the nuns of the Order of the Teachers of the Children of God at its convent in Tucson. Over the years, I have served in New York and throughout the Southwest. Currently, I am Mother Superior with the Order of the Teachers of the Children of God, but I return periodically to visit the Church of the Holy Apostles and members of my family who still reside on the reservation and in its environs.

Pearl Schuyler McLester: Recollections about the Oneida Episcopal Mission

I was married to Lee G. McLester II in 1939 at the Church of the Holy Apostles, better known at the time as the Oneida Indian Mission. Even though I was raised in the Methodist Church on the Wisconsin Oneida Reservation, I joined the Episcopal church after my marriage and have been involved in church activities ever since. I became a steadfast member, consistent volunteer and tireless worker at the church working with over 26 priests, especially Father Dewey Silas and Deacons Edmund Powless and Deborah Heckel. Now in my nineties, I have memories about the church's history over the past seventy-five years. Indeed, I remember when the Episcopal Mission Hospital still was serving my community. I raised my six children to become active members in the rituals, events, and programs that the church offers.

I look fondly back to the days of the Oneida Mission School when our church community was flourishing. Several of my memories stand out. I remember the outstanding work of the Sisters of St. Anne, who came to the Oneida Episcopal Mission to teach in January, 1946. We referred to them as "Women Warriors." The Sisters were also assisted by Ms. Clara D. Abbott, a missionary who taught the 7th and 8th grades. Father William Christian served eighteen years at the mission during this period and worked hand in hand with the Sisters of St. Anne; they combined to be a dynamic positive force influencing the lives of our congregation and our children. Well-beloved William H. Brady, the Bishop of Fond du Lac, assisted the mission in its educational work.

The mission was always busy with numerous activities going on. These included hosting church dinners and picnics, Boy Scouts, Cub Scouts, Girl Scouts, May Day carnivals, talent shows, women's guild activities, Young People's Fellowship [YPF] meetings, as well as sponsoring dart ball teams and card parties. Various church vigils and other religious activities were vital parts of the mission.

Clergy made their home visits to the sick or to those who were grieving a family loss. They also mentored children. Our priests and nuns were true evangelists and we were blessed to have had them within the Oneida Indian community. They were dedicated to serving our Oneida community in tireless fashion. As Jesus taught and a saying points out: "love is a verb."

Deacon Deborah Heckel: Father R. Dewey Silas

For much of his life, R. Dewey Silas, affectionately known as "Father Dewey" by his parishioners, was a prominent member of the "other Oneida," namely the large Wisconsin Oneida community living in Milwaukee. He was employed for many years as a machinist and attended St. Luke's Episcopal Church in the city. Because of his commitment to this church and his deep religious beliefs, he was approached by clergy from the Milwaukee Diocese to consider becoming an Episcopal deacon. His wife Marlene supported this path and encouraged Father Dewey to follow his heart. On May 21, 1994, he was ordained as a deacon at the St. Luke's Episcopal Church. Father Dewey continued his religious education and was ordained a priest in May of 1998 in Milwaukee. In 2001 Father Dewey was called to serve as vicar at Oneida at the Church of the Holy Apostles. He would spend the next six years as a dedicated, hard-working spiritual counselor. His desire was to share the words and knowledge of the Scripture with his parishioners and serve the church and surrounding community. He had a deep passion in his heart for God and "The Word" which he shared with all who knew him. Father Dewey died on May 22, 2007, and was subsequently buried in the courtyard of the Oneidas' Church of the Holy Apostles. The word of God and the splendid work of two

Oneidas—Father Dewey and Deacon Edmund [Powless]—guide me today in my role as a deacon at Oneida.

Judy Cornelius-Hawk: As I Remember the Women of the Oneida Mission

We have lists of priests as well as nuns, their orders, and their titles who have served at Holy Apostles; however it is next to impossible to name all of the women, both Native and non-Native, who worked side by side with the male clergy. Their work and love for our church and community still reverberate at Oneida. Indeed, the women were and continue to be the backbone of every effort, challenge, and responsibility that has followed our church's history.

Warm memories about these women have flooded my consciousness since my teenage years as an eighth grader at the Oneida Mission School. I was incredibly fortunate to be mentored by these amazing women who were strong, courageous, dedicated, and hardworking, and who I grew to love. I miss them all. I miss hearing the church bells on Sunday morning, at noon every day, and sadly when someone in our community had passed away. We could also tell whether it was a death of a young person or elder by how long the bells tolled. I miss the quiet days, the "Watch" on Maunday Thursday, the Benediction on Sunday evenings. I miss knowing there was a "place" for those who needed and desired to walk into church any time of the day and just "be."

I believe that, besides my parents, those wonderful women affiliated with our church who were so nurturing had the greatest influence on me. I wanted to emulate them and model my behavior on their respectful and loving manner. In my mind, Jesus' message about "love" has always been a verb, meaning action. The women of the church followed this message of the Gospel.

I grew up being educated by the nuns. We shared Quiet Days and they taught us, but we were also taught by Miss Abbott, our 7th and 8th grade teacher at the Episcopal Mission, who was not a nun. Women were involved in promoting the Church's YPF (Young People's Fellowship). It was our main source of organized recreation. It met on Wednesday evenings, although it also helped make all the arrangements for our activities on the weekends—ice skating on Duck Creek in the back of the church; sledding on John Rice's Hill; ping pong, dances and sock hops. Most of the teens who attended YPF would help out when the church sponsored dinners, breakfasts, picnics, cedar bough making, church school, card parties, May Day carnivals, Bishop's Day, and other events and celebrations.

Our church was not alone in developing a place for teens and teen activities. The Methodist Church on "the other end," or southern portion of the reservation, had what was known as MYF (Methodist Youth Fellowship). On more than one occasion, the Episcopal and Methodist Church would merge for joint activities. At some point the Mormons would actively seek out and recruit our youth as well.

Once our nuns were no longer at the Oneida Mission, the activities and programs for youth described above and the upkeep of the church building and the Parish Hall declined. The church school, which had a fair amount of enrollment, continued until about three years ago. Recent years [have] seen a dramatic decline in children eight and under and virtually no teens within the church. My interpretation of this decline is that it was caused in part by not having schools for Episcopal children, unlike Catholic, Lutheran, and Baptist churches in our region. I fear our church membership will decline even more than it has in the last twenty-five years. I do hope this situation improves, but without those wonderful women that taught me so much, I fear for the future. Faith is what I cling to.

Betty McLester and Judy Skenandore: Oneida Lace-Making, Then and Now

The Order of the Sisters of Holy Nativity, Fond du Lac always provided assistance to the church, especially in their teaching at the Oneida Mission School. In 1898, the National Episcopal Church sent nuns for the first time to the Oneida Reservation. At this time Deaconess Sybil Carter, an Episcopal missionary, sent a representative to the reservation to start a profitable industry of lace and beadwork. In August 1898, about a dozen Oneida women started working with beads. They were assisted by the Sisters of the Holy Nativity. Subsequently, Carter sent a lace teacher who helped the women in their work. Soon, the first lace was shipped off to New York and the women were paid for their work.

By September of 1899, 75 Oneidas were involved in lace-making. Over 500 pieces of lace had been made, including 600 yards of lace edging in strips of two and three yards each, and many doilies. These pieces brought $425.00 back to the Reservation. The women did all of the work in their homes, wrapping the braid and thread work in paper napkins and carrying it back and forth in pasteboard oyster pails, which could easily be hung on the cabin walls, away from their curious children. The women often repeated the phrase, "Jiot Kout sa-tso-bulon" or "Be always washing your hands." Both the bobbin lace and Italian Cut Work Lace were done by the Oneida women, and all materials were furnished by the Sybil Carter Indian Lace Association of the Episcopal Church.

After the sisters had supervised the lace industry for about five years, Josephine Hill [Webster], daughter of Chief Cornelius Hill, began administering the project. Miss Hill had just returned from school [Hampton Institute] in the East where she had already learned the art of making bobbin lace. Miss Hemmingway, a representative of the Sybil Carter Indian Mission, taught her the Italian Cut Work. The Oneidas also made lace bedspreads, cushions and doilies.

At its height, the lace-making project included 150 women and brought $200.00 a week into Oneida. Among the outstanding pieces made by the Oneidas was a set of altar lace, presented to Cathedral of St. John the Divine, in New York City, by Miss Amy Townsend, upon its opening in 1911. In the fall of 1926, the Sybil Carter Indian Lace Association was discontinued, but the Oneidas kept up their art independently.

Lace-making by hand pretty much died out with the invention of machines that could mass produce lace in a fraction of the time and at a lower cost. However, several years ago Elizabeth Benson McLester, an Oneida, decided to bring back the craft and has practically single handedly rejuvenated the interest in handmade bobbin lace. She worked tirelessly trying to get people interested in learning to make bobbin lace. Now a craft group is made up of mostly women who meet weekly to work on a variety of crafts. In addition to lace-making, they do traditional Oneida beadwork, corn husk dolls, basketmaking, knitting and crocheting.

L. Gordon McLester III: The Oneida Hymn Singers

The singing of Christian hymns in the Oneida language goes back more than two hundred years. Major Joseph Bloomfield, subsequently the fourth Governor of New Jersey, noted its use during church services conducted in the Mohawk Valley of New York by Reverend Samuel Kirkland during the American Revolution. Both Bloomfield in 1776 and visiting Quakers to Oneida Country in the mid-1790s commented favorably about Native Americans' hymn singing. In the 1820s, the Oneidas were pressured to leave their New York homeland and soon many migrated to the area of Green Bay, then a part of Michigan Territory. In 1825, they established their "Log Church," the first Protestant Church in the Old Northwest. As early as the mid-1830s, they began to use a hymnal brought into the community by Eleazer Williams. The hymnal was in Mohawk, an Iroquoian language closely related to Oneida, which they used in their church rituals. Encouraged by Bishop Kemper, Oneida hymn singing became a fixture in services at the Episcopal Church on their Duck Creek reservation. They continued this tradition, singing in churches throughout the Midwest, and at Oneida tribal ceremonies and funerals. Although the original singers were members of the Episcopal Church when they arrived in the Green Bay area, over the years the organization became an ecumenical group, adding Oneida members from the Methodist Church and other house of worships.

The Oneida Hymn Singers have adapted to the changing times. In 1987, they performed in Germany in 1987, in Finland in 1989, and at the National Cathedral in Washington, DC, in 1992. In 2004, they performed at the grand opening of the Smithsonian's National Museum of the American Indian. In the same year, their singing was included in "Beautiful Beyond," a Smithsonian Folkways recording. Although today few Oneidas are fluent speakers and the language survival is greatly in danger, Gerald L. Hill, an Oneida judge and president of the Indigenous Language Institute, has stated that the Oneida Hymn Singers are carrying forward a wonderful tradition of worship and song that could only benefit efforts at Oneida language preservation efforts in the present and the future. The National Endowment of the Arts agreed with Hill's statement and, in 2008, bestowed on the Oneida Hymn Singers its National Heritage Fellowship Award in a ceremony in Washington, DC.

PART IV

REFLECTIONS ON WISCONSIN ONEIDA EPISCOPAL CHURCH RELATIONS

10

PUTTING ONEIDA EPISCOPAL HISTORY IN PERSPECTIVE

American Indian Encounters with Christianity

Christopher Vecsey

FROM THE 1960S ONWARD, SCHOLARSHIP ON MISSIONARY ENCOUNTERS with
Native peoples has shifted in focus from analysis of Christian missionaries to
understanding the indigenous communities being proselytized. Scholars asked
themselves, why write another work on the American mainstream, including
Christian missionaries, when there were peoples—African Americans, Indians,
and so forth—relatively neglected by scholarship whose lives were worth knowing
about and whose ideas and behaviors, perhaps, were even worth learning from?
To see American Indians and other subalterns (as they have come to be called in
postcolonial studies) as actors in their own history, to grant them their agency, and
to listen to their testimonies was the new goal of the age, and I subscribed to it.

In my dissertation "Traditional Ojibwa Religion and Its Historical Changes,"
which was revised and published in 1983, my conclusion was that Ojibwa people
had been so crushed by white control, including that of missionaries, that they lost
their religious agency. I saw the Ojibwas as victims of circumstances, abiding no
longer in their traditions and still unallied to Christianity.[1] In my more mature
writings about American Indian Catholics, I made up for the error of seeing
Native peoples as passive victims. Instead, I described their active adaptations to
Christianity for their own purposes over time in particular historical and cultural
circumstances.[2] After centuries of contact with Spanish, French, American, and
Canadian forms of Catholicism, American Indian Catholics have brought together
their indigenous and Catholic identities, sometimes accomplishing a cultural
and religious melding within their tribal and personal lives. Individual Catholic

Indians have recorded their utterances of spiritual adaptation and participation.[3] The most famous Native convert to Catholicism, the Mohawk Kateri Tekakwitha in the 1600s, left no written records; however, she has served as a model of sanctity for generations of devotees, both Indian and non-Indian.[4]

Back in the 1970s, I perceived two types of studies regarding Christian missions to American Indians: congratulatory and condemnatory. The former were written by chroniclers in the employ of religious denominations, historians of American religions, and biographers of American religious figures. Their work uncritically praised the self-sacrifice, devotion, and determination of the missionaries, although on occasion there was a mild chiding of the missionaries for not ordaining more Native ministers or for chronic interdenominational squabbling. There was almost no attempt in these writings at understanding Native Americans.

As for the condemnatory studies—by historians, journalists, and others— their objective was to enumerate the wrongs committed by American society and government against the Indians. Their focus was perhaps on the values and institutions of white people in the United States, which had been influential in bringing about the wrongs, but more often than not the focus was on the wrongs themselves, with special emphasis given to the contrast between Indian virtues and white sins. In these studies, the missionaries were presented either as pious, but rather unwitting, dupes of the government conspiracy to eradicate or assimilate the Indians, or as deceitful, bigoted, self-serving, conscious organs of the same. This latter viewpoint was put forward in most strident terms by Vine Deloria Jr. (Dakota), the son and grandson of Episcopalian clergymen. Deloria indicted missionaries for shattering the cohesiveness of the American Indian communities, for introducing a religion that served to deteriorate Indian ethical standards, for using Indians as a means of obtaining personal or denominational power, and for deceiving Indians into selling their lands to whites, all while making a profit besides.[5]

Of course, there were exceptions back then to these two approaches. Even as early as 1962, Verne Dusenberry, author of *The Montana Cree: A Study in Religious Persistence*, published in Sweden, presented an alternate view. His book would prove to be the template for focused tribal studies of American Indian religious persistence under missionary duress; however, it is a work still virtually unknown in the United States, despite its excellence.[6] Robert Pierce Beaver's writings, especially *Church, State, and the American Indians*, enumerated the contours of Christian missionary efforts across North America, focusing primarily on theological motivation and church–state relationships.[7] More significant was Robert F. Berkhofer Jr.'s *Salvation and the Savage*, which analyzed missionaries as mirrors of white American society, stressing social rather than religious motivations. Berkhofer's work was path breaking, for he examined the effects of Christian missions on Indian society, especially the factionalism engendered by Christian inroads.[8] He was the first scholar to scrutinize the societal effects of missions among American

Indians in a social-scientific manner, and his work led to the many fine works that followed, including studies by Howard L. Harrod, Henry Warner Bowden, John Webster Grant, and James Axtell, who presented panoramic, nuanced portraits of Native American adaptations to Christianity, causing their readers to consider the ambiguities in the processes of "conversion" and "syncretism."[9] In the late 1970s, James P. Ronda and James Axtell also provided a critical bibliography of Christian missions among American Indians, as the literature on the subject grew.[10] These authors dwelt on the question of how Native American "converts" adopted Christianity. Were they spiritually conquered? Did they only appear to acquiesce in the Christian faith while persisting in aboriginal religious forms? Did they accept the new religious matrix without dropping the old? Or, did they combine the aboriginal and the Christian into something innovative? Were Indian "converts" passive recipients of evangelization, or did they actively mold the religious culture of their colonizers in ways that fit their own purposes?

There are now hundreds of books that examine those ambiguities and questions throughout the Americas, in Spanish, Portuguese, Dutch, French, English, Russian, and other European colonies from the outset—Catholic, Protestant, and Russian Orthodox missions—and in the settler states of North America: Mexico, the United States, and Canada, not to mention throughout Latin America. The list now includes *A Chain Linking Two Traditions: The Wisconsin Oneidas and the Episcopal Church.*

This book uses a traditional Iroquoian metaphor to describe how the relationship between a Native people and a church came about and how the chain has been maintained and polished for over two centuries. Indeed, there is so much amity between the two that the Oneidas' Church of the Holy Apostles and the Episcopal diocese of Fond du Lac are jointly invested in this worthy book project.

The book does not deny the rough edges to the abiding relationship, including societal strains caused by Christian missionizing, manipulations by Eleazer Williams (Mohawk), intrusions by other Episcopal ministers, assimilationist pressures by chauvinistic white Christian do-gooders, and the sense of Hodinöhsö:ni´ cultural loss over time. Nonetheless, the reader discerns elements that have made the story of Oneida Episcopal faith a cause for greater appreciation than resentment. This book is less about historical injustices felt or the current quest for spiritual self-determination—typical themes in the study of Indian–Christian encounters—and more about a special bond between a people and an institutional church. It is an atypical narrative—one might even call it unique—perhaps reflecting the confident resilience of the Oneidas, despite acculturation, and the big-heartedness of the editors and authors of this tome. Equally, it may draw on the mutual respect and support of several prominent players in these chapters: Bishop Jackson Kemper, Chief Daniel Bread, Chief Cornelius Hill, for certain, but many others, too. Oneidas may have been put off by the assimilationist agenda and stiff-necked moralism of Episcopal evangelists, but they also appreciated their support as go-betweens, economic benefactors, and protectors of tribal territory. Personal attachments cemented the chain of friendship. Episcopal ritualism was grafted onto traditional Condolence ceremonies. Oneida language played a role in Episcopal hymn singing and prayers, thus enhancing the sense of Oneidas' agency in choosing their spiritual path. There was even a melding of mythological figures, for example, the Good-Minded Twin, the Peacemaker, and Jesus Christ, as well as Sky Woman and the Virgin Mary.

The ambiguous figure of Eleazer Williams cannot be overemphasized. His latitudinarian flexibility and his Hodinöhsö:ni´ identity both greatly affected Oneida acceptance of Episcopal Christianity. Despite his questionable ethics, he let Oneidas engage in selective adaptation of Christian aspects. The Oneidas' so-called Pagan Party as well as the Presbyterians were attracted by his preaching. His eloquence, sacramental elaborations, musical expression, and allowance for gradualism all had their effect on Oneidas seeking attachment to Christians and their powerful God. He gave them assurance that their sins would be forgiven; he also emphasized their need for relationship with a caring, almighty deity. He identified their suffering with Christ's. The same silver-tongued persuasiveness that Williams employed in cajoling Oneidas to emigrate to Wisconsin played a role in getting them to shift toward identification with the Episcopal Church. By the middle of the 1800s, the Wisconsin Oneidas were Episcopalians, thanks in large part to Williams, even as they came to reject him as an untoward influence.

Wisconsin Oneidas were blessed by association with good Christian mission-aries and their wives, such as the extraordinary Ellen Goodnough. These mission-aries provided protections during crises. Edward A. Goodnough and Solomon S. Burleson were busybodies in tribal politics, but their benevolence was unmistak-able, especially in their resistance to white land-grabbers or in their promotion of better health care. The Oneidas did not forget—and have not forgotten—these Christians' good deeds: the building of a mission hospital, the establishment of a lace-making economy, the gifts of clothing, the musical accomplishments, the per-sonal friendships, the encouragement of temperance, the building and rebuilding of church edifices, and much more.

Many Oneidas came to identify themselves as Episcopalians because of their personal attachment to white Episcopalians; they also defended their Episcopal identity against other Christian denominations: Catholic, Mormon, and even to some degree Methodist. They took hold of Protestant Reformation antipathies and made them their own. Then in the twentieth century they shared in the trend toward Christian ecumenism, especially in hymn singing. In many ways, Oneidas became mainline Protestants.

Oneida Episcopalians combined political and religious leadership, espe-cially Cornelius Hill, who was a "spiritual chief," coupling Oneida chieftaincy with Episcopal priesthood. Even political rivals among the Oneidas, such as Bread and Hill, were secure in their shared Episcopal identity. Church members became societal leaders. Their religion had become the basis of goodwill, loyalty, authority, and respect among their people. Their church sponsored social events: picnics, dances, dinners, and the like. Their church committees provided the fixative that held social organization together. One can see the conjoining of religious and social amelioration in the work of the Sisters of the Holy Nativity, in the life of Deacon Deborah Heckel, and in general in church women who served as upholders of Oneida community—just as women have always been in Hodinöhsö:ni´ life. *Ekklesia* means "community" as much as it means "church." Oneida Episcopalians exemplified both meanings at once.

How does this portrait of Oneida Episcopalians match the experiences of many other American Indians who have encountered forms of Christianity and made adjustments to its presence? Let us see the Oneidas in the context of Episcopal history.

Building on the Anglican presence (the Church of England's Society for the Propagation of the Gospel in Foreign Parts having been founded in 1701) in the English colonies, prominently among the Mohawks,[11] the Episcopal Church began its proselytizing in the new United States of the early nineteenth century by engaging the Oneidas in New York. From there, Episcopal efforts reached many corners of the United States, among Minnesota Ojibwes, South Dakota Sioux, Oklahoma Choctaws, Alaska Tanana, Four Corners Navajo, and more.[12] This outreach netted converts (although today only 1 percent of American Indians are Episcopalians, whereas 20 percent are Baptists and 14 percent are Roman Catholics). The effort also produced leaders, including Enmegahbowh (Ojibwe), the first Native American Episcopal priest; David Pendleton Oakerhater (Southern Cheyenne); Vine Deloria Jr.'s Dakota forebears; missionary priest Philip Joseph Deloria and his son Vine Deloria, archdeacon among the Lakota. Today there are over half a dozen Native Episcopal bishops, including the first, Harold S. Jones (Santee Sioux),[13] Steven Charleston (Choctaw), and the first female Native Episcopal bishop, Carol J. Gallagher (Cherokee). Indigenous Ministries is an active branch of Episcopal administration, with many Native clergy. The Episcopal liturgical calendar of saints features not only Cornelius Hill, priest and chief among the Oneida (June 27), but also fellow Natives Mary (Molly) Brant, witness to the faith among the Mohawks (April 16); Enmegahbowh, priest and missionary (June 12); Samson Occom, Presbyterian Mohegan witness to the faith in New England (July 14); David Pendleton Oakerhater, deacon and missionary (September 1); and Kamehameha and Emma, king and queen of Hawai'i (November 28).

In Canada, the Anglican Church has conducted an indigenous ministry since the 1700s, from the Mi'kmaq of the Maritimes, to the Métis of the Prairies, the Tsimshian of the Northwest Coast, and the Inuit of the Arctic. Today, First Nations people make up 4 percent of Canadian Anglicans. There are over a hundred Native Anglican priests and nine bishops, including Rt. Rev. Mark MacDonald (nonstatus Indian), national indigenous Anglican bishop. Anglican Church participation in the system of Indian residential schools for a century following Confederation— Anglicans conducted over one-third of the eighty church-run boarding schools, with as many as one hundred thousand Native children over time[14]—has proven to be a source of regret and shame. The neglect and abuse of the children has been called "a national crime" and a perversion of Christian responsibility[15] and led to a 1993 apology to First Nations people by Michael Peers, then primate of the Anglican Church of Canada, as part of a process of national reconciliation. Still, the Anglican role in the residential school system is perceived as villainous, for example, in Ojibwe Drew Hayden Taylor's recent play, *God and the Indian*.[16]

Indeed, across five centuries of encounters and relationships, Christians and Indians in the Americas have engaged each other in all manner of incursion, avoidance, invitation, aggression, assertion, intrigue, sermonizing, debate, resistance, acquiescence, amalgamation, instruction, misunderstanding, usurpation, coercion, revolt, reconquest, adoption, adaptation, displacement, friendship, solidarity, intermarriage, betrayal, abuse, control, reinterpretation, spiritual power seeking, dialogue, silence, accommodation, subterfuge, assimilation, acculturation, syncretism, and inculturation. These are some of the major themes found in the hundreds of books about Native–Christian encounters produced in recent decades. The interplay between the two (Christians and Indians) is multifaceted and still in flux. Any taking stock of the relationship must remain open-ended, leaving way for rebuttal and reconsideration.

Half a century ago, scholars of the Native–Christian encounter shifted their focus from missionaries to Indians. Over time, Native Christians have come to speak for themselves. The ambivalent views of contemporary Native Christians regarding their identity and history are readily available on today's printed page. Muscogee scholar James Treat has gathered many of their "autobiographical narratives," both "problematic" and "enigmatic" in their stances and loyalties.[17] He has also edited the trenchant critiques of Christianity penned by Vine Deloria Jr. and gathered Native fiction about the white man's Christian "Cross Culture."[18] In addition, Treat has written a history of the Indian Ecumenical Conference, from the 1970s to the 1990s, whose participants hoped to overcome the "antagonisms between tribal and Christian traditions—a problem as old as the European colonization of the Americas."[19]

Part Osage, part Cherokee, and part Lutheran, Rev. George E. Tinker has excoriated Christian missionaries for their "cultural genocide" in the Americas.[20] He has dared to produce a Native American theology that arises from Native experience and culture and addresses contemporary Native existence apart from Christianity.[21] He has called for American Indian "liberation" from Christian hegemonic structures, a project of spiritual decolonization.[22] With Native coauthors Clara Sue Kidwell, Homer Noley, and Jace Weaver, Tinker has addressed the contentious interface between American Indian religions and American legal structures.[23]

Other American Indian Christians, such as Lakota Richard Twiss, are content to extol the virtues of present-day Native Christians whom "almighty God has raised up . . . as a new wave of ambassadors for the gospel of Jesus Christ."[24] In "rescuing the gospel from the cowboys," Twiss holds up Native hospitality as a model to all Christian peoples.[25] Randy Woodley, Keetowah Cherokee descendant, wants to overcome the "pain" of Christian colonialism by proclaiming "the real Jesus"—"not the one who was used to take our land and rob us of our cultures."[26] He finds "Christlike" Indian role models; indeed, he states, "There are marks of Jesus in every culture," including that of white Americans.[27] Thus, Woodley encourages Indian people to aim for "forgiveness" in order to attain "restoration" between Indians and whites.[28] He sees this as a form of Native agency, an "indigenous vision" for "the community of creation."[29]

These evangelical Protestant Indians eschew missionary rhetoric, which exhorts Natives to become *Christians*, or to identify with *Christianity*, but rather implore their audience to "follow Christ."[30] This may be one resolution to the longstanding disharmony between so many Native people and Christian institutions. In a recent reflection—"hard questions about Christian mission"—Indians have expressed disillusionment with the evangelization process and skepticism about "whether Christianity is compatible with the Indian Way."[31]

Contemporary Episcopalian Indians seem to take a more moderate tone in assessing their relationship with Christianity. In addressing the trauma that has constituted the Christian colonization of the indigenes of North America, Carol J. Gallagher—the Cherokee Episcopal bishop—has endorsed a "family theology" that draws on the tribal (as well as Christian) value of kinship duty, thus "finding God in very human relationships."[32] She writes, "My people have been Christian for many generations and my family and people have found ways to interweave our traditions with our embrace of Christ, and the heritage that comes with our acceptance of Christianity."[33] Lakota Episcopal priest Rev. Canon Dr. Martin Brokenleg comes to the same conclusion about the congruent vitality of making relationships in Native and Christian systems of spirituality. Despite a record of white Episcopal racism, he writes, "We are who we are as Lakota Episcopalians because Ye'sus has always been our good relative, a member of our family."[34] Choctaw Episcopal bishop Steven Charleston says that it is healthy to move beyond "'deconstructive' theory . . . that offers a critical analysis of Christianity from the historical trauma suffered by Native people." He recommends a more "constructive" view of Christianity, one that sees its goodness, "without glossing over the trauma of colonialism, assimilation, racism, and/or oppression."[35]

A Chain Linking Two Traditions follows this measured path. It is a Native Episcopal statement about an abiding collegiality, despite it all, between an Indian nation and a church.

Notes

1. Christopher Vecsey, *Traditional Ojibwa Religion and Its Historical Changes* (Philadelphia, PA: American Philosophical Society, 1983).

2. Christopher Vecsey, *On the Padres' Trail* (Notre Dame, IN: University of Notre Dame Press, 1996); *The Paths of Kateri's Kin* (Notre Dame, IN: University of Notre Dame Press, 1997); *Where the Two Roads Meet* (Notre Dame, IN: University of Notre Dame Press, 1999).

3. Marie Therese Archambault, Mark G. Thiel, and Christopher Vecsey, eds., *The Crossing of Two Roads: Being Catholic and Native in the United States* (Maryknoll, NY: Orbis, 2003).

4. Mark G. Thiel and Christopher Vecsey, eds., *Native Footsteps Along the Path of Saint Kateri Tekakwitha* (Milwaukee, WI: Marquette University Press, 2012). See also Henri Béchard, S.J., *Kaia'tanó:ron Kateri Tekakwitha*, trans. Antoinette Kinlough (Kahnawake, QC: International, 1994); Darren Bonaparte, *A Lily among Thorns: The Mohawk Repatriation of Kateri Tekahkwí:tha* (Akwesásne Mohawk Territory, QC: Wampum Chronicles, 2009); Allan Greer, *Mohawk Saint: Catherine Tekakwitha and the Jesuits* (New York: Oxford University Press, 2005); Michelle M. Jacob, *Indian Pilgrims: Indigenous Journeys of Activism and Healing with Saint Kateri Tekakwitha* (Tucson: University of Arizona Press, 2016).

5. Vine Deloria Jr., *Custer Died for Your Sins: An Indian Manifesto* (New York: Macmillan, 1969), 105–27.

6. Verne Dusenberry, *The Montana Cree: A Study in Religious Persistence* (Stockholm: Almqvist & Wiksell, 1962).

7. R. Pierce Beaver, *Church, State, and the American Indians* (St. Louis, MO: Concordia, 1966).

8. Robert F. Berkhofer Jr., *Salvation and the Savage: An Analysis of Protestant Missions and American Indian Response, 1787–1862* (Lexington: University of Kentucky Press, 1965).

9. James Axtell, *The Invasion Within: The Contest of Cultures in Colonial North America* (New York: Oxford University Press, 1985); Henry W. Bowden, *American Indians and Christian Missions: Studies in Cultural Conflict* (Chicago, IL: University of Chicago Press, 1981); John W. Grant, *Moon of Wintertime: Missionaries and the Indians of Canada in Encounter since 1534* (Toronto: University of Toronto Press, 1984); Howard L. Harrod, *Mission among the Blackfeet* (Norman: University of Oklahoma Press, 1971).

10. James P. Ronda and James Axtell, *Indian Missions: A Critical Bibliography* (Bloomington: Indiana University Press, 1978).

11. William Bryan Hart, "For the Good of Our Souls: Mohawk Authority, Accommodation, and Resistance to Protestant Evangelism, 1700–1780" (PhD diss., Brown University, 1998).

12. Owanah Anderson, *Jamestown Commitment: The Episcopal Church and the American Indian* (Cincinnati, OH: Forward Movement, 1988); and her *400 Years: Anglican/Episcopal Mission among American Indians* (Cincinnati, OH: Forward Movement, 1997).

13. Mary E. Cochran, *Dakota Cross-Bearer: The Life and World of a Native American Bishop* (Lincoln: University of Nebraska Press, 2000).

14. Eric Taylor Woods, *Cultural Sociology of Anglican Mission and the Indian Residential Schools in Canada: The Long Road to Apology* (New York: Palgrave Macmillan, 2016).

15. John S. Milloy, *"A National Crime": The Canadian Government and the Residential School System, 1879 to 1986* (Winnipeg: University of Manitoba Press, 1999).

16. Drew Hayden Taylor, *God and the Indian: A Play* (Vancouver: Talonbooks, 2014).

17. James Treat, ed., *Native and Christian: Indigenous Voices on Religious Identity in the United States and Canada* (New York: Routledge, 1996), 2, 9.

18. Vine Deloria Jr., *For This Land: Writings on Religion in America*, ed. James Treat (New York: Routledge, 1999); James Treat, ed., *Writing the Cross Culture: Native Fiction on the White Man's Religion* (Golden, CO: Fulcrum, 2006).

19. James Treat, *Around the Sacred Fire: Native American Activism in the Red Power Era* (New York: Palgrave Macmillan, 2003), 2.

20. George E. Tinker, *Missionary Conquest: The Gospel and Native American Cultural Genocide* (Minneapolis, MN: Fortress, 1993).

21. George E. Tinker, *Spirit and Resistance: Political Theology and American Indian Liberation* (Minneapolis, MN: Fortress, 2004).

22. Ibid.

23. Clara Sue Kidwell, Homer Noley, George E. "Tink" Tinker [and Jace Weaver], *A Native American Theology* (Maryknoll, NY: Orbis, 2001).

24. Richard Twiss, *One Church Many Tribes* (Ventura, CA: Regal/Gospel Light, 2000), 20.

25. Richard Twiss, *Rescuing the Gospel from the Cowboy: A Native American Expression of the Jesus Way* (Madison, WI: InterVarsity, 2015).

26. Randy Woodley, *When Going to Church Is Sin and Other Essays on Native American Christian Missions* (Scotland, PA: Healing the Land, 2007), xii, xiii.

27. Randy Woodley, *Living in Color: Embracing God's Passion for Ethnic Diversity* (Downers Grove, IL: InterVarsity, 2001), 89, 91.

28. Randy Woodley, *Mixed Blood, Not Mixed Up: Finding God-given Identity in a Multicultural World* (Hayden, AL: Randy Woodley, 2004), 142.

29. Randy Woodley, *Shalom and the Community of Creation: An Indigenous Vision* (Grand Rapids, MI: Wm. B. Eerdmans, 2012).

30. Andrea Smith, *Native Americans and the Christian Right: The Gendered Politics of Unlikely Alliances* (Durham, NC: Duke University Press, 2008), 86.

31. Amos Yong and Barbara Brown Zikmund, eds., *Remembering Jamestown: Hard Questions about Christian Missions* (Eugene, OR: Pickwick, 2010), 151.

32. Carol J. Gallagher, *Family Theology: Finding God in Very Human Relationships* (New York: Morehouse, 2012).

33. Steven Charleston and Elaine A. Robinson, eds., *Coming Full Circle: Constructing Native Christian Theology* (Minneapolis, MN: Fortress, 2015), 77–78.

34. Ibid., 149.

35. Ibid., viii. See also Steven Charleston, *Four Vision Quests of Jesus* (New York: Morehouse, 2015).

11

THE WISCONSIN ONEIDAS AND THE EPISCOPAL CHURCH

Then and Now

L. Gordon McLester III, Laurence M. Hauptman,
Judy Cornelius-Hawk, and Kenneth Hoyan House

IN 1907, JULIA KEEN BLOOMFIELD PUBLISHED THE FIRST edition of her classic, *The Oneidas*. Her book was largely derived from the extensive published and unpublished writings on the Oneidas by Susan Fenimore Cooper, nature writer, philanthropist, and the daughter of the United States' first great novelist, as well as notes and a diary loaned to her by Edward A. Goodnough and Frank W. Merrill, two missionaries to the Oneidas. Bloomfield traced the history of the Oneidas from the seventeenth century until the first decade of the twentieth century. As reflected in the quotation at the beginning of this book, she recognized the existence of a special link between the church and the Oneidas. She provided important information about one side of the chain—namely, the church and its clergy. Because of her limited knowledge of the culture and beliefs of the Oneidas, she ignored the other side—namely, what led the Oneidas to link arms with the Episcopal clergy and accept their mission, one that is now over two hundred years old. Hence, what the editors attempted to accomplish in *The Wisconsin Oneidas and the Episcopal Church: A Chain That Links Two Traditions* was to tell both sides of the story and update Bloomfield's book, carrying the analysis into the twenty-first century.

We have seen that Oneida Christianity had its roots with Jesuit and Anglican missionaries in the second half of the seventeenth century and first decades of the eighteenth century. While the Presbyterian missionary Samuel Kirkland made major inroads from the 1760s onward, his efforts were sullied after the American Revolution by his cooperation with land jobbers, which brought him personal rewards, and by his singular focus on establishing the Hamilton-Oneida Academy. In this vacuum, the Anglican tradition reappeared in Oneida Country, now branded as the Protestant Episcopal Church to avoid the stigma caused by its support of the British side in the American Revolution. By establishing the Oneida mission in 1816 and encouraging these Native peoples' emigration to the west, Bishop John Henry Hobart hoped to rebuild the church by spreading the faith to the frontier and meeting the challenge caused by competition with other faiths, especially by Catholic missionaries who had a century and a half head start in their proselytizing. Importantly, Hobart's efforts coincided with federal policies of the time, set in motion at the end of the War of 1812, that were aimed at countering British influences in the area of the western Great Lakes by relocating American-allied Indians to the frontier.

Indeed, the hierarchy of the Protestant Episcopal Church saw the opportunity to use the Oneida mission as the prototype, the model for extending its influence westward into Indian Country. Consequently, Hobart sent Eleazer Williams to head this effort, first as catechist and lay reader and then as an ordained deacon, believing that Williams, a charismatic Mohawk, would be better listened to by the Oneidas because of his Iroquoian heritage and Native language abilities. Although he initially successfully converted a significant number of Oneidas and established a ritual framework for future church services, the eccentric Williams, who subsequently claimed to be the "lost dauphin of France," brokered deals for himself, including ones with the Ogden Land Company, married a thirteen-year-old Menominee girl, and ignored his church responsibilities by staying at his residence at Little Kakalin instead of with his congregation of Oneidas along Duck Creek just south of today's Green Bay. It was no wonder that by the early 1830s, the Oneidas officially ostracized him from their community.

By the mid-1830s, the chain connecting the Episcopal Church to the Oneidas had been tarnished by Williams's misdeeds. It was at this time that Bishop Jackson Kemper made his first visit to Duck Creek. For the Oneidas, this new bishop's arrival occurred at just the right time because they needed allies to stand with them against the threat of Jacksonian removal policies. Despite the missing links in the chain caused by Williams's actions, and soon after by missionary Richard Cadle's physical abuse of students at the mission school, the relationship/alliance between the Episcopal clergy and the Oneidas had to be recast.

From 1834 to 1870, Bishop Kemper, a remarkable churchman, was a fervent advocate for the Oneidas. He was to restore the chain. Indeed, besides encouraging the important work of others on behalf of the Oneida Episcopal mission, the bishop was without doubt the primary force in creating a lasting special relationship between the church and this Native community. Kemper and Oneida chief Daniel Bread understood their reciprocal obligations to each other. Importantly, as shown in the quotation at the beginning of this book, the chain metaphor symbolizing the church's and the Oneidas' relationship with each other was even used when the bishop visited and consecrated the new Hobart Church in 1839. He cultivated this relationship through his frequent visits to Oneida, by conducting mass on numerous occasions at the Oneidas' Hobart Church, by providing tribal leaders with an honored place at church convocations, and by personally concerning himself with the education, religious training, and welfare of Oneidas sent to Nashotah House Seminary. Later, during his long tenure as bishop, Kemper defended the Oneidas against those who wanted to remove them from Wisconsin. He also encouraged Susan Fenimore Cooper to write about the Oneidas and raise money for construction of a new church at the Oneida mission.

After Kemper's death in 1870, the Episcopal mission–Oneida link was once again tested. Episcopal missionaries Edward A. Goodnough and Solomon S. Burleson achieved positive results for the Wisconsin Oneidas; nevertheless, they were criticized for meddling in internal Oneida politics. In 1898, ten years before the federal government founded the predecessor to the Indian Health Service, Bishop Charles Grafton, at the recommendation of missionary Burleson, established a hospital on the Wisconsin Oneida reservation. In the same year as the founding of this hospital, Episcopal missionary Sybil Carter established the Oneida lace-making project that eventually included 150 tribal members, mostly women, in a cooperative guild. They produced twenty-five altarpieces that were featured when the Cathedral of Saint John the Divine in New York City was opened and consecrated in April 1911.

An Oneida himself was to help strengthen the chain. In 1895, Chief Cornelius Hill, also known as Onan-gwa-at-go or Great Medicine, the most prominent Oneida of the late nineteenth and early twentieth century, was ordained as a deacon. Eight years later, he was the first Oneida to be ordained as an Episcopal priest. Other Wisconsin Oneidas were to later follow Hill's path. They included deacons Edmund Powless and Deborah Heckel and priests R. Dewey Silas and Edmund Webster, all who have served in the Episcopal clergy in more recent times. The interviews found in the WPA Oneida Language and Folklore Project from 1938 to 1942 and the reminiscences of contemporary Oneidas further reveal the importance of the bond created.

Today, the Hodinöhsö:ni´ teach their children about the *Kaswentha*, the Two Row Wampum. The belt contains two parallel purple rows of shell with three white rows of shell interspersed. To the Oneidas as well as to other members of the Six Nations in the United States and Canada, the two purple strands represent two vessels, an Iroquois canoe and a Euro-American ship, symbolic of two distinct peoples going down the river. One vessel, the canoe, represents the Iroquois world, while the other, the ship, represents the Euro-Americans and their laws, mores, and values. In order to successfully navigate the river, the vessels must not interfere with each other, meaning that the Indians and non-Indians need to respect each other's way of life.

Modern-day Hodinöhsö:ni' often add a further meaning to the Two Row Wampum, warning their people that it is nearly impossible to go down the river with one foot in the Indian canoe and the other in the Euro-American ship. They explain that the failure of certain missionaries, including the Mohawk Eleazer Williams, was their inability to understand that it is impossible to bridge the gap between two worlds by standing in one vessel as you navigate the rapids. Yet, other Hodinöhsö:ni' did succeed in doing so, including Chief Hill. His was not a story of failure but one of cultural adaptation, persistence, and survival in the face of overwhelming odds. Other more contemporary Oneidas, such as Deacon Ed, understood this lesson. Some non-Indian Episcopal churchmen serving the Oneidas learned this lesson of reciprocity and equality as well. Without question, the best at it were Rt. Rev. Jackson Kemper at the diocesan level and Rev. William Christian at the parish level. After all, good works along with mutual respect contributed to an Episcopal bond that has lasted decades despite internal and external pressures.

What is the future of this chain link between the Episcopal Church and the Wisconsin Oneidas? Since the late 1950s, Oneida leadership has not just emanated out of the Episcopal Church. Because of the expansion of Oneida-owned lands and greater economic opportunities in and around the reservation, especially over the last four decades, more Oneidas from different parts of the United States have returned to live, work, and bring their new faiths and ideas home. Moreover, besides the long-standing Methodist congregation on the reservation and the Catholic Church established in 1909, Oneida Episcopalians face the challenge of other fast-growing congregations and sects, including evangelical Protestant movements and the Longhouse founded in the late 1960s and early 1970s.

The walls of the stone church were strong enough to survive the great fire caused by a lightning bolt in 1920. Today they and the rest of the church stand as a monument not only to Oneida Christianity but also to Wisconsin Oneida survival as a distinct Native American community in the face of overwhelming odds.

CONTRIBUTORS

Editors

L. Gordon McLester III is the former secretary of the Oneida Nation of Indians of Wisconsin and director of the Oneida Indian Historical Society. Since 1986, he has coordinated more than a dozen conferences on Oneida history and has interviewed more than five hundred elders; these resources have been digitized for use in the schools and by the community at large. He is the coauthor of *Chief Daniel Bread and the Oneida Nation of Indians of Wisconsin* (2002) and has coedited three previous books on the history of the Oneidas. McLester has also coauthored a children's book, *The Oneida* (2001).

Laurence M. Hauptman is SUNY Distinguished Professor Emeritus of History. He is the author of numerous articles and books over the past forty years. His most recent book on Oneida history, *An Oneida Indian in Foreign Waters: The Life of Chief Chapman Scanandoah*, was published in 2016 by Syracuse University Press. Dr. Hauptman has testified as an expert witness before committees of both houses of Congress and in the federal courts and has served as a historical consultant for the Wisconsin Oneidas, the Cayugas, the Mashantucket Pequots, and the Senecas.

Judy Cornelius-Hawk is the former treasurer, tribal librarian, and member of the Land Claims Committee of the Oneida Nation of Indians of Wisconsin. She was also the cofounder of the Oneida Arts program. Cornelius-Hawk is a past recipient of the Clarion Award for Women in Communication and held a D'Arcy McNickle Fellowship from the Newberry Library Center for the History of the American Indian in Chicago. She has authored articles on missionaries among the Oneidas and coauthored an article on Susan Fenimore Cooper. For more than twenty years, she served as a teacher at the Episcopal Church school and as a member of the church's Altar Guild.

Kenneth Hoyan House is the chaplain of the Wisconsin Oneida Veterans of Foreign Wars. He was born on the Wisconsin Oneida reservation. When his uncle Robert L. Bennett served as US commissioner of Indian Affairs in the mid-1960s, House worked with him in Washington, DC. He later joined the US Navy and served for twenty-eight years before his retirement and return to Wisconsin.

Authors

Deborah Heckel, an Oneida, is the deacon of the Oneida Church of the Holy Apostles.

Kathy Powless Hughes, an Oneida, is the former vice-chairperson and former treasurer of the Oneida Nation of Indians of Wisconsin.

Betty McLester, an Oneida, is a member of the Church of the Holy Apostles and the church's Altar Guild. By her talks and demonstrations of lace-making techniques, she is actively involved today in promoting this artistic tradition introduced by missionary Sybil Carter and the Episcopal Church in the late nineteenth century. She is also a member of the Oneida Hymn Singers.

Pearl Schuyler McLester, an Oneida, has been an active member of the Church of the Holy Apostles for nearly seventy-five years. She has served on numerous church committees and was a member of the Altar Guild for many years.

Michael Leroy Oberg is SUNY Distinguished Professor of History at Geneseo. His many publications include *Professional Indian: The American Odyssey of Eleazer Williams* (2015) and *Peacemakers: The Iroquois, the United States, and the Treaty of Canandaigua, 1794* (2016). His textbook, *Native America: A History*, published by Wiley-Blackwell, is now in its second edition (2017).

Matthew Payne is the historiographer and diocesan archivist of the diocese of Fond du Lac and the author of *A Diocese, a Sovereign Nation and a Government: It's Whose Land?* (2011). His extensive research has focused on land issues surrounding the Episcopal mission on the Oneida reservation. He serves on the board of the National Episcopal Historians and Archivists, as director of operations of the Historical Society of the Episcopal Church, and on the archives committee of Nashotah House.

Very Rev. Steven Peay is the former president of Nashotah House Theological Seminary. He is also professor of homiletics and church history there. Father Peay holds a doctorate in history from St. Louis University. His articles have appeared in *The Congregationalist*, *Catholic Historical Review*, and in other journals and magazines.

Blanche Powless, an Oneida and descendant of Chief Cornelius Hill, has been an active member of the Church of the Holy Apostles for over half a century. She helped lead the United Thank Offering that raised funds for the church and served as the director of the Altar Guild for twenty years. Her late husband, Edmund, served as the church's deacon, and her daughter Theresa Rose is an

Episcopal nun in the Order of the Teachers of the Children of God. In 2007, she received the Bishop's Cross for her work on behalf of the church.

Sister Theresa Rose, an Oneida nun, is a member of the Order of the Teachers of the Children of God.

Judy Skenandore, an Oneida, works in the offices of the Church of Holy Apostles and is a member of the church's Altar Guild. She is also a member of the Oneida Arts Board and, as a lace maker, is one of the Oneidas helping to preserve and revive this art form.

Karim M. Tiro is professor of history at Xavier University. He is the author of *The People of the Standing Stone: The Oneida Nation from the Revolution through the Era of Removal* (2011), coeditor of *Along the Hudson and Mohawk: The 1790 Journey of Count Paolo Andreani* (2006), and coeditor of the recent new edition of Cadwallader Colden's *History of the Five Indian Nations*, first published in 1727.

Mother Alicia Torres, an Oneida nun, is a member of the Order of the Teachers of the Children of God.

Christopher Vecsey is Harry Emerson Fosdick Professor of the Humanities and Native American Studies in the Department of Religion at Colgate University. He has written or edited fourteen books on Native American religions, including the standard three-volume history of American Indian Catholicism: *On the Padres' Trail* (1996), *The Paths of Kateri's Kin* (1997), and *Where the Two Roads Meet* (1999). He is the editor of the Iroquois and Their Neighbors book series for Syracuse University Press.

WPA Storytellers

By Oneidas—Oscar Archiquette, Sarah Cornelius, Guy Elm, Pearl House, Lena Silas, David Skenandore. The WPA Oneida Language and Folklore Project, administered by Morris Swadesh, Floyd Lounsbury, and Harry Basehart, collected hundreds of stories from Oneidas between 1938 and 1942, which today are part of the curriculum used in the schools. Unlike other WPA projects at the time, these stories provide a unique portrait of an American Indian community because they were collected, translated, and transcribed by the Oneidas themselves.

Writings by Past Episcopal Clergy

Missionaries Solomon S. Burleson and Frank Wesley Merrill, Rev. G. P Schetky, Bishop William Ingraham Kip, and missionary wife Ellen Saxton Goodnough.

APPENDIX A: TIMELINE

1667:   Jesuit Jacques Bruyas establishes the Saint Francis Xavier mission in
            Oneida Country.
1685:   Jesuits end their mission in Oneida Country because of growing
            tensions between the French and the Five Nations.
1701:   King William III establishes the Society for the Propagation of the
            Gospel in Foreign Parts (SPG).
1704:   Queen Anne of England, through the Society of the Propagation of the
            Faith, sends Anglican missionaries to Mohawk and Oneida Country.
1709:   SPG missionary Thomas Barclay arrives in Albany to proselytize mem-
            bers of the Five Nations.
1767:   Samuel Kirkland establishes a Presbyterian mission to the Oneidas. It
            continues until his death in 1808.
1776–1783: Most Oneidas serve as allies of General Washington in the American
            Revolution; some Oneidas follow Mohawk war chief Joseph Brant into
            British Canada along Grand River (Ohsweken, Ontario).
1784:   US treaty with the Six Nations at Fort Stanwix. The federal government
            recognizes and demarcates the Oneidas' territorial lands in central
            New York.
1785–1846: Oneidas dispossessed of over 5 million acres in a series of treaties with
            New York State.
1794:   US treaty of friendship and alliance at Canandaigua with the Six
            Nations.
1794:   US treaty with the Oneidas.
1805:   Oneidas in New York partition lands; increasingly divided.
1808:   Samuel Kirkland dies.
1811:   John Henry Hobart, consecrated bishop of New York in the Protestant
            Episcopal Church, reaches out to the Oneidas.
1816:   First Episcopal mission among the Oneidas established; Eleazer
            Williams sent as a catechist to the Oneidas.
1817–1818: Williams converts members of the so-called Oneida Pagan Party to the
            Episcopal faith. They become known as the Second Christian Party.
1820s: Migration of Oneidas out of New York State begins.
1821–1822: Two Oneida treaties with Menominees and Ho Chunks. The Oneidas
            and other "New York Indians" allowed to "spread their blankets" in the
            western part of Michigan Territory.
1822:   First Oneida settlement along Duck Creek.
1824:   Eleazer Williams ordained a deacon in the Protestant Episcopal
            Church.
1825:   Oneida Log Church built, the first non-Catholic church in the Old
            Northwest.

1832:   Oneida Chiefs' Council ostracize and end all ties to Eleazer Williams.
1834:   Migration of Oneida Orchard Party out of New York led by Chief Jacob
               Cornelius; established the Methodist Church on the Oneida reservation.
1834:   Bishop Jackson Kemper makes his first visit to the Oneida mission.
1837:   The Hobart Church, a wood-frame, Gothic-style church, is built on the
               Oneida Indian reservation.
1838:   US treaty of Buffalo Creek; Oneidas set aside fifty-three acres at Duck
               Creek for the Episcopal mission.
1838–1839:   Bishop Kemper visits Oneida mission on two occasions, establishes a
               chain of friendship with the Wisconsin Oneidas.
1839–1846:   Migration of some Oneidas to Canada; establish themselves as the
               Oneida Band of the Thames at Southwold Ontario.
1842:   Bishop Kemper ordains James Breck and William Adams as Episcopal
               priests at the Oneida mission.
1842:   Nashotah House Episcopal Seminary established by James Breck
               and William Adams with the help of Bishop Kemper; three Oneidas,
               including Cornelius Hill, attend the seminary in the 1840s.
1847:   Episcopal diocese of Wisconsin formed with the Oneidas' Hobart
               Church being one of the three founding congregations; Oneida chief
               Daniel Bread given the seat of honor next to Bishop Kemper at the
               ceremony held in Milwaukee.
1853:   Bishop Kemper sends missionary Edward A. Goodnough (and his wife
               Ellen Saxton Goodnough) to the Oneidas.
1870:   Bishop Kemper and Ellen Goodnough die.
1884:   Sisters of the Holy Nativity come to Oneida.
1885–1886:   Susan Fenimore Cooper publishes fourteen articles on the history
               and current concerns facing Wisconsin Oneidas in *The Living Church*;
               helps raise money for church-building project.
1886:   New Hobart Church, the "Stone Church," completed.
1887:   Dawes General Allotment Act is passed; the Wisconsin Oneidas
               lose almost all of their 65,400 acres; regain approximately ninety
               tribally owned and seven hundred Oneida individually owned
               acres by 1933.
1895:   Chancel of Hobart Stone Church added.
1895:   Chief Cornelius Hill made a deacon by Bishop Charles Chapman Graf-
               ton at a ceremony at the Hobart Stone Church.
1897:   Hobart Stone Church consecrated by Bishop John Henry Hobart
               Brown; "Holy Apostles" is added to the church's name
1898:   Oneida Episcopal Mission Hospital opens; Oneidas Dr. Josiah Powless,
               the first Oneida-trained physician, and nurses Nancy Cornelius and
               Lavinia Cornelius, the first Oneida-trained nurses, work there. Later,
               the hospital is converted to a dispensary in 1905. It is eventually closed
               because of the lack of funding in the 1940s.
1898:   A branch of the Sybil Carter Indian Mission Lace Association is
               established on the Wisconsin Oneida reservation. As many as 150
               Oneidas, mostly women, involved in this project.

1899:	Frank Wesley Merrill publishes first history of the Episcopal mission to the Oneidas.
1903:	Bishop Charles Chapman Grafton ordains Chief Cornelius Hill as the first Oneida Episcopal priest.
1904:	Josiah Powless, encouraged by Bishop Grafton and missionaries Burleson and Merrill and whose education is funded by the Episcopal Church, is graduated from the Milwaukee Medical College; he is later killed while serving in the American Expeditionary Force's Medical Corps in World War I.
1906:	Bishop Grafton Parish Hall built.
1907:	Chief Cornelius Hill dies.
1907:	Julia Keen Bloomfield publishes *The Oneidas*.
1909:	Catholic Church built on Oneida reservation.
1911:	Cathedral of Saint John the Divine opens in New York City; Oneida women's lace altarpieces featured.
1920:	The Stone Church struck by lightning and gutted except for its stone walls and foundation.
1922:	The Stone Church is rebuilt and opens as the Church of the Holy Apostles, consecrated by Bishop Reginald H. Weller.
1930:	Rectory is erected at the Church of the Holy Apostles.
1934:	Indian Reorganization Act. Wisconsin Oneida government organized under new constitution and bylaws; leads to repurchase of some former tribal lands.
1938–1942:	WPA Oneida Language and Folklore Project.
1940:	Diocese of Fond du Lac provides ecclesiastical and financial support for the Oneida mission when support from the National Episcopal Church's Board of Missions comes to an end.
1946:	Sisters of the Order of Saint Anne replace the Sisters of the Holy Nativity at the Oneida Episcopal mission.
1948:	Church of the Holy Apostles and the diocese of Fond du Lac provide ten acres of its land for Oneida recreational purposes.
1961:	National Episcopal Church provides funding for addition to Grafton Parish Hall for school needs.
1966:	Church of the Holy Apostles and the diocese of Fond du Lac provide fifteen acres of its land for the Oneidas' forty-four-unit Site 1 HUD housing project.
1967:	Oneida mission school closes; sisters from the Teachers of the Children of God leave Oneida; Sisters of the Nativity return.
1970:	The diocese of Fond du Lac awards five acres of its church to the Oneida Nation of Indians of Wisconsin for athletic fields and recreational facilities.
1972:	The 150th Celebration of the Episcopal Mission.
1978:	American Indian Religious Freedom Act passed by Congress; National Episcopal Church adopts resolution calling for Congress to respect Native American sovereignty.
1984:	Remodeling of Episcopal convent building begins.

1986:   The 112th Annual Council of the diocese of Fond du Lac passes resolution denouncing Brown and Outagamie counties in their attempts to extend its jurisdiction over Wisconsin Oneida lands.

1996:   Church of the Holy Apostles hosts Eighth Annual Paths Crossing, a gathering of representatives from fifteen Native American Episcopal congregations.

1997:   Diocese of Fond du Lac reaches agreement with Wisconsin Oneida on transferring two acres and the Grafton Parish Hall in exchange for the Oneidas commitment to restore the building.

1997:   Jamestown Covenant: Edmond Browning, presiding bishop of the National Episcopal Church, asks forgiveness from Native Americans for some past abusive church policies starting in 1607. The church and Native American leaders agree to a new covenant of faith and reconciliation.

2008:   The National Endowment for the Arts' National Heritage Fellowship Award bestowed on the Oneida Hymn Singers.

2010:   For the third time over six decades, the diocese of Fond du Lac supports Oneida efforts to resist taxation of its cemetery lands by the town of Hobart.

2011:   Rt. Rev. Katherine Jefferts Schori, presiding bishop of the National Episcopal Church, visits the Church of the Holy Apostles.

2013:   Diocese of Fond du Lac transfers land to the Wisconsin Oneidas to allow the development of a recreational trail connecting two shores of Duck Creek for biking and jogging.

2014:   Conference celebrating the 175th anniversary of the consecration of the Oneida Episcopal Church; Matthew Gunter, bishop of Fond du Lac, pays tribute to the Wisconsin Oneidas.

2016:   Tri-County History Conference, sponsored by the diocese of Fond du Lac in cooperation with the Oneida Nation of Indians of Wisconsin, is held at the Oneida Radisson Hotel on the Oneida reservation. Church historians and clergy from all over Canada and the United States attend. Mass is performed at the Church of the Holy Apostles.

APPENDIX B: EPISCOPAL PRIESTS, VICARS, AND DEACONS WHO HAVE SERVED THE ONEIDAS IN WISCONSIN

Date of Appointment	Name
1822	Eleazer Williams
1830	Richard Fish Cadle
1835	Solomon Davis
1847	Franklin R. Huff
1853	Edward A. Goodnough
1890	Solomon S. Burleson
1898	Frank Wesley Merrill
1903	Cornelius Hill
1906	A. Parker Curtiss
1908	William B. Thorn
1920	William Watson
1924	Harry Kerstetter
1925	F. W. Sherman
1937	W. F. Christian (vicar)
1957	Philip I. Livingston (priest in charge)
1957	G. Colyn Brittain (vicar)
1960	C. B. Russell (assistant)
1960	H. I. Goetz (vicar)
1963	Nelson Skinner
1964	Harry C. Vedder (vicar)
1967	Philip I. Livingston (priest in charge)
1967	Robert Goode (assistant)
1968	Larry A. Westlund (vicar)
1970	John E. Hanshaw (assistant)
1974	John E. Walker III (assistant)
1975	Michael W. Minter (assistant)
1976	Paul A. Cheek (assistant)
1977	Charles P. Wallis (vicar)
1978	Thomas K. Sewall (priest in charge)
1978	Paul A. Cheek (vicar)
1979	Russell S. Northway (assistant)
1980	James H. Dolan (assistant)
1983	James H. Dolan (vicar)
1983	William J. M. Smith

1990	Edmund Powless (deacon)
1994	John F. Splinter
1998	Brad McIntyre
2002	Dewey Silas
2005	Deborah Heckel (deacon)
2008	Kristina Henning
2011	Robert Clark
2017	Rodger Patience (vicar)

APPENDIX C: BISHOPS
WHO HAVE HEADED THE DIOCESE

These are the bishops who served the diocese of Wisconsin prior to the creation of the diocese of Fond du Lac:

Jackson Kemper (1847–1870)
William Edmond Armitage (1870–1873)
Edward Randolph Welles (1874–1888)

These are the bishops who served the diocese of Fond du Lac:

John Henry Hobart Brown (1875–1888)
Charles Chapman Grafton (1889–1912)
Reginald Heber Weller, coadjutor bishop (consecrated 1900)
Reginald Heber Weller, (1912–1933)
Harwood Sturtevant, coadjutor bishop (consecrated 1929)
Harwood Sturtevant (1933–1956)
William Hampton Brady, coadjutor bishop (consecrated 1953)
William Hampton Brady (1956–1980)
William Louis Stevens (1980–1994)
Russell Edward Jacobus (1994–2013)
Matthew Alan Gunter (2014–)

BIBLIOGRAPHY

Archival Records and Manuscript Collections

Cathedral of Saint John the Divine
    Oneida lace altarpieces
Diocese of Fond du Lac
    Oneida Episcopal Mission Collection
Episcopal Church Archives, Austin, Texas
    Archival Holdings Relating to American Indians and Native Americans
Hamilton College
    Allen, Hope E. MSS
    Kirkland, Samuel MSS
Massachusetts Historical Society, Boston
    Pickering, Timothy MSS
Mathers Museum of World Cultures, University of Indiana, Bloomington
    Wanamaker Collection: Joseph Dixon Interviews of American Indian Veterans of
        World War I
Miscellaneous Manuscript Collections
    Jennings, Francis, et al., eds., *Iroquois Indians. A Documentary History of the*
        Six Nations and Their League. 50 microfilm reels. Woodbridge, CT: Research
        Publications, 1985.
Nashotah House Theological Seminary
    Blackburn, Imri. *Nashotah House; A History of Seventy-five Years* MSS.
    The Spirit of Missions, 1836–1900
National Archives, Washington, DC
    Cartographic Records—Archives II
    Correspondence of the Office of Indian Affairs. Letters Received, 1824–1881.
    M234, RG75.

        1. Records of the New York Agency, 1829–1880
           Microfilm Reels 583–596
        2. Records of the New York Agency Emigration, 1829–1851
           Microfilm Reel 597
        3. Seneca Agency in New York, 1824–1832
           Microfilm Reel 808
        4. Six Nations Agency, 1824–1834
           Microfilm Reel 832
        5. Green Bay Agency, 1824–1880
           Microfilm Reels 315–336
        6. Neosho Agency, 1831–1875
           Microfilm Reels 530–537

Office of the Secretary of War. Letters Received by the Secretary of War Relating to Indian Affairs, 1800–1823. M.271. Microfilm Reels 1–4.
Records Relating to Indian Treaties

1. Ratified Indian Treaties, 1722–1869. M668. Microfilm Reels 2, 3, 9, 12
2. Documents Relating to the Negotiation of Ratified and Unratified Treaties . . . , 1801–1869. T494. Microfilm Reels 1, 2, 4, 6, 8

New York Public Library
Morse, Jedidiah MSS
Schuyler, Philip MSS
New York State Archives, Albany, New York
[Schoolcraft Population] New York State Census of Indian Reservations, 1845
Records of Indian Deeds and Treaties, 1748–1847
Records of the New York State Land Office, Office of the New York State Surveyor-General, Series I and II
Records of the New York State Canals
Records of the New York State Legislature. Assembly Papers.
Indian Affairs.
Records of State Comptroller's Indian Annuity Claims, Receipts and Related Documents, 1796–1925
Records of the War of 1812—Certificates of Claims by War of 1812 Veterans
New York State Historical Association, Cooperstown, New York
Eulogy of Ellen Goodnough, Cooper Family MSS
New York State Library, Manuscript Division
Beauchamp, William MSS
Hough, Franklin Benjamin MSS
Holland Land Company MSS
Hutchinson, Holmes MSS
Parker, Arthur C. MSS
Schuyler Family MSS
Scriba, George MSS
Seymour, Horatio MSS
Stillman, Lulu MSS
Watson, Elkanah MSS
Wright, Benjamin MSS
Oneida Historical Society, Oneida, Wisconsin
The Autobiography of Chief Cornelius Hill
Oneida Nation of Indians of Wisconsin
WPA Oneida Language and Folklore Project Stories and Interviews
Onondaga Historical Association
Beauchamp, William MSS
New York State Comptroller Records (Albany Papers)
Vertical Files on Oneida Indians
Rutgers University
Records of the Northern Missionary Society of New York
Saint John Fisher College
Decker, George P. MSS

[Smithsonian] Cooper-Hewitt, Museum of Textiles
    Sybil Carter Indian Lace Association Collection of Pamphlets and Lace
Syracuse University, Bird Library
    DeWitt Family MSS
    Smith, Peter MSS
University of Rochester, Rush Rhees Library
    Morgan, Lewis Henry MSS
    Parker, Arthur C. MSS
Wisconsin Area Research Center, University of Wisconsin, Green Bay
    Oneida Holy Apostles Episcopal Church Records
    Powless-Archiquette Diaries
    Williams, Eleazer MSS
Wisconsin Historical Society
    Draper, Lyman C. MSS
    Kemper, Jackson MSS
Yale University
    Archiquette, John MSS
    James Fenimore Cooper Coll. [includes Susan Fenimore Cooper MSS]

Government Publications

American State Papers: Documents, Legislative and Executive of the Congress of the United States. 38 vols. [Class 2: Indian Affairs. 2 vols. 1832–1834] Washington, DC: Gales & Seaton, 1832–1861.
Carter, Clarence E., and John Porter Bloom, eds. *The Territorial Papers of the United States*. 28 vols. Washington, DC: U.S. Government Printing Office, 1934–1956.
Donaldson, Thomas, comp. *The Six Nations of New York. Extra Census Bulletin of the 11th Census [1890] of the United States*. Washington, DC: U.S. Census Printing Office, 1892.
Johnson, Sir William. *The Papers of Sir William Johnson*. Edited by James Sullivan, Alexander Clarence Flick, Almon W. Lauber, Milton W. Hamilton, and Albert B. Corey. 14 vols. Albany: University of the State of New York, 1921–1965.
Kappler, Charles J., comp. *Indian Affairs: Laws and Treaties*. 5 vols. Washington, DC: U.S. Government Printing Office, 1903–1941.
Morse, Jedidiah. *A Report to the Secretary of War of the United States on Indian Affairs, Comprising a Narrative of a Tour Performed in the Summer of 1820. . . .* New Haven, CT: S. Converse, 1822.
New York State Legislature, Assembly. Document No. 51: *Report of the Special Committee to Investigate the Indian Problem of the State of New York*. Appointed by the Assembly of 1888. 2 vols. Albany, NY: Troy, 1889. [Popularly known as the Whipple Report.]
New York State Secretary of State. *Census of the State of New York, 1825*. Albany, 1826.
New York State Secretary of State. *Census of the State of New York for 1835*. Albany, NY: Croswell, Van Benthuysen & Burt, 1836.
New York State Secretary of State. *Census of the State of New York for 1855*. Compiled by Franklin B. Hough. Albany, NY: Charles Van Benthuysen & Sons, 1857.
Royce, Charles C., comp. *Indian Land Cessions in the United States*. 18th Annual Report of the Bureau of American Ethnology, 1896–1897, Part 2. Washington, DC: U.S. Government Printing Office, 1899.

Truth and Reconciliation Commission of Canada. *Honouring the Truth and Reconciling the Future: Summary of the Final Report of the Truth and Reconciliation Commission of Canada.* Ottawa, Ontario, Canada, 2015.
U.S. Bureau of the Census. *United States Census of Population 1790–1940*
U.S. Interior Department. Commissioner of Indian Affairs, *Annual Reports*, 1849–present

Church Publications

Christian Advocate and Zion Herald
Christian Century
Christian Challenge
Christian Herald
Christian Journal and Literary Register
Christian Visitant
Churchman's Magazine
Forth
The Living Church
Religious Intelligencer
The Spirit of Missions
Witness

Newspapers and Magazines

Appleton (WI) Post-Crescent
Daily Inter Ocean (Chicago)
De Pere Journal-Democrat
Fond du Lac Commonwealth
Freeman's Journal
Green Bay Advocate
Green Bay Press-Gazette
Independent
Indian Country Today
Indian Helper
Indian Truth
Milwaukee Journal
Milwaukee Sentinel
News from Indian Country
New York Herald
New York Times
New York Tribune
Niles Register
Oneida (NY) Daily Dispatch
Onondaga Gazette
Oshkosh Northwestern
Oswego Daily Times
Otsego Republican
Red Man
Southern Workman

Syracuse Post-Standard
The Indian Friend
Utica Patriot and Patrol
Washington Post
Wisconsin [Daily] State Gazette
Wisconsin State Journal

Books, Booklets, and Pamphlets

Abbott, Clifford. *Iroquois Language Manuscripts, ca. 1768–1803*. Clinton, NY: Richard W.
    Couper Press of Burke Library Hamilton College, 2016.
Adams, David Wallace. *Education for Extinction: American Indians and the Boarding School
    Experience, 1875–1928*. Lawrence: University Press of Kansas, 1995.
Addison, James Thayer. *The Episcopal Church in the United States, 1789–1931*. New York:
    Charles Scribner's Sons, 1951.
Anderson, Owanah. *400 Years: Anglican/Episcopal Mission among American Indians*.
    Cincinnati, OH: Forward Movement, 1997.
Andreani, Paolo. *Along the Hudson and Mohawk: The 1790 Journey of Count Paolo Andreani*.
    Edited and translated by Karim M. Tiro and Cesare Marino. Philadelphia: University
    of Pennsylvania Press, 2006.
Archambault, Marie Theresa, Mark G. Thiel, and Christopher Vecsey, eds. *The Crossing
    of Two Roads: Being Catholic and Native in the United States*. Maryknoll, NY:
    Orbis, 2003.
Axtell, James. *The Invasion Within: The Contest of Cultures in Colonial North America*. New
    York. Oxford University Press, 1985.
Baltzell, E. Digby. *The Protestant Establishment: Aristocracy and Caste in America*. New York:
    Random House, 1964.
Beaver, R. Pierce. *Church, State, and the American Indians*. St. Louis, MO: Concordia, 1966.
Béchard, Henri S. J. *Kaia'tanó:ron Kateri Tekakwitha*. Translated by Antoinette Kinlough.
    Kahnawake, QC: International, 1994.
Belknap, Jeremy. *Journal of a Tour from Boston to Oneida, June 1796*. Edited by George
    Dexter. Cambridge, MA: John Wilson, 1882.
Belknap, Jeremy, and Jedidiah Morse. *Report on the Oneida, Stockbridge and Brothertown*
    [1796], *Notes and Monographs*, No. 54. Reprint edition. New York: Museum of the
    American Indian, 1955.
Berkhofer, Robert F. Jr. *Salvation and the Savage: An Analysis of Protestant Missions and
    American Indian Response, 1787–1862*. Lexington: University of Kentucky Press, 1965.
Bieder, Robert E. *Native American Communities in Wisconsin, 1600–1960: A Study of
    Tradition and Change*. Madison: University of Wisconsin Press, 1995.
Birdsall, Ralph. *The Story of Cooperstown*. New York: Charles Scribner's Sons, 1925.
Blatchford, Samuel. *An Address Delivered to the Oneida Indians, September 24, 1810,
    Translated at the Request of the Board of Directors of the Northern Missionary Society to
    Eleazer Williams*. Albany, NY: Churchill and Abbey, 1815.
Bloomfield, Joseph. *Citizen Soldier: The Revolutionary War Journal of Joseph Bloomfield*. Edited
    by Mark Leader and James Kirby Smith. Newark: New Jersey Historical Society, 1982.
Bloomfield, Julia. *The Oneidas*. New York: Alden, 1907 and 1909.
Bonaparte, Darren. *A Lily among Thorns: The Mohawk Repatriation of Kateri Tekahkwí:tha*.
    Ahkwesásne Mohawk Territory, QC: Wampum Chronicles, 2009.

Bowden, Henry W. *American Indians and Christian Missions: Studies in Cultural Conflict.* Chicago, IL: University of Chicago Press, 1981.

Bradford, Tolly, and Chelsea Horton, eds. *Mixed Blessings: Indigenous Encounters with Christianity in Canada.* Vancouver: University of British Columbia Press, 2016.

Branch, Michael P., ed. *Reading the Roots: American Nature Writing before* Walden. Athens: University of Georgia Press, 2004.

Brandão, Jose Antonio, and K. Janet Ritch, eds. and trans. *Nation Iroquoise: A Seventeenth-Century Ethnography of the Iroquois.* Lincoln: University of Nebraska Press, 2003.

Breck, James Lloyd. *James Lloyd Breck: Apostle of the Wilderness as Excerpted from the Life of the Reverend James Lloyd Breck.* Compiled by Charles Breck and edited by Thomas Reeves. Nashotah, WI: Nashotah House Theological Seminary, 1992.

Breck, James Lloyd. *The Life of the Reverend James Lloyd Breck, D.D. Chiefly from His Letters Written by Himself.* Compiled by Charles Breck. New York: E. and J. B. Young, 1883.

Burleson, Hugh L. *An Officer of the Line in the Conquest of the Continent.* Hartford, CT: Church Missions, 1911.

Calloway, Colin. *The American Revolution in Indian Country: Crisis and Diversity in Native American Communities.* New York: Cambridge University Press, 1995.

Campisi, Jack, Michael Foster, and Marianne Mithun, eds. *Extending the Rafters: Interdisciplinary Approaches to Iroquoian Studies.* Albany: SUNY Press, 1984.

Campisi, Jack, and Laurence M. Hauptman, eds. *The Oneida Indian Experience: Two Perspectives.* Syracuse, NY: Syracuse University Press, 1988.

Charleston, Steven. *Four Vision Quests of Jesus.* New York: Morehouse, 2015.

Charleston, Steven, and Elaine A. Robinson, eds. *Coming Full Circle: Constructing Native Christian Theology.* Minneapolis, MN: Fortress, 2015.

Christjohn, Amos, and Maria Hinton. *An Oneida Dictionary.* Edited by Clifford Abbott. Green Bay: University of Wisconsin at Green Bay, 1996.

Cochran, Mary E. *Dakota Cross-Bearer: The Life and World of a Native American Bishop.* Lincoln: University of Nebraska Press, 2000.

Cooper, Susan Fenimore. *Rural Hours.* Reprint edition with introduction by Rochelle Johnson and Daniel Patterson. Athens: University of Georgia Press, 1998.

Cooper, Susan Fenimore [written anonymously as "By a Lady"]. *Rural Hours.* New York: G. P. Putnam, 1850. Paperback reprint edition. Syracuse, NY: Syracuse University Press, 1968.

Cooper, Susan Fenimore. *Susan Fenimore Cooper: Essays on Nature and Landscape.* Edited by Rochelle L. Johnson and David Patterson. Athens: University of Georgia Press, 2002.

Cooper, Susan Fenimore, ed. *William West Skiles: A Sketch of a Missionary Life at Valley Crucis in Western Carolina.* New York: J. Pott. 1890.

Crosswell, George W. *The Sermon at the Consecration of the Right Reverend Jackson Kemper, D.D., Missionary Bishop for Missouri and Indians in St. Peter's Church, Philadelphia, September 25, 1835.* Burlington, NJ: J. L. Powell, 1835.

Current, Richard N. *The History of Wisconsin.* Vol. 2, *The Civil War Era, 1848–1873.* Madison: State Historical Society of Wisconsin, 1976.

Current, Richard N. *Wisconsin: A Bicentennial History.* New York: W. W. Norton, 1977.

Curtiss, Alonzo Parker. *History of the Diocese of Fond du Lac and Its Several Congregations.* Fond du Lac, WI: P. B. Haber, 1925.

Deloria, Vine Jr. *Custer Died for Your Sins: An Indian Manifesto.* New York: Macmillan, 1969.

Deloria, Vine Jr. *For This Land: Writings on Religion in America*. Edited by James Treat. New York: Routledge, 1999.

Deloria, Vine Jr. *God Is Red*. New York: Grosset and Dunlap, 1974.

Demos, John. *The Unredeemed Captive: A Family Story from Early America*. New York: Knopf, 1994.

Dennis, Matthew. *Cultivating a Landscape of Peace: Iroquois-European Encounters in Seventeenth-Century America*. Ithaca, NY: Cornell University Press, 1995.

Doxtator, Antonio J., and Renee J. Zakhar, comp. *American Indians in Milwaukee*. Charleston, SC: Arcadia, 2011.

Dusenberry, Verne. *The Montana Cree: A Study in Religious Persistence*. Stockholm: Almqvist & Wiksell, 1962.

Egar, John H. *The Story of Nashotah House*. Milwaukee, WI: Burdick and Armitage, 1874.

Elm, Demus, and Harvey Antone. *The Oneida Creation Story*. Translated and edited by Floyd G. Lounsbury and Bryan Gick. Lincoln: University of Nebraska Press, 2000.

Fenton, William N. *The Great Law and the Longhouse: A Political History of the Iroquois Confederacy*. Norman: University of Oklahoma Press, 1998.

Finke, Roger, and Rodney Stark. *The Churching of America, 1776–1990: Winners and Losers in Our Religious Economy*. New Brunswick, NJ: Rutgers University Press, 1990.

Fischer, David Hackett. *Champlain's Dream*. New York: Knopf, 2008.

Gallagher, Carol J. *Family Theology: Finding God in Very Human Relationships*. New York: Morehouse, 2012.

Gianquitto, Tina. *"Good Observers of Nature": American Women and the Scientific Study of the Natural World, 1820–1885*. Athens: University of Georgia Press, 2007.

Glatthaar, Joseph P., and James Kirby Martin. *Forgotten Allies: The Oneida Indians and the American Revolution*. New York: Hill and Wang, 2006.

Grafton, Charles Chapman. *A Journey Godward of a Servant of Jesus Christ from the Words of Rt. Rev. Charles C. Grafton*. Vol. 4. Edited by B. Talbot Rogers. New York: Longman, Green, 1914.

Grant, John W. *Moon of Wintertime: Missionaries and the Indians of Canada in Encounter since 1534*. Toronto: University of Toronto Press, 1984.

Graymont, Barbara. *The Iroquois in the American Revolution*. Syracuse, NY: Syracuse University Press, 1972.

Greer, Allan. *Mohawk Saint: Catherine Tekakwitha and the Jesuits*. New York: Oxford University Press, 2005.

Hagan, William T. *The Indian Rights Association*. Tucson: University of Arizona Press, 1985.

Hale, Horatio E. *The Iroquois Book of Rites*. 2 vols. Philadelphia, PA: D. G. Brinton, 1883.

Hammond, Luna M. (Whitney). *History of Madison County, State of New York*. Syracuse, NY: Truair Smith, 1872.

Harrod, Howard L. *Mission among the Blackfeet*. Norman: University of Oklahoma Press, 1971.

Hauptman, Laurence M. *Between Two Fires: American Indians in the Civil War*. New York: The Free Press, 1995.

Hauptman, Laurence M. *Conspiracy of Interests: Iroquois Dispossession and the Rise of New York State*. Syracuse, NY: Syracuse University Press, 1999.

Hauptman, Laurence M. *The Iroquois and the New Deal*. Syracuse, NY: Syracuse University Press, 1981.

Hauptman, Laurence M. *The Iroquois in the Civil War: From Battlefield to Reservation.* Syracuse, NY: Syracuse University Press, 1993.

Hauptman, Laurence M. *The Iroquois Struggle for Survival: World War II to Red Power.* Syracuse, NY: Syracuse University Press, 1986.

Hauptman, Laurence M. *An Oneida Indian in Foreign Waters: The Life of Chief Chapman Scanandoah, 1870–1953.* Syracuse, NY: Syracuse University Press, 2016.

Hauptman, Laurence M. *Seven Generations of Iroquois Leadership: The Six Nations since 1800.* Syracuse, NY: Syracuse University Press, 2008.

Hauptman, Laurence M., and L. Gordon McLester III. *Chief Daniel Bread and the Oneida Nation of Indians of Wisconsin.* Norman: University of Oklahoma Press, 2005.

Hauptman, Laurence M., and L. Gordon McLester III, eds. *The Oneida Indian Journey: From New York to Wisconsin, 1784–1860.* Madison: University of Wisconsin Press, 1999.

Hauptman, Laurence M., and L. Gordon McLester III, eds. *The Oneida Indians in the Age of Allotment, 1860–1920.* Norman: University of Oklahoma Press, 2006.

Hayes, Charles Wells. *The Diocese of Western New York: History and Recollections.* 2nd edition. Rochester, NY: Scranton, Wetmore, 1905.

Hein, David, and Gardiner H. Shattuck Jr. *The Episcopalians.* New York: Oxford University Press, 2004.

Henery, Charles, ed. *Beyond the Horizon: Frontiers for Mission: The Jackson Kemper Conference.* Nashotah, WI: Nashotah House, 1985.

Hewitt, J. N. B. *Iroquoian Cosmology.* Part I. Bureau of American Ethnology, *21st Annual Report.* Washington, DC: U.S. Government Printing Office, 1899–1900.

Hewitt, J. N. B. *Iroquoian Cosmology.* Part II. Bureau of American Ethnology, *43rd Annual Report.* Washington, DC: Bureau of American Ethnology, 1928.

Hinderaker, Eric. *The Two Hendricks: Unraveling a Mohawk Mystery.* Cambridge, MA: Harvard University Press, 2010.

Hobart, John Henry. *The Correspondence of John Henry Hobart.* New York: privately printed, 1911.

Holcombe, Theodore Isaac. *An Apostle of the Wilderness: James Lloyd Breck, D.D.: His Missions and His Schools.* New York: Thomas Whittaker, 1903.

Holmes, David L. *A Brief History of the Episcopal Church.* Valley Forge, PA: Trinity, 1993.

Hough, Franklin Benjamin. *A History of St. Lawrence and Franklin Counties, New York, from the Earliest Period to the Present Times.* Albany, NY: Little, 1853.

Hough, Franklin B. *Notices of Peter Penet and His Operations among the Oneida Indians.* Lowville, NY: Albany Institute, 1866.

Hough, Franklin Benjamin, comp. *Proceedings of the Commissioners of Indian Affairs Appointed by Law for the Extinguishment of Indian Titles in the State of New York.* 2 vols. Albany, NY: Munsell, 1861.

Hoxie, Fred. *A Final Promise: The Campaign to Assimilate the Indians, 1880–1920.* Lincoln: University of Nebraska Press, 1984.

Jackson, Helen Hunt. *A Century of Dishonor: A Sketch of United States Government's Dealing with Some of the Indian Tribes.* New York: Harper and Brothers, 1881.

Jacob, Michelle M. *Indian Pilgrims: Indigenous Journeys of Activism and Healing with Saint Kateri Tekakwitha.* Tucson: University of Arizona Press, 2016.

Jarvis, Brad D. E. *The Brothertown Nation of Indians: Land Ownership and Nationalism in Early America, 1740–1840.* Lincoln: University of Nebraska Press, 2010.

Jennings, Francis, William N. Fenton, Mary A. Druke, and David R. Miller, eds. *The History and Culture of Iroquois Diplomacy: An Interdisciplinary Guide to the Treaties of the Six Nations and Their League.* Syracuse, NY: Syracuse University Press, 1985.

Johnson, Rochelle L. *Passions for Nature: Nineteenth-Century America's Aesthetic of Alienation.* Athens: University of Georgia Press, 2009.

Kellogg, Laura Cornelius. *Our Democracy and the American Indian* [1920]. Edited by Kristina Ackley and Christina Stanciu. Reprint edition. Syracuse, NY: Syracuse University Press, 2015.

Kidwell, Clara Sue, Homer Noley, George E. "Tink" Tinker [and Jace Weaver]. *A Native American Theology.* Maryknoll, NY: Orbis, 2001.

Kip, William Ingraham. *A Few Days at Nashotah.* Albany, NY: J. Munsell, 1849.

Kirkland, Samuel. *The Journals of Samuel Kirkland: 18th-Century Missionary to the Iroquois, Government Agent, Father of Hamilton College.* Edited by Walter Pilkington. Clinton, NY: Hamilton College, 1980.

Lafitau, Joseph François. *Customs of the American Indians* (1724). Translated by Elizabeth Moore and edited by William N. Fenton. 2 vols. Toronto: Champlain Society, 1974.

Lewis, Bonnie Sue. *Creating Christian Indians: Native Clergy in the Presbyterian Church.* Norman: University of Oklahoma Press, 2003.

Lewis, Herbert S., ed. *Oneida Lives: Long-Lost Voices of the Wisconsin Oneidas.* Lincoln: University of Nebraska Press, 2005.

Linklaen, Jan [John]. *Travels in the Years 1791 and 1792 in Pennsylvania, New York and Vermont: Journals of John Linklaen, Agent of the Holland Land Company.* New York: G. P. Putnam's Sons, 1897.

Loew, Patty. *Indian Nations of Wisconsin: Histories of Endurance and Renewal.* 2nd ed. Madison: Wisconsin Historical Society, 2013.

Love, W. Deloss. *Samson Occom and the Christian Indians of New England.* Reprint edition. Syracuse, NY: Syracuse University Press, 2000.

Lurie, Nancy O. *Wisconsin Indians.* 2nd edition. Madison: Wisconsin Historical Society Press, 2002.

Lydekker, John Wolfe. *The Faithful Mohawks.* Cambridge, UK: Cambridge University Press, 1938.

Martin, Deborah B. *History of Brown County, Wisconsin: Past and Present.* 2 vols. Chicago, IL: S. J. Clarke, 1913.

Martin, Joel, and Mark Nicholas, eds. *Native Americans, Christianity, and the Reshaping of the American Religious Landscape.* Chapel Hill: University of North Carolina Press, 2010.

McCallum, James Dow, ed. *The Letters of Eleazar Wheelock's Indians.* Hanover, NH: Dartmouth College, 1932.

McLester, L. Gordon III, and Laurence M. Hauptman, eds. *A Nation within a Nation: Voices of the Oneidas in Wisconsin.* Madison: Wisconsin Historical Society Press, 2010.

McNally, Michael D. *Ojibwe Singers: Hymns, Grief, and a Native Culture in Motion.* New York: Oxford University Press, 2000.

Merrill, Frank W. *The Church's Mission to the Oneidas.* Wisconsin Oneida Reservation: Oneida Episcopal Mission, 1899.

Milloy, John S. *"A National Crime": The Canadian Government and the Residential School System, 1879 to 1986.* Winnipeg: University of Manitoba Press, 1999.

Morgan, Lewis Henry. *League of the Ho-de-no-sau-nee or Iroquois*. Rochester, NY: Sage and
    Bros., 1851. Paperback reprint edition. New York: Corinth Books, 1962.
Nashotah House Theological Seminary. *Our Anniversary Book: The Oneida Mission, 1822–*
    1942. Nashotah, WI: Nashotah House Theological Seminary, n.d.
Niobrara League of New York [of Protestant Episcopal Church]. *Second Annual Report of*
    the Niobrara League of New York: A Branch of the Women's Auxiliary of the Board of
    Missions, 1873–1874. New York: American Church Press, 1874.
Northern Missionary Society. *Report of the Directors of the Northern Missionary Society, 1814*.
    New York: Websters and Skinners, 1815.
Norton, David J. *Rebellious Younger Brother: Oneida Leadership and Diplomacy, 1750–1800*.
    DeKalb, IL: University of Northern Illinois Press, 2009.
Oberg, Michael Leroy. *Professional Indian: The American Odyssey of Eleazer Williams*.
    Philadelphia: University of Pennsylvania Press, 2015.
O'Connor, Daniel. *Three Centuries of Mission: The United Society for the Propagation of the*
    Gospel, 1701–2000. London: Continuum, 2000.
Parker, Arthur C. *Parker on the Iroquois*. Edited by William N. Fenton. Syracuse, NY:
    Syracuse University Press, 1968.
Parmenter, Jon. *The Edge of the Woods: Iroquoia, 1534–1701*. East Lansing, MI: Michigan State
    University Press, 2010.
Pascoe, C. F. *Two Hundred Years of the Society of the Propagation of the Gospel [SPG]: An*
    Historical Account of the Society for the Propagation of the Gospel in Foreign Parts.
    (Based on a Digest of the Society's Records). London: SPG, 1901.
Pascoe, C. F., comp. *Classified Digest of the Records of the Society of the Propagation of the*
    Gospel in Foreign Parts, 1701–1892. London: Society of the Propagation of the Gospel in
    Foreign Parts, 1893.
Preston, David. *The Texture of Contact: European and Indian Settler Communities on the*
    Frontiers of Iroquoia, 1667–1783. Lincoln: University of Nebraska Press, 2002.
Prichard, Robert. *A History of the Episcopal Church*. Harrisburg, PA: Morehouse, 1999.
Prucha, Francis Paul. *American Indian Policy in Crisis: Christian Reformers and the*
    American Indian, 1865–1900. Norman: University of Oklahoma Press, 1976.
Prucha, Francis Paul, ed. *"Americanizing" the American Indian: Writings by the "Friends of*
    the American Indian," 1880–1900. Cambridge, MA: Harvard University Press, 1973.
Prucha, Francis Paul. *The Churches and the Indian Schools, 1888–1912*. Lincoln: University of
    Nebraska Press, 1979.
Prucha, Francis Paul. *The Great Father: The United States Government and the American*
    Indians. 2 vols. Lincoln: University of Nebraska Press, 1984.
Rath, Richard Cullen. *How Early America Sounded*. Ithaca, NY: Cornell University Press,
    2003.
Richards, Cara E. *The Oneida People*. Phoenix, AZ: Indian Tribal Series, 1974.
Richter, Daniel K. *The Ordeal of the Longhouse: The Peoples of the Iroquois League in the Era*
    of European Colonization. Chapel Hill: University of North Carolina Press, 1992.
Richter, Daniel K., and James H. Merrell, eds. *Beyond the Covenant Chain: The Iroquois*
    and Their Neighbors in Indian North America, 1600–1800. Syracuse, NY: Syracuse
    University Press, 1987.
Ripley, Dorothy. *Bank of Faith and Works United*. Philadelphia, PA: J. H. Cunningham, 1819.
Ritzenthaler, Robert E. *The Oneida Indians of Wisconsin*. Bulletin 19. Milwaukee, WI: Public
    Museum of the City of Milwaukee, 1950.

Ronda, James P., and James Axtell. *Indian Missions: A Critical Bibliography*. Bloomington: Indiana University Press, 1978.

Shattuck, Gardiner H. Jr. *Episcopalians and Race: Civil War to Civil Rights*. Lexington: University Press of Kentucky, 2000.

Shattuck, George C. *The Oneida Indian Land Claims: A Legal History*. Syracuse, NY: Syracuse University Press, 1991.

Shoemaker, Nancy. *Negotiators of Change: Historical Perspectives on Native American Women*. New York: Routledge, 1994.

Silverman, Daniel J. *Red Brethren: The Brothertown and Stockbridge Indians and the Problem of Race in Early America*. Ithaca, NY: Cornell University Press, 2010.

Smith, Alice. *The History of Wisconsin*. Vol. 1, *From Exploration to Statehood*. Madison: State Historical Society of Wisconsin, 1973.

Smith, Andrea. *Native Americans and the Christian Right: The Gendered Politics of Unlikely Alliances*. Durham, NC: Duke University Press, 2008, 86.

Snow, Dean, Charles Gehring, and William A. Starna, eds. *In Mohawk Country: Early Narratives about a Native People*. Syracuse, NY: Syracuse University Press, 1996.

Society for the Propagation of the Gospel. *Classified Digest of the Records of the Society for the Propagation of the Faith in Foreign Parts, 1791–1802*. 5th edition. London: Society for the Propagation of the Gospel in Foreign Parts, 1802.

Steckley, John L. *De Religione: Telling the Seventeenth-Century Jesuit Story in Huron to the Iroquois*. Norman: University of Oklahoma Press, 2004.

Stevens, Laura M. *The Poor Indians: British Missionaries, Native Americans, and Colonial Sensibility*. Philadelphia: University of Pennsylvania Press, 2010.

Taylor, Alan S. *The Divided Ground: Indians, Settlers, and the Northern Borderlands of the American Revolution*. New York: Knopf, 2006.

Taylor, Alan S. *William Cooper's Town*. New York: Alfred A. Knopf, 1995.

Taylor, Drew Hayden. *God and the Indian: A Play*. Vancouver, BC: Talonbooks, 2014.

Thiel, Mark G., and Christopher Vecsey, eds. *Native Footsteps along the Path of Saint Kateri Tekakwitha*. Milwaukee, WI: Marquette University Press, 2012.

Thwaites, Reuben G., ed. *The Jesuit Relations and Allied Documents* [1896]. 73 vols. Reprint edition. New York: Pageant, 1959.

Tinker, George E. *Missionary Conquest: The Gospel and Native American Cultural Genocide*. Minneapolis, MN: Fortress, 1993.

Tinker, George E. *Spirit and Resistance: Political Theology and American Indian Liberation*. Minneapolis, MN: Fortress, 2004.

Tiro, Karim M. *The People of the Standing Stone: The Oneida Nation from the Revolution through the Era of Removal*. Amherst: University of Massachusetts Press, 2011.

Tooker, Elisabeth. *The Iroquois Ceremonial of Midwinter*. Syracuse, NY: Syracuse University Press, 1970.

Treat, James. *Around the Sacred Fire: Native American Activism in the Red Power Era*. New York: Palgrave Macmillan, 2003.

Treat, James, ed. *Native and Christian: Indigenous Voices on Religion and Identity in the United States and Canada*. New York: Routledge, 1996.

Treat, James. *Writing the Cross Culture: Native Fiction on the White Man's Religion*. Golden, CO: Fulcrum, 2006.

Trigger, Bruce G. *The Children of Aataentsic: A History of the Huron People to 1660*. 2 vols. Montreal: McGill–Queen's University Press, 1976.

Trigger, Bruce G., ed. *Handbook of North American Indians*. Vol. 15, *The Northeast*. Washington, DC: Smithsonian Institution, 1978.

Trigger, Bruce G. *Natives and Newcomers: Canada's "Heroic Age" Reconsidered*. Montreal: McGill–Queen's University Press, 1985.

Twiss, Richard. *One Church, Many Tribes*. Ventura, CA: Regal/ Gospel Light, 2000.

Twiss, Richard. *Rescuing the Gospel from the Cowboy: A Native American Expression of the Jesus Way*. Madison, WI: InterVarsity, 2015.

Van den Bogaert, Harmen Meyendertsz. *A Journey into the Mohawk and Oneida Country, 1634–1635*. Translated and edited by Charles Gehring and William A. Starna. Syracuse, NY: Syracuse University Press, 1988.

Vecsey, Christopher. *On the Padres' Trail*. Notre Dame, IN: Notre Dame University Press, 1996.

Vecsey, Christopher. *The Paths of Kateri's Kin*. 2nd edition. Notre Dame, IN: Notre Dame University Press, 2016.

Vecsey, Christopher. *Traditional Ojibwa Religion and Its Historical Changes*. Philadelphia, PA: American Philosophical Society, 1983.

Vecsey, Christopher. *Where the Two Roads Meet*. Notre Dame, IN: Notre Dame University Press, 1999.

Vecsey, Christopher, and William A. Starna, eds. *Iroquois Land Claims*. Syracuse, NY: Syracuse University Press, 1988.

Wagner, Harold E. *The Episcopal Church in Wisconsin, 1847–1947: A History of the Dioceses of Milwaukee*. Milwaukee, WI: Diocese of Milwaukee, 1947.

Wallace, Anthony F. C. *The Death and Rebirth of the Seneca*. New York: Knopf, 1969.

Walworth, Clarence E. *The Oxford Movement in America* (1895). Reprint edition. New York: United States Catholic Historical Society, *Monograph Series XXX*, 1974.

Whipple, Henry Benjamin. *Lights and Shadows of a Long Episcopate: Being the Reminiscences and Recollections of the Right Reverend Henry Benjamin Whipple, D.D., LL.D., Bishop of Minnesota*. New York: Macmillan, 1899.

Williams, Eleazer, trans. *Book of Common Prayer According to the Use of the Protestant Episcopal Church Translated into the Mohawk or Iroquois Language by the Request of the Domestic Committee of the Board of Missions of the Protestant Episcopal Church*. New York: H. B. Durand, 1867.

Williams, Eleazer. *Prayers for Families and for Particular Persons: Selected from the Book of Common Prayer*. Albany, NY: G. J. Loomis, 1816.

Wonderley, Anthony. *At the Font of the Marvelous; Exploring Oral Narrative and Mythic Imagery of the Iroquois and Their Neighbors*. Syracuse, NY: Syracuse University Press, 2009.

Wonderley, Anthony. *Oneida Iroquois Folklore, Myth, and History*. Syracuse, NY: Syracuse University Press, 2004.

Woodley, Randy. *Living in Color: Embracing God's Passion for Ethnic Diversity*. Downers Grove, IL: InterVarsity, 2001.

Woodley, Randy. *Mixed Blood, Not Mixed Up: Finding God-given Identity in a Multi-cultural World*. Hayden, AL: Randy Woodley, 2004.

Woodley, Randy. *Shalom and the Community of Creation: An Indigenous Vision*. Grand Rapids, MI: Wm. B. Eerdmans, 2012.

Woodley, Randy. *When Going to Church Is Sin and Other Essays on Native American Christian Missions*. Scotland, PA: Healing the Land, 2007.

Woods, Eric Taylor. *Cultural Sociology of Anglican Mission and the Indian Residential Schools in Canada: The Long Road to Apology*. New York: Palgrave Macmillan, 2016.

Yong, Amos, and Barbara Brown Zikmund, eds., *Remembering Jamestown: Hard Questions about Christian Mission*. Eugene, OR: Pickwick, 2010.

Contributed Articles and Chapters

Ackley, Kristina. "Haudenosaunee Genealogies: Conflict and Community in the Oneida Land Claim," *American Indian Quarterly* 33 (2009): 462–78.

Ackley, Kristina. "Renewing Haudenosaunee Identity: Laura Cornelius Kellogg and the Idea of Unity in the Oneida Land Claim," *American Indian Culture and Research Journal* 32 (2008): 57–81.

Buerger, Geoffrey E. "Eleazer Williams: Elitism and Multiple Identity on Two Frontiers." In *Being and Becoming Indian: Biographical Studies of North American Frontiers*, edited by James H. Clifton. Chicago, IL: Dorsey, 1989.

Campisi, Jack. "Consequences of the Kansas Claims to Oneida Tribal Identity." In *Proceedings of the First Congress, Canadian Ethnology Society*, edited by Jerome H. Barkow. Mercury Series 17 (1974): 35–47. Ottawa: Canada National Museum of Man, Ethnology Division.

Campisi, Jack. "New York-Oneida Treaty of 1795: A Finding of Fact." *American Indian Law Review* 4 (Summer 1976): 71–82.

Campisi, Jack. "Oneida." In *Handbook of North American Indians*. Vol 15, *The Northeast*, edited by Bruce G. Trigger, 481–90. Washington, DC: Smithsonian Institution, 1978.

Campisi, Jack, and Laurence M. Hauptman. "Talking Back: The Oneida Language and Folklore Project, 1938–1941." *Proceedings of the American Philosophical Society* 125 (December 1981): 441–48.

Clark, Jennifer. "'Church of Our Fathers': The Development of the Protestant Episcopal Church within the Changing Post–Revolutionary Anglo-American Relationship." *Journal of Religious History* 18, no. 1 (1994): 27–51.

Colman, Henry. "Recollections of Oneida Indians, 1840–1845." *Proceedings of the State Historical Society at Its Fifty-Ninth Annual Meeting*, 152–59. Madison, WI: State Historical Society, 1912.

Cope, Alfred. "Mission to the Menominee: A Quaker's Green Bay Diary." *Wisconsin Magazine of History* 49 (1966): 302–23; 50 (1966): 18–42, 120–44, 211–41.

Corwin, Charles E. "Efforts of the Dutch-American Colonial Pastors for the Conversion of the Indians." *Journal of the Presbyterian Historical Society* 12 (1925): 225–46.

Cummock, Thomas. "Sketch of the Brothertown Indians." *Wisconsin Historical Collections* 4 (1906): 292.

Davidson, John Nelson. "The Coming of the New York Indians to Wisconsin." *Proceedings of the State Historical Society of Wisconsin* 47: 153–85. Madison, WI: Democrat Printing Co., 1899.

Davis, Natalie Zemon. "Iroquois Women, European Women." In *Women,"Race," and Writing in the Early Modern Period*, edited by Margo Hendricks and Patricia Parker, 243–58. New York: Routledge, 1994.

Donovan, Mary S. "Women as Missionaries in the Episcopal Church, 1830–1920." *Anglican Episcopal History* 61 (1992): 16–35.

Draper, Lyman C. "Additional Notes on Eleazer Williams." *Wisconsin Historical Collections* 8 (1879): 353–69. Reprint edition. Madison: State Historical Society of Wisconsin, 1908.

Duncan, Kate. "American Indian Lace-making." *American Indian Art* 5 (Summer 1980): 28–35, 80.

Elbourne, Elizabeth. "Managing Alliance, Negotiating Christianity: Haudenosaunee Uses of Anglicanism in Northeastern North America, 1760s–1830s." In *Mixed Blessings: Indigenous Encounters with Christianity in Canada*, edited by Tolly Bradford and Chelsea Horton. Vancouver: University of British Columbia Press, 2016.

Ellis, Albert G. "Advent of the New York Indians into Wisconsin." *Wisconsin Historical Collections* 2 (1856): 415–49.

Ellis, Albert G. "Fifty-Four Years' Recollections of Men and Events in Wisconsin." *Wisconsin Historical Collections* 7 (1876): 207–68. Reprint edition. Madison: State Historical Society of Wisconsin, 1908.

Ellis, Albert G. "Recollections of Rev. Eleazer Williams." *Wisconsin Historical Collections* 8 (1879): 322–52. Reprint edition. Madison: State Historical Society of Wisconsin, 1908.

Ellis, Albert G. "Some Accounts of the Advent of the New York Indians into Wisconsin." *Wisconsin Historical Collections* 2 (1856): 415–49.

Emlen, James. "The Journal of James Emlen Kept on a Trip to Canandaigua, New York," edited by William N. Fenton. *Ethnohistory* 12, no. 4 (1965): 279–342.

Feister, Lois M. "Indian-Dutch Relations in the Upper Hudson Valley: A Study of Baptism Records in the Dutch Reformed Church, Albany, New York." *Man in the Northeast* 24 (1982): 89–113.

Fenton, William N. "Structure, Continuity, and Change in the Process of Treaty-making." In *The History and Culture of Iroquois Diplomacy: An Interdisciplinary Guide of the Treaties of the Six Nations and Their League*, edited by Francis Jennings, William N. Fenton, Mary A. Druke, and David R. Miller, 3–36. Syracuse, NY: Syracuse University Press, 1985.

Germic, Stephen. "Land Claims, Natives, and Nativism: Susan Fenimore Cooper's Fealty to Place." *American Literature* 79 (September 2007): 475–500.

Graymont, Barbara. "New York State Indian Policy after the Revolution." *New York History* 57 (October 1976): 438–74.

Hart, William Bryan. "Mohawk Schoolmasters and Catechists in Mid-Eighteenth Century Iroquoia: An Experiment in Fostering Literacy and Religious Change." In *The Language Encounter in the Americas, 1492–1800*, edited by Edward G. Gray and Noman Fiering, 233–44. New York: Berghahn, 2000.

Hauptman, Laurence M. "Refugee Havens: The Iroquois Villages of the Eighteenth Century." In *American Indian Environments: Ecological Issues in Native American History*, edited by Christopher Vecsey and Robert W. Venables, 128–39. Syracuse, NY: Syracuse University Press, 1980.

Hauptman, Laurence M., and L. Gordon McLester III. "Death in the Ardennes: Dr. Josiah A. Powless, Oneida Hero of World War I," *American Indian* [National Museum of the American Indian] (Spring 2015): 26–30.

Heller, Terry. "Sarah Orne Jewett's Transforming Visit: 'Tame Indians' and One Writer's Professionalization." *New England Quarterly* 86 (December 2013): 655–84.

Holmes, David L. "The Episcopal Church and the American Revolution." *Historical Magazine of the Protestant Episcopal Church* 79 (1978): 261–91.

Hopkins, Vivian C. "De Witt Clinton and the Iroquois." *Ethnohistory* 8 (Spring 1961): 213–41.

Horsman, Reginald. "The Origins of Oneida Removal to Wisconsin, 1815–1822." In *Oneida Indian Journey: From New York to Wisconsin, 1784–1860*, edited by Laurence M. Hauptman and L. Gordon McLester III, 53–69. Madison: University of Wisconsin Press, 1999.

Howard, Joy A. "Rebecca Kellogg Ashley: Negotiating Identity on the Early American Borderlands, 1704–1757." In *Women in Early America*, edited by Thomas A. Foster, 128–33. New York: New York University Press, 2015.

Huguenin, Charles A. "The Sacred Stone of the Oneidas." *New York Folklore Quarterly* 8 (1957): 16–22.

Johnson, Rochelle L. "Walden, *Rural Hours*, and the Dilemma of Representation." In *Thoreau's Sense of Place: Essays in American Environmental Writing*, edited by Richard L. Schneider. Iowa City: University of Iowa Press, 2000.

Kemper, Jackson. "Journal of an Episcopalian Missionary's Tour to Green Bay, 1834." *Wisconsin Historical Collections* 14 (1898): 394–49.

Kiel, Douglas. "Competing Visions of Empowerment: Oneida Progressive-Era Politics and Writing Tribal Histories." *Ethnohistory* 61 (Summer 2014): 419–44.

Kimball, Sue Leslie. "Cooper, Susan, Augusta Fenimore." In *American National Biography*, edited by John A. Garraty and Mark Carnes. Cary, NC: Oxford University Press, 1999.

Lehman, J. David. "The End of the Iroquois Mystique: The Oneida Land Cession Treaties of the 1780s." *William & Mary Quarterly*, 3rd ser., 47 (1990): 523–47.

Mandell, Daniel. "'Turned Their Minds to Religion': Oquaga and the First Iroquois Church, 1748–1776." *Early American Studies* 11 (2013): 211–42.

Marryat, Frederick. "An English Officer's Description of Wisconsin in 1837." *Wisconsin Historical Collections* 14 (1898): 137–54.

Martin, Morgan L. "Sketch and Narrative of Morgan L. Martin." *Wisconsin Historical Collections* 13 (1895): 163–246, edited by Reuben G. Thwaites.

Matteson, Patricia. "Sybil Carter and Her Legacy." In *A Nation Within a Nation: Voices of the Oneidas in Wisconsin*, edited by L. Gordon McLester III and Laurence M. Hauptman, 67–80. Madison: Wisconsin Historical Society Press, 2010.

McElwain, Thomas. "'The Rainbow Will Carry Me': The Language of Seneca Christianity as Reflected in Hymns." In *Religion in Native North America*, edited by Christopher Vecsey, 83–103. Moscow: University of Idaho Press, 1990.

McLester, Betty, and Debra Jenny. "Reviving Oneida Lace-making." In *A Nation Within a Nation: Voices of the Oneidas in Wisconsin*, edited by L. Gordon McLester III and Laurence M. Hauptman, 81–82. Madison: Wisconsin Historical Society Press, 2010.

McNally, Michael D. "The Practice of Native American Christianity," *Church History* 69 (2000): 834–59.

McNally, Michael D. "The Uses of Ojibwa Hymn-singing at White Earth." In *Toward a History of Practice Lived*, edited by David D. Hall, 133–59. Princeton, NJ: Princeton University Press, 1997.

Merritt, Jane T. "Dreaming in the Savior's Blood: Moravians and the Indian Great Awakening in Pennsylvania." *William and Mary Quarterly*, 3rd ser., 54 (1997): 723–46.

National Episcopal Church General Convention. "Resolution 2009-D 035." *Journal of the General Convention of . . . the Episcopal Church* (2009): 371–72.

O'Grady, Terence J. "The Singing Societies of the Oneida." *American Music* 9 (Spring 1991): 67–91.

Penfield, Lida. "Last of the Coopers of Cooperstown at Oswego." *Oswego County Historical Society Journal* (1948): 59–64.

Penfield, Lida. "Three Generations of Coopers in Oswego." *Oswego County Historical Society Journal* (1941): 1–7.

Prucha, Francis Paul. "A Friend of the Indian in Milwaukee: Mrs. O. J. [Oshia Jane Joselyn] Hiles and the Women's Indian Association." *Historical Messenger* 29 (August 1973): 78–95.

Richter, Daniel K. "Iroquois versus Iroquois: Jesuit Missions in Village Politics, 1642–1686." *Ethnohistory* 32 (1985): 1–16.

Richter, Daniel K. "'Some of Them . . . Would Always Have a Minister with Them': Mohawk Protestantism, 1683–1719." *American Indian Quarterly* 16 (Autumn 1992): 471–84.

Silverman, David J. "The Curse of God: An Idea and Its Origins among the Indians of New York's Revolutionary Frontier." *William and Mary Quarterly*, 3rd ser., 66 (July 2009): 495–534.

Simmons, Williams S. "Red Yankees: Narragansett Conversion in the Great Awakening." *American Ethnologist* 10 (May 1983): 253–71.

Smith, Robert, and Loretta Metoxen. "Oneida Traditions." In *The Oneida Indian Experience: Two Perspectives*, edited by Jack Campisi and Laurence M. Hauptman, 150–51. Syracuse, NY: Syracuse University Press, 1988.

Stambaugh, Samuel. "Report on the Quality and Condition of Wisconsin Territory, 1831." *Wisconsin Historical Collections* 15 (1900): 399–438.

Starna, William A. "The Oneida Homeland in the Seventeenth Century." In *The Oneida Indian Experience: Two Perspectives*, edited by Jack Campisi and Laurence M. Hauptman, 9–22. Syracuse, NY: Syracuse University Press, 1988.

Tiro, Karim M. "A 'Civil War'? Rethinking Iroquois Participation in the American Revolution." *Explorations in Early American Culture* 4 (2000): 148–65.

Tiro, Karim M. "The Emergence of Iroquois Literacy; Insights from the Samuel Kirkland Papers." In *Iroquois Language Manuscripts, ca 1768–1803*, edited by Clifford Abbott, 9–18. Clinton, NY: Richard W. Couper Press of Burke Library, Hamilton College, 2016.

Tiro, Karim M. "James Dean in Iroquoia." *New York History* 80 (October 1999): 391–422.

Tiro, Karim M. "'We Wish to Do You Good': The Quaker Mission to the Oneida Nation, 1790–1840." *Journal of the Early Republic* 26 (2006): 353–76.

Tooker, Elisabeth. "Women in Iroquois Society." In *Extending the Rafters: Interdisciplinary Approaches to Iroquoian Studies*, edited by Michael Foster, Jack Campisi, and Marianne Mithun, 109–23. Albany: SUNY Press, 1984.

Thwaites, Reuben G., ed. "Sketch and Narrative of Morgan L. Martin." *Wisconsin Historical Collections* 13 (1895): 163–246.

Wonderley, Anthony. "An Oneida Community in 1780: Study of an Inventory of Iroquois Property Losses during the American Revolutionary War." *Northeast Anthropology* 56 (1998): 19–41.

Dissertations

Ackley, Kristina. "'We Are Oneida Yet': Discourse in the Oneida Claim." PhD diss., SUNY Buffalo, 2005.

Basehart, Harry S. "Historical Changes in the Kinship System of the Oneida Indians." PhD diss., Harvard University, 1952.

Campisi, Jack. "Ethnic Identity and Boundary Maintenance in Three Oneida Communities." PhD diss., SUNY Albany, 1974.

Geier, Philip Otto. "A Peculiar Status: A History of the Oneida Indian Treaties and Claims: Jurisdictional Conflict within the American Government, 1775–1920." PhD diss., Syracuse University, 1980.

Green, Gretchen. "A New People in an Age of War: The Kahnawake Iroquois, 1667–1760." PhD diss., The College of William & Mary, 1991.

Hart, William Bryan. "For the Good of Our Souls: Mohawk Authority, Accommodation, and Resistance to Protestant Evangelism, 1700–1780." PhD diss., Brown University, 1998.

Kiel, Douglas. "The Oneida Resurgence: Modern Indian Renewal in the Heart of America." PhD diss., University of Wisconsin, 2012.

Kurth, Rosaly T. "Susan Fenimore Cooper: A Study of Her Life and Work." PhD diss., Fordham University, 1974.

Patrick, Christine Sternberg. "The Life and Times of Samuel Kirkland, 1741–1808: Missionary to the Oneida Indians, American Patriot, and Founder of Hamilton College." PhD diss., SUNY Buffalo, 1993.

INDEX

Page numbers in italics indicate illustrations.

www.ingramcontent.com/pod-product-compliance
Lightning Source LLC
Chambersburg PA
CBHW052001270326

41929CB00015B/2746